California

*Two Centuries of
Man, Land, and Growth
in the Golden State*

CALIFORNIA

Two Centuries of Man, Land, and Growth In the Golden State

BY W. H. HUTCHINSON

Illustrations selected and collated by John Barr Tompkins

AMERICAN WEST PUBLISHING COMPANY

PALO ALTO / CALIFORNIA

Library of Congress Catalog Card Number 77-77828

For John Barr Tomkins

With Reason . . .

Many individuals, institutions, organizations and reposi-
tories have over many years enlightened me to the fact that
California is sui generis. To list them all would be an un-
conscionable imposition upon both publisher and readers.
It is seemly, however, to mention Mr. Michael Harrison, Fair
Oaks, California; Professor Richard G. Lillard, California
State College, Los Angeles; and Professor Clarence F. McIn-
thosh, Chico State College—all of whom have made persistent
attempts to sharpen the pot metal of my sensitivities. As
should everyone who purports to write on California agriculture, I acknowledge my debt to the consistently accurate
reportage of Mr. Henry Schact, San Francisco.

I have specific obligations in this particular work to Professor David W. Lantis, Chico State College; Dr. Albert Shumate,
San Francisco; and Professor Gerald T. White, University of
California, Irvine. Chief among these obligations is to make
very plain their absolution from responsibility for my sins of
omission and commission.

The ill-fated California Exposition and State Fair Corporation provided the incentive to self-discipline that started me
on this work. As has been the case for more than a quarter-
century, Esther Ormsby Hutchinson made its completion
possible.

W. H. HUTCHINSON
Chico State College
Chico, California
January, 1969

7

Table of Contents

AMERICA SEPTENTRIO: NALIS.

CIRCULUS ARCT

New North Wales

NO

BR

California a prioribus Geographis semper
habita fuit quædam pars Continentis, at cepta per
Hollandos sub Hispanis tabula quædam Geographica
compertum est insulam esse et continere ubi latissima
est 500 leucas A Cap. Mendocino vero usq; ad C S Luca
repertum est testibus tabula prædicta et Francisco
Gauli extendi in longitudinem 1700 leucarum

S Thomas Button hybernans in portu
Nelson ad altitudinem grad 57 observavit
singulis 12 horis æstum maris accrescere
15 pedes aut ultra qui flante Zephyro
statas magnos flos plenilunij intumescebat
Sequenti Æste animadvertit quog ad
altitud grad 60 similes æstus maris sui nunc
Orientem versus nunc Occidentem vergebant

Annotationes in Iames Bay
detectum a Cap Thoma Iacobo Anglo 1631
in quo etiam hybernavit
1. Lord Westons Ile
2. Sr Thomas Roos Ile
3. Charlton Ile
4. Danby Ile
5. Cayes Ile

In Sinu Maris Nelson
a Hudson hybernans
non ultra dura pedum
D Thomas Iacobus
dictus in majori
excedebat

Buttons
Bay

A   M   E   R   I   C

SEPTENTRIONALI

INSULA CALIFORNIA

MARE VERMEIO

MARE DEL ZUR

Rey Coronado

Lago de oro

Pueblo de
Moqui

Las Playas

NUEVA
GRANADA

Real de Nueva
Mexico

VIRG

FLORID

Tegesta
Provincia

NUEVA BISCAIA.

GOLFO DE
MEXICO.

Zacatecas

NUE
Xalisco

VITLA

ESPAN
A

HONDURAS.

GOLFO DE HONDU
RAS.

NICARAGUA

COSTARICA

M   A   R   D   E   L   Z   U   R.

Mythic Island,
State of Mind

O
N THE RIGHT HAND of the Indies . . . very close to the Earthly Paradise" was the geographical location of the mythical island of California created by Garcí Ordóñez de Montalvo in his romantic confection, *Las Sergias de Esplandián*, published in Seville about 1510.

At this time, Cortés had not conquered Mexico, nor had anyone in Europe any accurate idea of what lay north, south or west beyond unnamed Cape Horn. Thus Señor Montalvo had no geographical basis from which to extract the name "California," and inasmuch as the setting of his romance was in the Mediterranean Levant, the name had no derivation that can be traced to the state which now bears it.

Montalvo peopled his island with black Amazons, ruled by a Queen Calafia. He studded it with griffins, creatures which were half-eagle, half-lion; and he filled it to overflowing with pearls, and precious metals, and all the wonders that an impecunious man-at-arms turned author could imagine. In the light of subsequent historical developments, Montalvo was a better prophet, perhaps, than novelist.

The name "California" was given by Cortés and his men to the land that lay to the west of Mexico across the Gulf of California (The "Sea of Cortés"), or what we know today as Baja California. In the wake of the first Spanish voyages up the unknown coast from Mexico, the name became applied to all of Spain's territorial claims from Cape San Lucas (Baja) into the shrouding Alaskan mists. Then, after Spain's settle-

I I

California as an island, from a map of North America by Henricus Hondius, 1642.

ment at San Diego, the name was split into "Alta California" and "Baja California" to reflect the two administrative provinces of Spain into which the territory of the original California had been divided.

Under the Mexican regime, 1822–46, the name "Alta California" encompassed generally the land mass between the Continental Divide and the Pacific, between 42° north latitude — the state's present northern boundary — and Mexico proper. Thus, it included the present states of California, Nevada, Utah, and Arizona, plus parts of Wyoming, Colorado, and New Mexico. With the foregoing in mind, it should be made clear that hereafter the name "California" refers only to the present territorial extent of the state, unless specifically noted otherwise.

Within this territorial area, the population has virtually doubled every twenty years since 1860, the year of the first accurate federal census in California. A state-conducted census in 1852, showing a population of 223,856, may be regarded as the first accurate tally of humanity in the American period. The state's population on July 1, 1968, was given by the Department of Finance as 19,662,000, and population projections into the year 2000 range between 38,471,000 and 41,321,000, which will comprise about 14 percent of the nation's total human burden in that year. This growth has been caused primarily by the second greatest voluntary migration in the history of mankind, being exceeded only by the massive and sustained emigration from Europe to the United States in the century between 1815 and 1914. Even today, with procreation outstripping immigration, which added only 477,000 residents to California in 1967, almost one-half of the state's inhabitants have been born elsewhere. This dramatic demonstration of the basic American freedom of personal mobility is continued within the state; especially in its urban centers where, in Richard G. Lillard's trenchant phrase, "spinsters move as often as call girls."

In-migrants know little about their new home, its history, or the causal forces that have made it their Mecca. The constrictions of urban living also prevent the native-born from knowing as much about their state as they should. Basic to both these lacks is the state's size, its 158,693 square miles making it third largest in the Union, and its geographical diversity, which spans ten degrees of latitude and includes 1,264 miles of coastline. This expanse of coastline facilitated smuggling during the Hispanic period and eased the task of rum-running during the Prohibition years. It has great potential, as well, for California's future. The authorial intention in the pages that follow is to bring Californians of all ages, races, creeds, and origins a sense of identity with their land by providing them with a very usable past in readily assimilable form.

California's remarkable ability to sustain an ever-accelerating growth since 1849 has been made possible through technological utilization of a most bounteous natural resource base. The various segments of this base have been developed in a sequence, which gives an illusion of design to what was more likely historical happenstance. As a result California's growth has been a chain reaction in which factors acting upon one another do not break sharply into clean compartments but interweave and interact. Until the turn of the century at least, this interaction gave California a self-generating and self-contained accumulation of surplus capital that made it unnecessary to seek outside financing for the state's continuing development and growth. In and of itself, this factor separated California from the rest of the trans-Missouri states and laid substantial foundations to support the "state of mind" that is an integral part of the state's inheritance from the past.

The Anatomy
of Plenty

CALIFORNIA ALWAYS HAS BEEN deficient in the major components of the Industrial Age—coal and iron. Even today, the Fontana operation of the Kaiser Steel complex depends upon coal imported from New Mexico and Utah. Too, California is as yet lacking in the wonder element of the twentieth century—uranium. Had she had these things, the imaginary riches of Señor Montalvo's mythical island would seem even more pallid by comparison than they do.

California's climate, even when it becomes unusual enough to be classed as *weather,* has been of incalculable direct and indirect value to the state's sustained growth. From immigrants to irrigation, from citrus fruits to cinema, from astronomical observatories to space-age hardware, climate is inseparable from growth.

In John Walton Caughey's words, "Gold is the Cornerstone" of California's growth. It provided the initial thrust of human energy that overcame a millennia-long inertia, and it vitally affected our national history as well.

Agriculture may seem inseparable from the climate. But its role as a bulwark of the state's commerce and industry, coupled with the stirring saga of its transition from post-Gold Rush days to the present, warrant its separation from the climate that has made it possible.

California's timber stands gave the state a self-contained supply of basic building material that was vital to the Gold

15

A view of the California Eden—in an age
before freeways, billboards, and megalopolis.

Rush and to initial urban development. Forests today are yielding tremendous returns from the chemical utilization of wood fibers, and the state's timberlands—private, state, and federal—are vital to watershed protection and recreational facilities.

The "black gold" of petroleum gave California a self-contained basic energy source that was expanded immeasurably by the utilization of natural gas. It was particularly important to the industrial growth of Southern California, which lacked the hydroelectric energy of Northern California; and this growth was vital to that section's rise to dominance in the state's affairs today.

The state was blessed with one of the world's few major sources of quicksilver, a matter of great importance to the early mining phases. The state also is secure in a tremendous supply of cement and silicates; while clays, and borates, and building aggregates, and rare earth compounds augment its arsenal of industrial minerals.

Silver, too, belongs in the California roster of resources because of the Comstock Lode. While physically within the political boundaries of Nevada, the Comstock belonged economically to California for its productive life, and it gave the state a renewed source of surplus investment capital as the impact of the Gold Rush waned. Economic control of the Comstock had political overtones of such magnitude that it was said for many years that California was the one state possessed of four United States Senators, two of whom just happened to maintain their residences in Nevada, converting it to the largest "rotten borough" known to history.

The major resources may be categorized simply as white gold, yellow gold, green gold, and black gold, with the Comstock weaving a silver thread among their twisting strands. These treasures were present for millions of years before the technological level of the mid-nineteenth century began to unlock them. They were created by the slow evolving of the California landscape—a landscape whose features strongly affect contemporary life in the state. The story of California begins with the formation of its physical features, continues with the aboriginal inhabitants, thence leads to the Hispanic colonizers and to the penetration of Hispanic California by the "foreigners" from east of the Sierra Nevada barrier.

IN THIS AGE of supersonic intrusions upon our nearest galactic neighbors and of preoccupation with the superficial in our daily lives, we take the landforms around us for granted or, far worse, for annoyances. Our short-term successes in tinkering with our physical environment have given us the dangerous belief that we control Nature. Yet for all our technological triumphs, California remains firmly influenced by certain physical factors which we have ameliorated but which we do not as yet control and are not likely to in man's foreseeable future.

In Cenozoic time, say sixty million years past, what is now the Sierra Nevada consisted of a corrugation of troughs and basins between elevated ridges, whose tops had been so badly eroded that they were almost inconspicuous. The Pacific Ocean lapped against the western base of this massif, and the ridge crests were so low that they did not squeeze dry the moisture-laden prevailing westerly winds as they swept inland in the immemorial pattern that still governs California's rainfall. Thus, oceanic moisture was carried several hundred miles inland, permitting luxuriant vegetation in what are now the arid lands of Nevada. In this same period, an older offshore landmass, known as Cascadia, marked the location of today's "continental shelf."

During Miocene time, perhaps sixteen million years past, a pattern of upheaval, subsidence, and erosion reduced Cascadia beneath the surface. Concurrently, the Sierra Nevada was upthrust enough, say to two thousand feet, that it cut off the moisture-laden winds moving inland (the "rain shadow" effect) and began the transition of the lush areas into aridity.

In early Pleistocene time, say one and a half million years

17

OVERLEAF: *Wrinkled by time and weather, the primordial hills of the Coast Range loom above the sea throughout much of California's length.*

past, more and very marked upheaval and subsidence took place, with Lake Tahoe appearing as the most spectacular visible evidence of this faulting in the Sierra Nevada. About eight hundred thousand years before the present, John Muir's magnificent "Range of Light" assumed the basic shape it has today. Among other dramatic charms, it offers the most magnificent example of "fault-block" mountains in the nation, as seen most vividly from its eastern base in Owens Valley.

The geologic process of upheaval and subsidence still continues, with some five thousand earth shocks occurring yearly, most of them known only to those interested in seismographs. They seldom are heeded by ordinary people until some substantial ripple of the earth's crust along the San Andreas Fault, the Garlock Fault, or one of the others compels a smashed-crockery awareness. This process, too, in eons past, cleft tremendous submarine canyons offshore, one of which led directly to the creation of Port Hueneme in Ventura County.

Volcanism has been prevalent in latter Pleistocene time, the period in which we live today, and the geysers of Sonoma County are a legacy from this fiery period. They currently are being tapped for steam, which already generates enough electricity to supply almost twenty thousand two-bedroom homes. Development of this energy source is continuing apace, to meet the needs of the ever-growing conurbation north of San Francisco Bay.

A more spiritually and aesthetically refreshing legacy from the days of volcanism is the jumbled mass known to the Maidu people as *the-long-high-mountain-that-was-broken-off*, which we know as Lassen Peak. Erupting sporadically between 1914 and 1917, Lassen Peak bears the distinction of being the most recently active volcano in the forty-eight contiguous states; and the vast lava flows of northeastern California, including the Lava Beds National Monument, bear witness to its activity down the unrecorded centuries.

Lassen is the southernmost peak of the Cascade Range, and its California neighbor in this same range is Mount Shasta, which at 14,161 feet above sea level is only 335 feet lower than Mount Whitney. "Lonely as God and white as a winter moon," wrote Joaquin Miller, "Mount Shasta starts up sudden and solitary from the heart of the great black forests of Northern California." Both Lassen Peak and Mount Shasta are reminders of California's place in the "Pacific Ring of Fire," that vast, horseshoe-shaped arc that extends from New Zealand to Japan and thence to Alaska, whence it stretches down the continental length of the Pacific Coast to Cape Horn.

Pleistocene time has been dubbed "one of the most remarkable interludes in earth's history," and it includes another remarkable shaper of the California landscape in the glacial stages it encompassed. Basically, there were four glacial and interglacial stages, perhaps but three in California, and they began about one million years before the present. Our primary concern here is the last glacial stage, which began about one hundred thousand years ago and which had two main periods: the first one being its culmination and arrest about fifty-five thousand years ago, and the second being the start of the last main ice retreat, about thirty thousand years later.

Between these periods, the level of the world's seas was reduced as much as three hundred feet; there was a land bridge, probably, across Bering Strait between Asia and North America, and San Francisco Bay virtually was a dry lake. Also between these periods, Southern California had truly different flora and fauna than have been known in historic time. The bones of extinct animals that then roamed where Los Angeles' Wilshire Boulevard now lies have been recovered from the La Brea Tar Pits. Other specimens of similar animals—the dire wolf and giant jaguar among them—have been retrieved from a "dig" near Maricopa and have been dated by the carbon 14 process as belonging almost fourteen thousand years before the present. The present physical features of Yosemite Valley are also a result of the forces of the last glacial movement.

Parenthetically, it should be noted that man-caused air pollution has contributed to the warming of the earth's surface over the past decade. Should the present Greenland and

Antarctic ice sheets melt, the level of the world's seas would be raised perhaps one hundred feet, embarrassing much of coastal California. For added emphasis on the glacial epochs, it should also be noted that during the glacial stage of 325,000-225,000 years past, Death Valley contained a lake some ninety miles in length and at least 600 feet deep, while Mono Lake was about 900 feet deep during this period. The contrast with today's conditions east of the High Sierra, especially in Death Valley, dramatizes the changes wrought by geologic time and forces.

As a result of Pleistocene happenings, California today is separated by geologists and geographers into distinct geomorphic provinces. For reference purposes, these provinces are tabulated as: Sierra Nevada, Basin Ranges, Mojave Desert, Colorado Desert, Modoc Plateau, Cascade Range, Klamath Mountains, Great Valley, Coast Ranges, and Transverse Ranges. In many respects, the Sierra Nevada province is the key to California's past, present, and future.

Extending some 430 miles as California's eastern wall, and ranging from forty to eighty miles in width, the Sierra Nevada held the gold of the Mother Lode, the *Veta Madre* of the Spaniards. It held, and still holds, most of the state's vast resources of coniferous timber—the "West Sierra Pine Forest" —and is said by professional foresters to be one of the world's most favored timber-growing regions, especially in its northern reaches on the west side of the range. More important than gold or timber or recreation, the vital water-tachment section of the Sierra Nevada in normal seasons receives between 30 and 40 feet of snowfall, with more than 60 feet in peak years and a record fall of 70 feet 4 inches recorded at the hamlet of Tamarack.

These peak years occur approximately every forty-two years, with rough fourteen-year intermediate swings within this span. The last peak snowfall year was the winter of 1951-52, when the streamliner *City of San Francisco* was marooned on Donner Pass for three days; an intermediate peak rainfall season occurred in 1966-67. The value of this snowpack to

The face of geologic time: Death Valley.

agriculture in the Great Valley goes without saying, and the value of the snowpack to the ever-increasing water needs of Los Angeles and all of urban California is illustrated directly by the just-completed Oroville Dam and the whole California Water Plan. This aspect of the Sierra Nevada's importance is one that cannot be overemphasized, especially to those of us who have no other knowledge of water than that it is a substance we get out of a faucet by turning the handle.

In the Great Valley, which is comprised of the San Joaquin and Sacramento valleys, the Sutter Buttes near Marysville make a distinct contrast to the valley floor. A volcanic mass rising some twenty-one hundred feet above the surrounding farmlands, the Buttes are often called "a miniature mountain range," which they are not. They mark roughly the northern limits of what was, when the Spaniards first came, one of the continent's great wintering grounds for migratory waterfowl. From the Buttes to below Stockton to Carquinez Strait, the land was a veritable marsh during most of every winter; and early fur trappers, including the organized brigades of the Hudson's Bay Company, found sanctuary at the Buttes when life became too waterlogged elsewhere. (Federal wildlife refuges in this region today provide a haven for thousands upon thousands of migratory ducks, geese, and similar sky-farers.) In this same Hispanic period, Tulare Lake in the upper San Joaquin Valley was an immense body of water resulting from the flow of the Kern River. Down the years, it has been reclaimed for agricultural purposes, but in the unusually wet spring of 1967, even the best of man's restraining devices could not prevent the flooding of thousands of acres of this old lake bed.

The basic forces of creation gave California certain natural barriers that contributed to its isolation, even into the Jet Age. They consisted of the arid expanse between the Rocky Mountains and the Sierra Nevada; the formidable barrier of the Sierra Nevada itself; the desert wastes stretching from San Gorgonio and Cajón passes to the Colorado River and onwards into Sonora, Mexico; and the adverse winds and cur-

Following almost tidal compulsions, a sea of summer fog boils through the Golden Gate.

rents offshore that hindered sea exploration and sea transportation northward from Mexico. These same forces, which include the terrestrial sweep of Pacific winds and currents, still shape one of California's greatest assets—its climate.

IN COMMON WITH Chile, parts of southern Africa and southern Australia, as well as countries ringing the Mediterranean, much of California enjoys the dry-summer, subtropical conditions that are popularly called a "Mediterranean-type" climate. While this classification has four major subtypes within the state, we are here concerned only with the basic Mediterranean climate that affects the area containing the bulk of the state's population.

Mediterranean climates occur between 30° and 40° of latitude, either south or north, and their basic characteristics are mild winters and dry summers, with a high percentage of sunny days the year round. They are unique among the world's climates for their winter rainy season, and California's political boundaries encompass the only region in North America of summer drouth and winter rainfall. Because evaporation losses naturally are less during the winter season, these winter rains and snows are more lastingly beneficial than equal amounts in climates where precipitation occurs throughout the year.

The first requirement for this climate is the presence of a large body of water to windward, with its consequent cool, high-barometric-pressure area in summer. The Pacific High in summer generally dominates the ocean between California and Hawaii, extending well to northwards of the latitude of San Francisco. It acts as a buffer, shunting middle latitude storms toward the Pole. In winter, the ocean to our west becomes warmer than the land; the Pacific High weakens and retreats southward toward the equator, and the storm track moves south, bringing the winter rains and snows upon which California's life depends. The general effect of Cali-

The mining town of Johnsville endures a Sierran winter, ca. 1890.

*A scrub oak clings to one of the rolling hills
of the Mother Lode country.*

fornia's latitudinal length is to reduce average annual precipitation amounts from north to south along the coast: Crescent City receives 74 inches annually and San Francisco but 22 inches, while Los Angeles receives 11 inches and San Diego only 9 inches.

Air movements develop around the Pacific High and, under the influence of the earth's rotation, circulate in a clockwise direction in the Northern Hemisphere. Flowing in the same direction day after day after day, the air currents that directly affect California—the so-called "trade winds" and "prevailing westerlies"—set ocean currents in motion parallel to the air currents. This mass movement of air and water is almost beyond individual comprehension and may be approached by realizing that the great oceanic river we call the "California Current" is known in Japan as the *kurashio,* or "black current." Hence the dry-summer, subtropical climate not only experiences cool, dry winds blowing equatorwards in summer, but has a cool-water current flowing equatorwards offshore. This "cool-water coast" is the second major ingredient in the creation of a Mediterranean climate.

It is typical for the "cool-water coasts" to be enveloped in prolonged fog in summer. Relatively warm, moisture-laden oceanic air flowing shoreward is cooled as it passes over the upwelling, colder "California Current" near the land. The moisture in the air is condensed into fog, and then, as the marine air moves inland, it is warmed and reabsorbs its moisture. This phenomenon may be observed nearly any normal summer day in Northern California on Interstate Highway 80 between the Nut Tree roadside restaurant and Vallejo.

Our basic Mediterranean climate has both "coastal" and "interior" aspects. Along the coast, the cold offshore current acts as a climate-tempering device. Almost daily fog affects the daily temperatures—ask any tourist who drives across the sweltering Great Valley in July and then finds himself and family shivering an hour later on the Bay Bridge! The fog also delays the seasonal cycle by slowing the earth's warming by the sun. The characteristics of this coastal-type Mediter-

28

ranean climate are cool summer weather that reaches maximum warmth in September; mild, almost frost-free winters; and minimal temperature fluctuations.

Inland, where marine air does not easily penetrate, the temperature range is more extreme. Clear, dry summer air permits maximum sunlight penetration, and days become hot. After sunset, this same clear, dry air permits maximum heat radiation and the nights are cool by comparison with the days; a drop of thirty degrees after sunset is not uncommon. Frost is frequent in winter, the growing season is shorter, and rainfall is less than along the coast.

The usual differences between coastal and interior Mediterranean climate types are greater and more evident in the central portions of the Great Valley. This intensification is due to the existence of the Coast Range, which virtually bars the movement of marine air into the interior except through the "wind gap" of Carquinez Strait, where the waters of the Sacramento and San Joaquin rivers enter San Francisco Bay. Engineers have estimated that shaving some hundreds of feet off the tops of the Coast Range ridges east of Richmond, Berkeley, and Oakland would change quite drastically the climate of the central Great Valley, and require a momentous shift in its agricultural economy. Thus we introduce the third major ingredient affecting California's climate—the mountains that bound the Great Valley.

Mountains make excellent moisture catchers, because their ascending slopes and summits are cooler than the valley or seacoast below. As masses of warm, moist air are pushed up the slopes of these mountains by storms, the air is cooled and its moisture content is precipitated in the form of rain or snow —a squeezing process like wringing out a sponge. After the storm mass has been relieved of its moisture and pushed over the mountains, its air then warms rapidly as it drops down the other side. Precipitation falls sharply, and the warmed air, as it expands, may even absorb existing moisture from the ground over which it passes. The resultant dry areas in the lee of the mountains are called "rain shadow" areas, and

California has them on the east side of all its mountain ranges. The pattern of rain shadow and squeezing is graphically demonstrated by the fact that Coalinga must haul its potable water from elsewhere, while Fresno just across the valley receives 12 inches annually; Blue Canyon on the ascending Sierran slope gets 60 inches annually, while Owens Valley is lucky to have 8 inches, and the Mojave Desert rejoices over but 2 inches.

Because of the normal storm track pattern out of the North Pacific, the rain shadow area in the Sacramento Valley is less arid than the rain shadow area of the western San Joaquin Valley. The rain shadow east of the Sierra is most pronounced in the Mono Basin-Owens Valley country, simply because the Sierra Nevada has higher elevations as you come down its crest from north to south.

It should be noted here that both the Los Angeles Lowlands —to use geographers' terminology—and the San Diego area have distinct variants of the basic Mediterranean climate. San Diego's is classified as "fog desert," wherein the scanty annual precipitation is compensated for in part by persistent fogs. The Los Angeles Lowlands, owing to their mountain-girt location, suffer an air-inversion pattern which makes itself felt in recurrent "smog alerts." Both regions endure sporadic invasions of air masses from the deserts to the east, which are most hazardous in the Los Angeles Lowlands.

Meteorologists do not fully understand why at times a tremendous mass of dry air becomes stalled above the Great Basin between the Rocky Mountains and the Sierra Nevada. It forms a stationary dome of high barometric pressure that may last for several days before collapsing with a tremendous surge in an inexorable search for a lower-pressure area. The towering barrier of the Sierra Nevada forces this collapsing mass southwestward towards the lower mountains that separate it from a low-pressure trough off the coast of Southern California.

This desert air is pushed through the mountain passes and across the Los Angeles Lowlands, where it is known as the

"And I brought you into a plentiful country, to eat the fruit thereof, and the goodness thereof . . ." Above, a barn and outbuildings near Santa Cruz. Below, cattle grazing in San Benito County.

"Santa Ana" because it rushes down Santa Ana Canyon at speeds up to one hundred miles per hour. As the air mass moves downward, it is heated and compressed, gaining five degrees for every thousand feet of descent. Humidity readings in the Lowlands have reached as low as 1 percent; this factor, plus the velocity of the Santa Ana, explains the horrendous fire damage that often results. This is a high price to pay for the fact that the Santa Ana does sweep away the smog shroud from the Lowlands.

Similar winds from similar causes are known as the *foehn* in Austria and Germany, as the *chinook* in Montana and Wyoming, and as the *khamsin* in Israel. Wherever they occur, by whatever name they are known, such winds have been charged with accentuating asthma, increasing high blood pressure, magnifying irrational behavior, and stimulating suicides, general lassitude, and crimes of passion. The behavior of freeway traffic while a Santa Ana is buffeting the Southland seems to support these charges. A similar equalization of tremendous barometric pressure differentials afflicts the Great Valley, albeit less dramatically than does the Santa Ana. This results in a parching, gusty north wind that seems to turn plums into prunes on the tree in just one day.

The climate of central and northern California holds the key to both the state's present level of development and its future prospects, simply because past, present, and future have been, are, and will be concerned most urgently with water. Today, as for a half-century past, San Francisco is dependent upon the Sierra Nevada for its water of life, which comes from Hetch Hetchy Valley, north of Yosemite, via aqueduct to San Francisco's peninsular appendage. The burgeoning East Bay conurbation draws its water requirements from Pardee Dam on the Mokelumne River. The City and County of Los Angeles would not, because it could not, have grown above five hundred thousand persons without Sierra Nevada water from Owens Valley; and subsequent growth required the Hoover Dam Project on the Colorado River. California agriculture, with its "Peach Bowl," and "Rice Bowl,"

The plentiful country is also earthquake country. In 1906, the
heaving earth ruptured San Francisco's Union Street (above);
in 1933, it disintegrated buildings in Compton (below).

and "Salad Bowl," aspects, has grown by the grace of water from the Sierra Nevada. Now California has lost, although the loss has not yet been felt, a sizable amount of Colorado River water to Arizona, and the Sierra Nevada has already been tapped for its major contributions to California's water needs. What now?

One more internally controlled major source of surplus water remains to California; and even as the Sierra Nevada, it stems from the evolution of the California landscape. California's North Coast region, which stretches from San Francisco to the Oregon border, between the main Coast Range massif and the sea, annually receives about 41 percent of the state's total natural water supply—a total that has been estimated at 71,000,000 acre-feet per annum. It should be understood that one acre-foot of water comprises 330,000 gallons, which will flush approximately 60,000 suburban toilets simultaneously. The North Coast region uses a miniscule portion of what it receives today, and most of this largesse flows unchecked and unused into the sea. Under the ultimate optimal development foreseen for the region, it will require not more than 4 percent of all the water consumed in California.

The first step in saving this presently wasted water has already been taken on the headwaters of the Trinity River, with the Lewiston-Whiskeytown dam-and-tunnel complex, which diverts water through the Coast Range into the Sacramento River for ultimate use along the west side of the San Joaquin Valley and in Southern California. The next steps in utilizing the surplus waters of the North Coast region require the damming and diverting of the waters of the Eel and Russian rivers in the same manner.

A summary of the effect upon California's water resources of its physical geography makes a simple equation: north of Sacramento two-thirds of our rainfall blesses one-third of our land mass; south of Sacramento two-thirds of our people receive one-third of our rainfall. This natural maldistribution explains more clearly than any political oratory the interdependence of the state's sections, inasmuch as the area south of

Sacramento, primarily because of the urban complex in Southern California, furnishes the major portion of the state's taxes. Herein is found the taproot of the conflict between urban needs and agricultural needs, between megalopolis and "cow county," in developing water allocations within the state.

Desalination of ocean water is one possible answer to supplying Southern California's needs without exhausting the northern water supply. A major plant for this purpose is in the planning stage, to be constructed at Huntington Beach by a consortium of private utility companies and the federal government. The widespread popular view of desalination as the millennial answer to California's water problems, upon which its future growth depends, is open to question because of the enormous costs and ecological factors involved.

California's future growth, even if at a lesser rate than in the past, depends upon the zealous protection of its watersheds, coupled with the procurement of outside water resources. The latter already has gone far beyond any local, or state, or even interstate solution. It is a national matter, and will be discussed more fully in the chapter on the growth of Southern California in general and Los Angeles in particular —a growth that is the most significant historical, political, economic, and cultural development in the saga of California in this century.

California's First Immigrants

CALIFORNIA'S TREASURE TROVE of resources demanded an industrial technology to unlock them that was not possessed by her first human inhabitants and her first in-migrants, the California Indians. Passive in all its potential plenty, the environment we have described made no demands upon them; neither did it impose obstacles. Nature was passive and man was the determinant. And in California the first humans responded to this passivity with passivity in themselves. Lo, the poor Indian of California! Rarely ever has a good word been said about him, and in all candor it must be admitted that the California Indians were culturally backward—cultural laggards if you like.

They lacked the dash and derring-do of the Cheyenne, and Comanche, and Sioux; they were without the fierce cruelty and political organization of the Iroquoian peoples of the eastern woodlands; the Hopi and Zuñi of the Southwest were far above them in social organization and cultural accomplishments. Between the Indians of California and the Mayan and Aztec civilizations, the cultural, social, and political gulf yawns gapingly. Yet these people had a harmony with, and a stability within, their environment that would stand modern man in good stead.

To the Indian of California, he and all the plants and animals around him were members of the same one world; each and all were a part of nature. When he came to the inexplicable in this natural world, he did precisely what man has

37

Portrait of a Pomo Indian.

always done: he invented myths and legends to explain the inexplicable, so that he and all the unknowns all about him could live harmoniously together. Perhaps this mystico-religious structure, which kept intact the psychic envelope of being, explains the lag in material cultural accomplishments.

Given the ethnic writhings in the nation's viscera today, it may be impolitic to present the California Indians as they actually were. Compounding the problem of presenting them in their true light, without malice or rancor but in the pursuit of ethno-historical truth, is the hard matter of myth. Every American Indian—come hell, high water, or the Immaculate Conception—is too often pictured riding an ear-notched war pony, wearing a double-tailed, eagle-feather war bonnet, and living in a skin tipi surrounded by herds of buffalo. We simply have to face the facts that there were no horses, as we know them, in California until the Spanish arrived in 1769. There were no buffalo in California in historic time; and the pre-historic mammals were gone, as far as we know, before the first human wanderers came across from Asia.

Depending upon what anthropologist you hear or what book you read, the erratic migrations out of Asia to North America range from 10,000 to 40,000 years past. Sometime during the last glacial stage, probably between 55,000 and 25,000 years ago, small bands of nomadic hunters came by way of Bering Strait, either on a land bridge caused by glacial with-drawal of water, or on an ice bridge, or by paddling crude rafts between closely situated islands. The date at which the first of these immigrants entered California is moot, to say the least. Shell mounds around San Francisco Bay indicate, through carbon dating, that inhabitants were there at least three thousand to four thousand years ago.

What is regarded as the most reliable estimate of their number—and it *is* an estimate—places the total number of Indians in California at about one hundred fifty thousand when the Spanish first encountered them. Some current esti-mates increase this number to exceed two hundred thousand. Whatever figure is used, California was one of the most

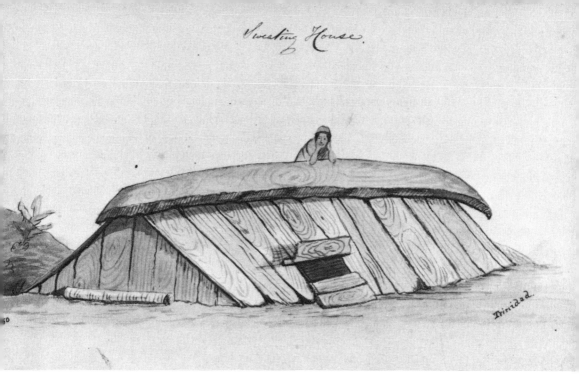

(Above): Long before Americans began to install Finnish Sauna baths in split-level homes, the communal sweat house was common to the cultures of many northern California "tribelets." (Below): An Indian house near Trinidad Bay.

densely populated Indian areas in the entire North American continent north of Mexico, with perhaps four times the human density per square mile of any other aboriginal population in what is now the United States.

Diversity is the key word to remember about the Indians of California. Their total population, about enough to fill two college football stadiums today, spoke 135 dialects of some twenty basic linguistic families—language grouping being the commonly accepted means of classifying the "Amerinds." Thus, we have about one thousand human beings, on an average, sharing a common dialect. Communication between these linguistic fragments was about as difficult as it might have been between a Greek of Periclean Athens and a courtier of Kublai Khan.

The usual Indian village, or *ranchería* in Spanish idiom, contained about 130 persons. The method of constructing dwellings varied as widely as did their dialectical differences. The Karok along the Klamath River made houses of crudely split planks, using stone axes and elk-horn chisels to cleave the redwood, which runs true to its grain for many lineal feet at a stretch. The Maidu in the Sacramento Valley made houses sunk half into the earth with a thatched framework above-ground. The Cahuilleño people of the southeastern deserts made a crude wickiup, little more than a windbreak. This diversity in shelters was repeated in differences of dress, customs, and artifacts.

The words "tribe" and "chief" are to be used sparingly, if at all, in relation to these peoples. Perhaps the Mojave along the Colorado River near Needles, Arizona, were the only ones to whom the political connotation of "tribe" could be applied. The numerous bands of the Yokuts in the San Joaquin Valley also had a proper tribal structure based upon a common clan, or totemic name, but the word "tribelets" seems more appropriate for the various dialectic groups.

Each tribelet shared a common dialect and a common geographical use territory, or range. This use territory usually was so circumscribed that an individual could be born, live his allotted span, and die without ever leaving the boundaries of his tribelet's use range, perhaps as much as one hundred square miles. One Indian woman moved at least eight times during her life-span of more than sixty years and yet stayed within an area six miles in diameter. Socially and economically, the tribelets were self-sufficient, and whatever warfare occurred between them generally stemmed from trespass upon one another's use range to hunt, or fish, or gather seeds and acorns. Such trespass, or food stealing, was serious inasmuch as the exigencies of life within the ancestral territory did not permit the luxury of sharing its productive capacity with outsiders.

With all their diversities, the naturally fragmented California Indians had certain common characteristics. They were a Stone Age people, who did not have the wheel, or beasts of burden, or written records. They all were hunters and gatherers, except on the borders of California along the lower Colorado River, where both the Yuma and the Mojave Indians were flood-plain agriculturists. Most of them practiced a crude form of public sanitation by the simple expedient of leaving their fouled dwellings when they became too noisome, often burning them, and then constructing new dwellings within their territory. The use of the *temescal,* or sweathouse, was widespread, and many of the first Californians bathed each day, which was far more frequently than European or white-American custom dictated for many and many a year.

The California Indians by and large made superior baskets, the Pomo of Lake County excelling in this craft; and this skill in basketry is advanced as one reason for the lack of any skill at all in pottery-making. Another reason offered is the absence of suitable kaolin which their level of technology could employ. The Chumash of the Santa Barbara Channel made seagoing canoes out of split planks caulked with asphaltum, and the Yurok and Karok of the Trinity-Klamath river complex made dugout canoes by fire-hollowing windfall tree trunks.

A complex system of mystico-religious cults was widespread, and Jimsonweed and wild tobacco were the counter-

parts of today's cultist fascination with LSD and "pot." Their religious leaders were shamans, individuals with a personal pipeline to their pantheon of supernaturals, who cured disease by dancing and incantations, and by feats of sleight of hand. The greatest cultural accomplishment, perhaps, was the widespread use of acorns as a dietary staple, those from the foothill species of oaks being favored over those from the Great Valley's grasslands. This involved the leaching-out of the tannic acid in the acorns, which boasted a fat content that gave acorn mush or cakes a high caloric value. It may be said that the lowly acorn was indeed the corn-bean-squash of the California Indians.

Within a tribelet's use territory, the land generally provided its hunting-and-gathering culture with abundance: salmon and trout in the streams, sky-darkening flocks of waterfowl, acorns, grass seeds, grasshoppers, the larva of flies and insects, stately elk if they were lucky, fleet antelope if they were luckier, and grizzly bears so numerous as to be a daily hazard. Only rarely did the Indians tackle "Old Ephraim," and then generally when he was found asleep. They then would ring the sleeping monster with fire and arrow him to death.

With such natural largesse in all save abnormal years, the land made no demands upon them and imposed no obstacles. Why seek "progress" such as agriculture when for millenia your ancestral people had been able to survive, generally at a comfortable subsistence level, simply by harvesting what Nature provided in her seasons? It has been suggested that California's physical environment, rather than cultural forces, inhibited the adoption of agriculture by the Indians. This suggestion holds that the winter rain-summer drouth pattern would not permit the introduction of crops from the lower Colorado River agricultural complex. My own feeling is that the beneficent environment of California did not present a challenge requiring such an innovative response.

Another factor in the culture lag was the isolation imposed by the desert and mountain barriers. It should be remembered, however, that the California Indians did not know

43

The architecture of a life reduced to comfortable simplicities: the interior of a Maidu lodge in the Sacramento Valley. OVERLEAF: *A sweat house of the Peewan Klamath.*

that they were isolated. It is known that the Paiute of Owens Valley raided the Chumash of the Santa Barbara Channel, and that the Washo of the Lake Tahoe region traded pine nuts with the tribelets of the Great Valley. These contacts produced no measurable cultural explosion, simply because all of those involved were at the same general level of accomplishment.

By and large, the Indians of California were short and squat, flat-nosed, broad-faced, and roundheaded. They did not practice scalping as an indigenous custom, or human sacrifice, or torture. Only the lower Colorado River peoples had a specific war weapon in the form of a club. Slavery based upon debt was practiced along California's northwest coast; and the Modoc of extreme northeastern California were slave raiders for profit; trading their captives into the trade route that ran northward east of the Cascade Range to Celilo Falls on the Columbia River. With these exceptions, the California Indians did not wage aggressive warfare; and none of them rode horses, or lived in skin tipis, or wore flowing feather bonnets, or hunted the buffalo. And it should be pointed out that there is no such thing as a "Digger" Indian. The word is a derisive epithet to be shunned.

Spain's contacts with these people were confined, as were her settlements, to the coastal strip between Napa-Sonoma and San Diego. Some thirty-one thousand more-or-less Christianized Indians were said to be in the care of the missions in 1834, the year that the missions were secularized (disbanded). There is no record of how many Indian lives were lost during smallpox epidemics in 1827-28 and 1837-39. Another disease, believed to have been malaria, killed an estimated thirty thousand Indians in the Great Valley between 1832-33. The full force of the Gold Rush influx fell upon those peoples who had been beyond Spanish or Mexican influence or control. The impact was made more brutal by the fact that the California Indians did not have the cultural level to provide a cushion against the arrival of tens of thousands of gold-seekers bearing the Industrial Age.

46

A Yokuts Indian woman.

The human warmth of the history of the California Indian is learned best perhaps through the story of Ishi, the last of the Yahi, who were a subgroup of the Yana tribelet that ranged the foothills east of Red Bluff. Ishi, about fifty years of age and still living in the Stone Age, was captured in the corral of a slaughterhouse near Oroville, California, in 1911.

During the next five years, until his death from tuberculosis in 1916, he was a ward of the University of California, working as a janitor at the University of California Hospital in San Francisco. The great story in his life, its urgent message to modern man, is the manner in which he made the transition from his Stone Age milieu into the twentieth century, for he made it with great dignity and unafraid. This was the aspect I stressed in a brief telling of his story for the American Museum of Natural History in 1948. A full-scale treatment of his life, *Ishi in Two Worlds,* appeared several years ago, written by Mrs. Theodora Kroeber, widow of the distinguished anthropologist A. L. Kroeber, and is well worth your reading.

Today, the most tangible legacy from the California Indians to mark their long existence here is found in place names, including those of nine California counties: Colusa, Modoc, Mono, Napa, Shasta, Tehama, Tuolumne, Yolo, and Yuba. An intangible legacy surrounds Mount Rubidoux in Southern California, which is said to have been sacred to the peoples of the San Gabriel Valley as their altar to the Sun, which gave their whole world life. The first Easter sunrise service in Southern California made its joyous way to the summit of Mount Rubidoux on Easter Sunday, 1909.

The social, political, and linguistic fragmentation of the California Indians prevented their making any unified or sustained opposition to Spain's penetration and settlement. Their lack of cultural skills, including that of applied homicide, also worked in Spain's favor. Evidence of this is to be found in the fact that the total strength of Spain's military forces, to protect the province from Napa-Sonoma to San Diego, often fell below one hundred soldiers.

On the other side of the coin, the Indians' ability to absorb simple instructions, to learn and to execute the basic tasks associated with the society that Spain transplanted to California, made them the basic labor force upon which Spain's colonization was built. In appraising the Indians' role in the three phases of the Europeanization of California, it may be said that they were vital to Spain, useful to Mexico, and an annoyance to the United States. For the record, it seems worth noting that the United States has reimbursed the California Indians in the amount of some forty million dollars for the lands they lost. Those of Indian descent eligible to share in this reimbursement numbered about thirty-three thousand. So far as is known, neither Spain nor Mexico has even considered such reimbursement for their acquisition of land in California. Irrespective of this fact, it must stand that without *los Indios* Spain would have been unable to transform California into the isolated outpost of empire on the very "Rim of Christendom" that it became.

Spain's
Farthest North

ALTA CALIFORNIA made a final sunburst of accomplishment in the deepening twilight of Spain's imperial glory. Two and a half centuries elapsed between the beginning of Cortés' conquest of Mexico and the raising of Spain's brilliant banners above the site of San Diego in 1769. Interestingly enough, these same banners had been raised over what became Santa Fé, New Mexico, between 1598 and 1606. When one considers that California was admitted to the Union in 1850, sixty-two years before this same privilege was accorded the Territory of New Mexico, the impact of the Gold Rush upon California's destiny becomes apparent.

By 1540, less than twenty years after Cortés had conquered Mexico, Spanish mariners had sailed to the head of the Gulf of California, and one of them had ventured some distance up the turbulent Colorado River. In 1542, Joao Rodriguéz Cabrilho (a Portuguese, which fact irks Hispanophiles, who have changed his name to the Spanish *Juan Cabrillo*), set forth on a voyage of discovery from Navidad, a vanished port which in its glory days lay about twenty miles up the coast from the present-day city of Manzanillo, Mexico.

He discovered and landed at San Diego Bay and battled the adverse winds and currents as far north as Monterey Bay before turning back to Cuyler's Harbor on San Miguel Island, off Santa Barbara. There he died from a fall and was buried about January 3, 1543. His successor, a Levantine named

The bells of Mission San Gabriel, 1897.

Ferrelo, resumed the voyage northwards to about Cape Mendocino before turning back for Navidad. Spain's northward voyages from Navidad—then from Acapulco, and then from San Blás—took between thirty-five and fifty days against the winds and currents. Rolling home before the prevailing winds and with the currents, the voyage consumed only about one-third of this time.

It should be remembered that these ships were not the *Queen Mary* nor yet the *Lurline*. They were built on the west coast of Mexico from native timber, designed in accordance with marine architecture then prevalent, which called for three feet of length to one of beam. Thus, a vessel sixty feet long would be about twenty feet wide at the waist. Ships were undecked for the most part, sat low in the water, combined square and lateen sails, and generally were unhandy, and uncomfortable, and all too often, unsound. The galleon type of vessel, of course, was larger and relatively more comfortable and more seaworthy.

In 1565 a monk-turned-mariner, Urdaneta, pioneered the round trip from Acapulco to Manila. Thereafter, Spain's artery of communication with Manila pulsed via the Atlantic and Caribbean to Vera Cruz, thence by a Royal road across Mexico to Acapulco, and thence across the lone leagues of sea to Manila. On the return voyage—the *tornaviaje*—Spain's galleons utilized the wind and current pattern of the North Pacific to raise the North American mainland at about Cape Mendocino and then roll down the offshore swells to Mexico.

The "master thief of the unknown world," the not-yet-knighted Francis Drake, appeared on the California coast in July, 1579, seeking what he might appropriate, and he did rather well. He also gave England its first knowledge as to the approximate width of North America, and when the Virginia (London) Company was given its charter, it was granted land all the way to the Pacific. The controversy over Drake's alleged landing place on the California coast still rages with subdued ferocity among certain scholars. It appears safe, however, to accept it as the present Drake's Bay,

"By the grace of God and in the name of Her
Majesty Queen Elizabeth of England . . ."
Francis Drake's plate of brass, 1579.

north of San Francisco, and to accept the "plate of brasse" that Drake affixed to a "greate poste" above the beach to claim the land for England as New Albion.

The need for a safe harbor on the California coast, where "the lonely horror that was the Manila galleon" could obtain fresh water and anything that would combat the ravages of scurvy, brought about the next Spanish contact. This occurred in 1587 when Unamuño anchored in today's Morro Bay, near San Luis Obispo, and explored a short distance inland. This resulted in the first known skirmish between Europeans and California Indians, the first opening of the time capsule that contained the conflict between Stone and Iron.

In 1595 a Manila galleon under the command of Sebastián Cermeño, a Portuguese merchant-adventurer in Spain's service, was exploring the California coastline on its home-ward voyage when it was wrecked near Point Reyes. In a superb feat of seamanship, Cermeño and his survivors sailed a small open boat to Acapulco, continuing coastal explorations as they went. The loss of the galleon and its cargo put an end to using these vessels for coastwise probings, probably to the great relief of Spain's mariners.

In 1602 Sebastián Vizcaíno, a Basque, rediscovered San Diego Bay and gave it the name it bears today. He then voyaged northward, giving the names we now use to many of the points and headlands that he passed. He rediscovered Monterey Bay and described it with such exaggeration, as a fine harbor, that when Portolá viewed it more than a century later he was unable to recognize it from Vizcaíno's description. For all practical purposes, Vizcaíno's voyage ended Spains efforts to establish a place of succor for the Manila galleon on the California coast. There are no known voyages thereafter until the settlement of San Diego in 1769. The best explanation for this hiatus is the morass of problems, both at home and in the New World, in which Spain found herself, coupled with a slow but steady rundown of her imperial energy under the Hapsburgs.

The hazards of sea voyages northward from the west coast

of Mexico have been demonstrated. The exploring vessels, as well as the Manila galleon, often returned home with half their crews dead and the other half so weak from scurvy as to be unable to stand on deck. These difficulties—and the word seems inadequate at best—operated throughout the age of sail, although the toll from scurvy was later reduced by the use of citrus fruits and juices.

The other isolating barrier, the Colorado and Sonoran deserts, began to be breached in 1691 when Fray Eusebio Kino commenced his years of missionary labors in *Pimería Alta*, which included present-day southern Arizona, that ended with his death in 1711. Kino was a Jesuit, and that order was expelled from the New World by order of the Crown in 1767. Kino's pioneer work in unlocking the geography of the deserts, however, was carried on in 1768 by Fray Francisco Garcés, a Franciscan, and it was on their findings that Juan Bautista de Anza built when he established an overland route from Sonora to California in 1774-76. This was done after Spain became suddenly galvanized into action regarding California, an action stemming from dramatic international developments.

In 1740-42, Vitus Bering, a Dane in the service of the Russian government, began his voyages from Siberia toward Alaska and the Arctic. In 1763 as a result of the Seven Years War in Europe, for which the great French and Indian War in America was the trigger, England replaced France as master of the eastern Mississippi River Valley. Thus, despite her possession of Texas and French Louisiana—a buffer against England in physical mass only—Spain was in danger of having her New World empire outflanked on both the northeast and the northwest. This threat loomed at a time when Carlos III was seeking valiantly to revivify Spain's fading glory. Pursuant to his instructions, the Viceroy in Mexico organized an expedition to colonize California.

The entire colonial party—both the two groups by land and the vessels by sea—was under the general command of Gaspar de Portolá. Fray Junípero Serra, a Franciscan who was chap-

lain of the land expedition, was charged with overseeing the
establishment of religious activities in the new colony. However, so strong has been the religious motif in the writing and
teaching of California history that poor old Portolá, a brave
man, competent and loyal, has been frequently overshadowed
by Fray Serra. Certainly, the mission role in establishing
Spain's farthest north settlement in the New World, can
hardly be overstated, but it was Portolá who was the overall
commander of the first expedition.

Spain's plan of settlement for California essentially was a
plan tested and proven effective on Spain's frontier in Mexico.
It rested upon three legs, each with its own special function—
the "presidio," the "mission," and the "pueblo."

The presidio was the military leg and comprised the fort
or garrison. Its function was to defend California against
external aggression, to quell Indian uprisings, and to suppress
civil insurrections should such occur. Spain's presidios were
established at Monterey, San Francisco, Santa Barbara, and
San Diego, and military towns grew up around them in time.
Each of these presidios fought a losing battle against apathy
and the elements under both Spain and Mexico, and that at
San Francisco boasts the distinction of never having had a
shot fired in anger from its batteries to this day.

The mission was the religious leg of the tripod of settlement.
Its functions were to convert the heathen *Indios* and train
them in useful skills; about 55,000 converts is the estimated
harvest from Franciscan labors during the heyday of the missions. The missions also became the granary of the province,
thus freeing the presidial forces for their primary defense
functions, which included protecting the missions and en-
forcing discipline in cases which the religious could not
handle. Civilian towns grew up around the mission nucleus
at San Luis Obispo, Sonoma, San Juan Bautista and San Juan
Capistrano.

Mission Santa Barbara has been in the hands of the Franciscans since its founding, and is the *only* one continuously
in use for religious services despite earthquakes, uprisings,

and revolutions. Santa Barbara is also distinctive in that it reflects the earliest phase of Spanish Renaissance architecture and thus differs from the exuberant and lavishly ornamented *churrigueresque* of Old Mexico, which is said to have influenced the general mission style. The latter style influenced the design of the buildings for the San Diego Exposition of 1915 and spread from there into general California use between the world wars.

The *campo santo* at Mission Santa Barbara contains some four thousand graves of Indians, and has led to charges that the Franciscans were guilty of coercion, brutality, and genocide. The record of history disproves these charges. There never were enough Franciscans, even reinforced by soldiers, to coerce the Indian population of California in such a manner as charged, let alone to practice genocide, which was in all truth contrary to the teachings of the Church of both Franciscan and soldier. Smallpox took a heavy toll, as did the dread strangling of diphtheria *(el garrotillo)*. Perhaps even more deaths were caused by the lack of even such primitive sanitation methods as the Indians had practiced in moving and burning their houses at sporadic intervals, which were not possible in the fixed abodes of the missions.

The pueblo was the civil leg of the tripod, designed to attract civilian colonists. Each pueblo was granted four square leagues of land—about 17,600 acres—with which to provide its residents with homes, garden plots, and common grazing grounds. Only two true pueblos became operational in California: San Jose and Los Angeles. A third, Branciforte, was contemplated near present-day Santa Cruz, but it did not materialize as a functional civic unit. Other pueblos grew up around both presidios and missions, and were granted lands as noted above; but these pueblos were outgrowths of the initial nuclei of settlement provided by presidio and mission, and were not originally established as parts of the civil leg of Spain's plan.

Founded as a pueblo on November 29, 1777, the city of San Jose is the oldest continuously inhabited civilian community in the state. Its initial settlers were nine *soldados*, five *pobladores* (settlers) with their families, and one *vaquero*. Every settler was given two each of cows, oxen, mules, sheep, and goats, plus some seeds and crude farming implements, and was promised the equivalent of ten dollars per month for the first two years of residence. It was a notably independent community, exemplified by the fact that its citizens did not recognize Mexico's independence from Spain until May 10, 1825, three years after the formal act of allegiance to Mexico had been taken by the Spanish government of California. Prickly with independence though it was, San Jose's European population grew slowly, numbering but 524 persons by 1831.

This growth rate supports the statement that the mission was the most effective and certainly the most important segment of civilization in California during the Spanish regime, 1769–1821. The mission complex not only became the granary of the province but served as the educational center, the religious center, and the cultural center. The mission chain also became the main arm of Spanish expansion in California. It has been said too often in California history that the missions were established a day's horseback ride apart. They came to be about this distance apart, given a good horse and a durable seat, but the dates and locations of their foundings show clearly that they were not a day's ride apart in the beginning. The missions were established where there were Indians, and the Indians were found where natural conditions were most favorable for their way of life. In this indirect way, perhaps, the Indians of California laid the base for many of the state's modern coastal communities.

Out of the twenty-one missions in California, only one, Sonoma, was founded during the Mexican regime, 1822–46; all the rest were born under Spain. All of the missions were established by the Franciscan order, and from its beginnings until final secularization in 1834, the mission record is one of friction between the Franciscans and the military. The friars felt that the soldiers corrupted their converts, and the military

Inner court of Mission San Juan Capistrano, 1900.

felt that the religious encouraged their charges to be insubordinate to military authority. Mission San Diego was moved five miles from its original site to escape the pernicious influence of the garrison troops, and Mission San Carlos Borromeo was moved from Monterey to the Carmel Valley for the same reason.

Added to the basic friction was a matter of practical economics. While Spain was willing to make the down payment of men and materials to establish the first settlement of California, she did not make the subsequent installments that might have made California what she intended it to become: a sturdy defense bastion on the northwest flank of her New World empire. Until the missions attained adequate food production, about 1780, the struggling colony was dependent upon supply ships from Mexico. These often were long delayed by the hazards of navigation; many were lost at sea, and there were times when the infant colony was on the brink of starvation. Dependence upon maritime communication forced the search for an overland route between California and Spain's outposts in northern Sonora, and this is where De Anza built upon the desert explorations of Fray Kino and Fray Garcés.

In 1774–75 De Anza blazed an overland trail from Sonora to Mission San Gabriel, near Los Angeles, and used it in 1775–76 to lead 240 colonists (of whom 166 were women and children) and livestock to California. This movement resulted in the founding of San Francisco around Mission Dolores and of the Presidio of San Francisco, although it is worth noting that De Anza himself did not actually select the precise presidial site. De Anza's journey must rank as one of the epic feats of travel on this continent, if for no other reason than that he arrived in California with more people than had left Sonora: births along the way more than offset the few deaths. The first white child born in California, Salvador Ignacio Linares, arrived on Christmas Eve, 1775, while the expedition was encamped at Coyote Canyon in today's Riverside County.

The key to the overland route was the Yuma Crossing of

the Colorado River, for as long as the Yuma Indians remained friendly, the crossing was usable. However, relations between Spaniard and Yuman worsened. In 1787 the Yuma warriors, jealous of their gardens and their women, wiped out the Spanish garrison and missionaries at the crossing and closed the overland link with California for many years. This step apparently had a most deleterious effect upon Spain's ability to reinforce the California colony with civilian settlers. For the rest of California's period of control by both Spain and Mexico, its stoutest lifeline with, and window upon, the outside world was the sea.

Dependence upon the sea, coupled with the availability of substantial Indian populations along the coast and accentuated by the lack of population pressures owing to the lack of colonists, explain why neither Spain nor Mexico expanded its perimeter of settlement inland. There simply was no compelling pressure to do so.

The Franciscans, zealous in the quest for souls to be saved, did make many journeys into the San Joaquin Valley seeking possible mission sites. Several such seem to have been selected where the Indian populations promised a harvest of souls and a source of labor, but no missions ever were established within the Great Valley. The present-day community of Los Banos acquired its name from Fray Arroyo de la Cuesta's habit of bathing himself there on his journeys from San Juan Bautista over Pacheco Pass to the valley. Impoundment behind the great San Luis Dam, latest link (1968) in the state's master water plan to slake Southern California's thirst, now hides the sturdy friar's bathing pool.

After the closing of the overland route from Mexico, the main source of civilian colonists was provided by several hundred ex-convicts from Mexico and discharged soldiers from the military garrisons, many of whom found wives among the Indian converts of the missions. Richard Henry Dana would note in later years that one drop of Spanish blood carried with it all the rights and privileges of Spanish subjects—and these were few enough by modern standards of

OVERLEAF: *Mission San Luis Rey in about 1890—a disintegrating remnant of Spanish empire on the "rim of Christendom."*

civil rights. The rate and quality of growth in Spanish California is eloquently portrayed by the fact that in 1820 the colony's total European population approximated 3,720 persons, including thirteen "foreigners," meaning non-Spanish.

Another reason for slow growth was the lack of any real economic incentive for individual free enterprise in Spanish California. The government in Mexico controlled all trade, and it forbade commercial intercourse with vessels of other countries. California's internal market for agricultural produce was the presidios and pueblos, and here the individual had to compete with mission production as well as with fixed prices established by the government. All imported goods were subject to this same price-fixing and regulation. So, under Spain, the residents of California were bound by rigid controls that provided no reward for individual economic initiative.

It must be remembered, too, that down all its days under both Spain and Mexico, California had no manufacturing, save simple handcrafts. The *Californio* was dependent upon importation for all the survival artifacts of western civilization: knives and axes, forks and spoons; soft cloth that did not scratch as did the home-loomed product; coffee and tobacco, salt and pepper, and the cones of hard sugar called *panocha*; mission bells, altar cloths, and priestly vestments; fireworks for *fiestas*, wine, and rum—everything that was needed came from outside, except for the basic, and limited, foodstuffs and rather rudimentary handcraft manufactures. It is not surprising, then, that smuggling by foreign vessels became common during Spain's tenure, and that under Mexico it changed to venal conniving with officialdom. It is in this context that the United States' maritime trade with California, immortalized in Richard Henry Dana's *Two Years Before the Mast*, must be considered.

Here it is well to dispose of another rampant figment of California mythology: the Spanish land grants. During Spain's entire tenure, less than twenty-five grants of land were made by the Crown to individuals, the bulk of them being in Southern California around Los Angeles and San Diego. Of the almost eight hundred land grants that were adjudicated by the United States after its acquisition of California, the overwhelming majority were made by Mexico between 1822 and 1846; and the preponderance of Mexican grants was made after the secularization of the missions in 1834. It should be noted here that grants of land by the Crown to the missions were not made to the Church per se. Rather, they were grants to be held in trust until such time as the Indians had been converted and trained in the simple survival tasks and skills of a feudal society. Then these lands were to be given to the Indians for their own subsistence. In this context the oft-made statement that the missions were despoiled of their rightful property by secularization falls apart.

In essence, Spain transplanted a feudal society to the beneficent wilderness that was California. It was a society lacking completely in the technology necessary to unlock California's resources, although if the placer (surface) gold that caused the Gold Rush had been found in the Spanish period, the mission dwellers could have handled it quite well. It was a society with agricultural techniques of the most primitive kind, a society without internal banking or commerce, and one lacking in the arts, in communications, and in libraries, to say nothing of schools as we know them.

In a very real sense, the following twenty-four years as a province of Mexico did little to change the basic nature of California's society, although at least one aspect of it was expanded greatly.

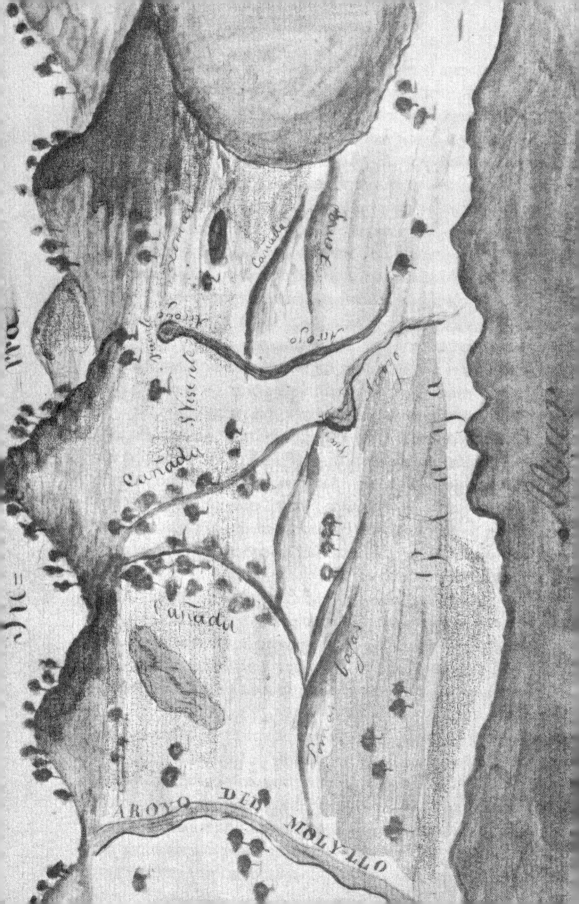

Ay! Ranchero!

THE ISOLATED PROVINCE CALLED Alta California played no part in the long years of struggle that culminated in the dissolving of Spain's New World empire into a congeries of sovereign nations from the Rio Grande to Cape Horn. California did experience one almost comic-opera incident in this period, when the Argentine privateer Hippolyte Bouchard seized Monterey for a few days and looted it of all that was usable, portable and potable.

During the Mexican period, 1822–46, California experienced what might be termed a "population explosion," in that its population grew from some 3,700 persons to slightly less than 8,000, including about 700 non-Hispanic foreigners. This "foreign" element at first was comprised of British and American deserters from trading, naval, and whaling vessels, and wandering trappers from Canada and "the States." Beginning in 1841, a very thin trickle of emigrants from the United States seeped across the natural barriers.

Secularization of the missions—that is, stripping them of all functions except that of parish church—was the most significant internal development of the Mexican period. Using the missions' livestock as a foundation, the *rancho* system flourished apace. Bereft of the only cultural and psychic stability many of them had ever known, the Indian population around the missions declined from 30,000 to about 10,000 in a scant ten years. Those that were left made the labor force for the *rancho*, which became the basic social, cultural, and

A diseño *(grant-map) of Rancho San Vicente; 10,802 acres near Santa Cruz granted to Blas Escamilla in 1846.*

economic unit of Mexican California. This was the period of "pastoral Arcadia," which gave California the gauzy and nostalgic heritage of dashing *caballeros,* beautiful *señoritas,* and the "cattle on a thousand hills." In all truth, this was one of the largest non-nomadic pastoral societies the world ever has known.

Independence from Spain removed the interdiction against trade with foreign countries, although rather high import and export taxes were levied at Monterey, the only legal port of entry, to finance the provincial government. Mexico virtually insisted that California's costs of government be met internally, and taxes upon foreign commerce were the principal means to this end. A miniscule tax on each head of livestock slaughtered was the only internal revenue measure, and the lack of real property taxes was most appealing to the earliest emigrants from the States. The emphasis upon import taxes in all their nuances brought about the switch from illicit smuggling under Spain, to venal conniving with officialdom to gain more favorable treatment in the matter of levying duties and tonnage taxes upon cargoes and vessels.

The relaxing of trade restrictions enabled the *rancheros* to dispose of their principal commercial product: hides and tallow; and this period coincided with the growth of industry in New England. The infant United States needed hides for leather and tallow for soaps and candles, particularly the latter. It also needed a market in which to dispose of its manufactured products. Although the English had been the first to trade legally with California after it gained independence from Spain, it was not long before American vessels out of New England and Middle Atlantic ports, especially Boston, dominated the California trade. San Diego became the principal place for collecting and curing the hides obtained all up and down the coast, and the "hide houses" there contained a polyglot assortment of the world's seafarers.

The hide-and-tallow trade was the mainstay of the California economy during the Mexican period. Estimates of the total number of hides exported from California during the twenty-five years of Mexican tenure veer wildly from 600,000 to 1,250,000. The peak year appears to have been 1838, when it is believed that 200,000 hides were shipped to Boston alone. There were other aspects of commerce that became prominent in this period as well. American whalers plied the coast and reaped a rich harvest from the migrations of the California gray whale. Livestock from California were exported to Tahiti, while cattle and horses from California, with *vaqueros* to instruct the Hawaiians, laid the foundation of the cattle industry on the Big Island of Hawaii. An early trade in lumber developed during this period and is dealt with in a subsequent section.

In the beginning of the hide-and-tallow trade, each ship traded for itself along the coast, sending a supercargo riding inland to persuade the *rancheros* to bring their produce to the nearest beach. Under these conditions, a vessel might be all of two years on the coast getting a full cargo of forty thousand hides. This evolved into a resident-merchant system, the most prominent members being Americans such as Henry Delano *"Enrique"* Fitch in San Diego, Abel Stearns in Los Angeles, and Thomas Oliver Larkin in Monterey. These men purchased whole cargoes of imported goods and acted as purchasers of produce the year round, centralizing the business and providing California with a steady market, as well as a constant supply of goods. A concomitant of this arrangement was the beginning of California's first banking system, in that the merchants provided credit and advanced funds against future production by the *rancheros,* whose word was indeed their honor, not alone their bond.

One result of the rise of the *rancho* system was the eruption of violent sectionalism between Northern and Southern California, an item that has modern connotations. Monterey always had been the capital of California under Spain, and it remained so under Mexico. With secularization of the missions, the most rapid growth in both population and livestock occurred between Santa Barbara and San Diego, and inland toward today's San Bernardino. It was the modern cry of "the most people need the most attention," and for the last decade of California's existence as a Mexican province, it was racked by sectional political strife.

Compounding this internal turmoil, California felt herself to be the unloved, idiot stepchild, so to speak, of the Mexican Republic. She resented having the governor appointed from Mexico, and she resented even more the quality of the soldiers (all too often ex-convicts whom the *Californios* dubbed *rateros* and *cholos*) that Mexico sent north to protect the province. What California wanted was home rule, and in 1836 Juan Bautista Alvarado actually declared California to be an independent republic. This status did not become permanent, but California remained unimpressed with Mexico's appointed officials right up to the Mexican War and her acquisition by the United States. This governmental instability within California, coupled with an even greater political chaos in Mexico proper, was a factor in the calculations that the United States, Great Britain, and France—especially the former two—made about California in the decade preceding the Mexican War.

The basic social unit in Mexican California was the *rancho* family, widely separated from its neighbors. It was a patriarchial unit, and respect for parents was so deeply ingrained that grown men of forty, with their own grandchildren, thought it proper to submit without protest to their parents' disciplinary measures. In a land and time unafraid of excess humanity, Secundino Robles and María Antonia García became the parents of twenty-nine children on their *rancho* where Stanford University stands today. William E. P. Hartnell, a young English trader who married the beauteous Teresa de la Guerra, sired nineteen progeny, and Tomás Sanchez, who married María Sepulveda in her thirteenth year, became the father of twenty-one offspring.

It was an isolated life on the *ranchos* but a life of boundless hospitality. It has been said that you could ride from one end of Hispanic California to the other, from San Diego to Napa-Sonoma, without a purse or a horse of your own and exist comfortably, and travel astride, simply from the bounty of

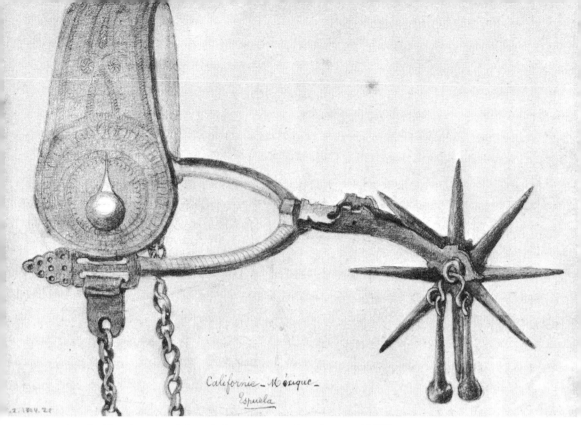

A caballero's *spur (sketch by Fritz Wikersheim, 1851).*

A *California* caretta *(Wikersheim sketch, 1851).*

the families along the way. It was a life of pastoral simplicity, incredibly simple by today's standards, but it was socially and culturally self-sufficient. Economically it was profitable, thanks to the hide-and-tallow trade.

In a very real sense, the land made no demands upon the *Californios* and imposed no obstacles in their lifeway. Man again was the determinant in California. As Sir George Simpson of the Hudson's Bay Company acidulously observed, "Idleness can find both subsistence and recreation" in California. The *Californio* rode superlatively, feared God, honored his parents, worried not about the morrow, and cherished his *dignidad*. What else was there?

The seemingly idyllic life style of the *Californios* survived the Mexican War intact, and the processes of history under normal conditions would seem to have favored its gradual, generational assimilation into the technologically superior culture of the conquering Americans. The best parts of both styles of living might have been combined thereby through progressive acculturation. But such a development was not to be. The lifeway of the *Californios* first was inundated, then swept away forever by the flood tide of gold seekers.

It is proper to note here that the Hispanic influence in contemporary California, where Los Angeles contains one of the largest Mexican centers in the world, is not due to California's slumberous days under Spain and Mexico, except in regard to place names and a bastard architectural style. Neither is it due to the influx of people from Mexico and Latin America during the first two years of the Gold Rush; most of these went home, willingly or for survival. Today's Hispanic influence stems primarily from the migration of people from Mexico during World War I and between the world wars, to meet the state's demand for unskilled labor. The *bracero* program, terminated in 1966, was a recent manifestation of this historic influx.

As a grace note to the above, it well may be that we speak glibly of "bulls" and "bears" today because of California's Hispanic heritage. Contests between wild bulls and ferocious

California—a good land, a gentle land, where the Californios *evolved a life of pastoral simplicity.*

A California rancheria *(sketch by Fritz Wikersheim, 1851).*

The "gente de razón": Southern California's Lugo family lines up for a turn-of-the-century portrait.

grizzly bears, both captured by skillful use of *la riata,* were a staple of the *Californios'* relaxations. Horace Greeley, the thunderous editor of the New York *Tribune,* is said to have witnessed one of these encounters while visiting California, and to have applied the names of the antagonists to the denizens of Wall Street's wilds after his return.

Los Extranjeros

THERE IS NO DOUBT of early visitations by Asiatics to the New World. A Chinese legend holds that a Buddhist monk visited Mexico before Cortés and remained among the Aztec several years before returning to Cathay. Juan Bautista de Anza saw the wreckage of a "foreign" (non-European) vessel on the rocks near Carmel in 1776. At least two Japanese trading voyages reached the west coast of Mexico during the early years of the seventeenth century. A Japanese vessel has been reported as drifting ashore near Santa Barbara in 1815, after a derelict year at sea, with three men still clinging to life aboard her battered hulk. Here again, the winds and currents of the North Pacific enter the picture, even as they do today when the glass floats of Japanese fishing nets wash ashore on Pacific Coast beaches. Too, a Spanish navigator in the Gulf of California in 1540 reportedly sighted "strange" vessels with golden pelican figureheads.

Despite the evidence of such voyages, the fact remains that nothing effective came of them. They belong in the same category as Thor Heyerdahl's drift voyage to Tahiti, which proved that it was possible. Nothing more. The outside world's first meaningful contacts with California, both by sea and by land, came about because of the quest for the pelts of fur-bearing animals.

The first of these animals to spur the avarice of the world was the mammalian sea otter, one of the most appealing of all the sea's creatures, which ranged the Pacific Coast from

77

Captain William A. Richardson, ex-seaman, trader, and founder of San Francisco's commercial beginnings.

the fog-shrouded Aleutian Islands to the slag-barren head-lands of Baja California. Its rich, lustrous pelt, a sensuous chocolatey blackish-brown, could yield a fur sixty inches long by half that wide. Captain James Cook, of the British navy, on one of his great voyages of discovery into the Pacific, brought the world's attention to the profits to be derived from marketing sea-otter pelts in China. By 1789 American vessels were trading with the seafaring Indians of the Pacific North-west around Vancouver Island; and in 1792 an American ship-master out of Boston, William Gray, gave the name of his vessel to the Columbia River. This was the United States' first claim to what became the "Oregon Country" and marks our first national interest in the western lands washed by the Pacific Ocean.

A round-the-world trade quickly developed for New Eng-landers, who brought out their crude manufactures, particu-larly iron products, and traded them on the Northwest Coast for sea otter pelts. Thence they sailed down the latitudes to the Hawaiian Islands to get fresh foodstuffs and fill their water casks, and to take on sandalwood, highly prized in China, in exchange for ironware. In Canton, the principal Chinese port, they traded sea otter and sandalwood for spices and silks and ceramics. Then they sailed down between the emerald islands set in the equatorial girdle, out into the Indian Ocean and the far South Pacific, around the Cape of Good Hope, and home to New England.

As the northern sea otter was hunted out, the California coast came into the picture, because one of the otter's favorite haunts was the kelp beds and rocky ledges of the Santa Bar-bara Channel. William Shaler, in the ship *Lelia Byrd*, traded so flagrantly for sea otter in San Diego, in violation of Spanish law, that he had to fight a bloodless battle with the *castillo* on Point Loma to win his way down the San Diego River to open sea. Captain Ebenezer Dorr in 1796 became the first American known to have landed officially in California when his ship *Otter* entered Monterey Bay, and he took advantage of international law to remain two days while getting wood for cooking and water. Dorr had come up from Australia, and when he departed surreptitiously, he left ashore some convicts from the Botany Bay penal colony "down under."

The sea-otter trade created one of the first peaceful collaborations between Americans and Russians on record. The Russian-American Fur Company in Alaska would supply a crew of fierce Aleut hunters, the "Cossacks of the North Pacific," to American shipmasters in return for a proportion of the catch. The men of this combined operation hunted down the California coast, fighting pitched battles whenever necessary along the Santa Barbara Channel with Indians hunting otter for the missions, and then returned to Sitka to divide the spoils.

A variant of this collaboration saw the American ship *Juno* bring the dashing Baron Rezánov to San Francisco for the purchase of foodstuffs to protect the Russian-American Fur Company's posts in Alaska from starvation. Spanish law, of course, prohibited all such purchases, but the beautiful Concepcíon Argüello, the teen-aged daughter of the *commandante* of the Presidio of San Francisco, fell in love with the Russian Baron. So the legend goes. Her father then shut one eye or winked it just long enough for the foodstuffs to be acquired. Rezánov and Concepcíon were betrothed when he sailed from San Francisco, but he was killed on his way across Siberia to seek the Czar's permission for his marriage. In due time, "Concha" Argüello became Sister Mary Dominica and ended her days on December 23, 1857, in a convent at Benicia, where she is buried.

Another outgrowth of this trade was the establishment by Russia of Fort Ross, an illegal settlement under international law, for the unlawful purpose of poaching sea otter. The fort also was expected to grow food for the Russian outposts in Alaska. Spain was powerless to prevent its establishment; Mexico was powerless to expel it. Fort Ross endured until its contents were purchased by John Sutter, the founder of New Helvetia, the compound that became today's Sacramento.

The Russian River, a favorite summer haunt of San Franciscans, commemorates the onetime Russian presence in the land. So does Mount St. Helena, brooding above the vineyards of the Napa Valley, which was named either for Princess Helena de Gargarin, the wife of the Russian governor of Alaska, or for the Empress of Russia. The Monroe Doctrine took warning notice of the Russian presence in California, and the California Poppy was given its botanical name *(Eschscholtzia californica)* to honor a German zoologist, Johann Friedrich Eschscholtzia, who visited California in 1816 while in the service of Russia.

The sea-otter trade passed its peak by 1822, although a brief flurry of renewed activity seems to have occurred during the early 1830's in and around San Francisco Bay. The sea otter now is a protected creature, and the 1967 report from the state's wildlife agency indicated a herd of about 575 animals, which ranges between Monterey–Carmel and the Santa Barbara Channel.

The quest for beaver skins brought the first Americans overland to California—"men with the bark on," who were able to surmount the formidable natural barriers, including the resident aborigines, that long had protected California's eastern marches. They came as a result of the brass-knuckled competition for beaver skins in the trapping grounds along the crest and the western slope of the Continental Divide. Their conquest of the mountain fastness gave a nasty shock to the then governor of California, a "thin and juiceless man" named Echéandia. What they represented was the cutting edge of the American frontier; and what they learned about the overland routes to California, what they learned about California's vast and untapped potential, contributed to the yeasty ferment bubbling in the collective consciousness of the American people. It was a ferment that would come to a head in the year of the War with Mexico, the year of "Manifest Destiny," the year 1846.

James Ohio Pattie, whose reminiscences are not to be believed as Holy Writ, trapped west-southwest from Taos, New Mexico, in 1826 and apparently reached as far west as the east bank of the Colorado River on this journey. He did not, so far as is known, then set foot on any part of what today is California. The first we know to have done so was unique among the mountain men.

Jedediah Strong Smith was a praying and fighting Methodist, who did not use profanity, who eschewed tobacco, who took wine only upon ceremonial occasions, and who did not follow the custom of the mountains in making temporary alliances with assorted Indian wives-by-courtesy-only. He first went to the Rocky Mountains in 1822 from St. Louis, headquarters of the emerging American segment of the fur trade of the Far West, and by the year 1826 he was a full partner with David Jackson and William Sublette in what became the Rocky Mountain Fur Company. Competition from the great Hudson's Bay Company for the fur riches west of the Continental Divide caused Smith to seek new beaver streams. With a small party of trappers, he left the vicinity of Bear Lake (Utah) in the midsummer of 1826 and made his way southward across Utah to the mouth of the Virgin River, where he crossed the Colorado. Recrossing this silt-laden stream near what is today Needles, Arizona, he traversed the waterless waste of the Mojave Desert and entered California by way of Cajón Pass, arriving at Mission San Gabriel. Here he and his men were received hospitably by the resident Franciscans, but his reception at San Diego was a different matter.

José María Echéandia, a man of astringent personality, was the Mexican governor of California; and he had established his personal headquarters at San Diego because the climate at Monterey was, he believed, injurious to his health. His ego had suffered in San Diego from the loss of his suit for Josefa Carillo to the dashing American seafarer-merchant Henry Delano Fitch. In the governor's jaundiced view, Smith was a spy, and he had him plunked into the local *juzgado* until he could decide his fate. American shipmasters then in San Diego interceded for Smith, and the governor released him on Smith's solemn promise to leave California by the way he had entered it. Rejoining his men at San Gabriel, which they were

81

OVERLEAF: Extranjeros *and entrepreneurs (left to right):*
Jacob P. Leese, Talbot Green, Thomas O. Larkin, Sam Brannan,
W. D. M. Howard.

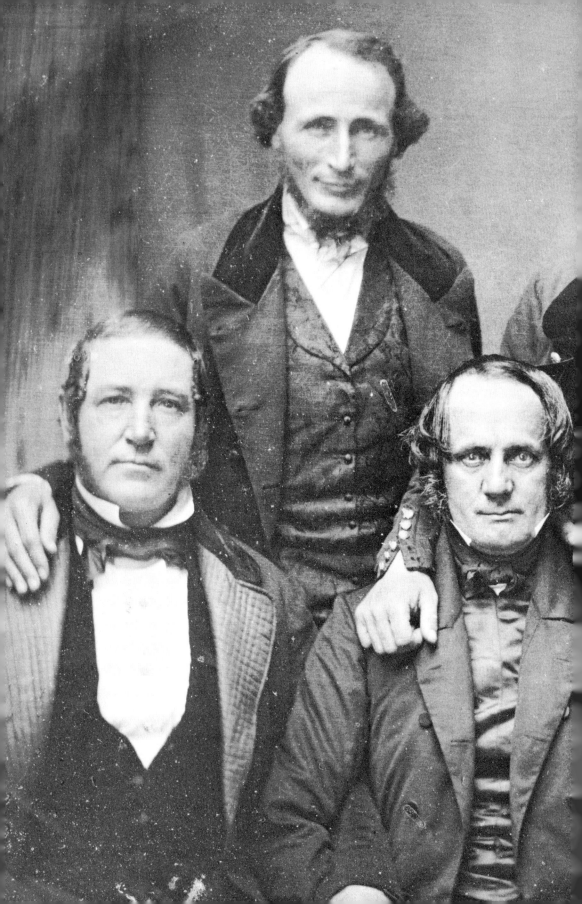

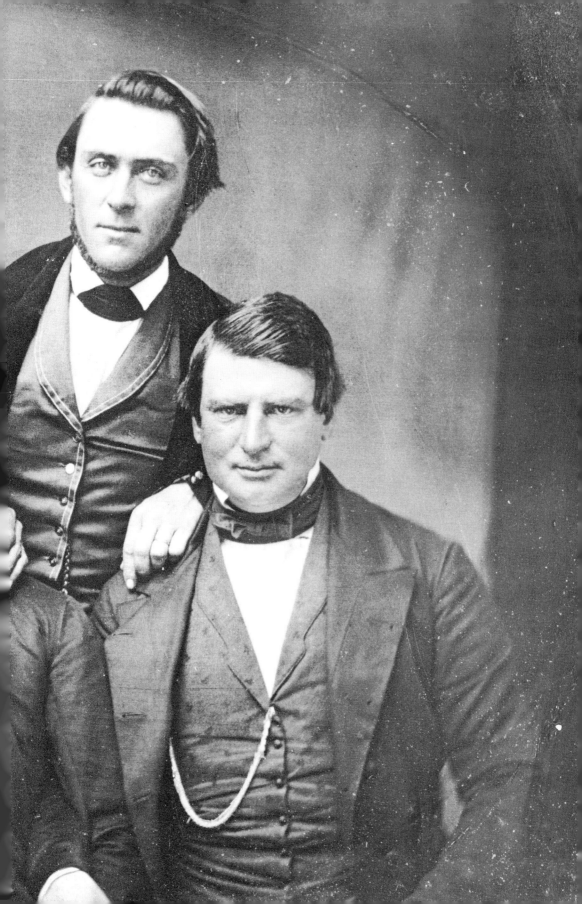

sorry to leave, so equable was the climate and so refreshing the wine made there, Smith led his little band back over Cajón Pass, thus seeming to follow his promise to the governor.

He then turned northwest across the Mojave Desert to Tehachapi Pass, crossed it, and entered the San Joaquin Valley early in 1827. Here he found rich beaver streams and trapped up the east side of the valley to the mouth of the Stanislaus River. Leaving the bulk of his party encamped there to trap, Smith and two companions made the first known crossing of the main range of the Sierra Nevada by Europeans. Then they traversed the unknown wastes of the Great Basin, almost dying of thirst, and were reunited with Smith's partners at Bear Lake, in the first week of July, 1827. Smith had proven that California could be reached overland, and even though his route did not become a major one in the later migrations to California, the information he had gained became most valuable to his country in its restless, westering urge.

Before July, 1827, had run its course, Smith had set out again for California with another party of trappers. Following his previous route, he came to the Mojave Indian villages on the Colorado without incident. These Indians, most peaceably inclined on his first trip, apparently had had a bitter encounter with American trappers from New Mexico shortly before Smith's second arrival in their lands. They avenged this encounter by surprising Smith's party and killing ten of its members. With the eight other survivors, Smith made his way to the men he had left encamped at the mouth of the Stanislaus River. Because the combined party needed supplies, Smith journeyed to Monterey to obtain them and again was incarcerated as a spy.

Again he was released through the intercessions of American merchants and shipmasters on his promise to the governor to leave California. This time he kept his promise. Obtaining the supplies he needed, he led his party from the Stanislaus up the east side of the Great Valley to above Sacramento. Here he turned westward, at about today's Chico Landing, and crossed the Coast Range folds to the ocean. Turning northward along the coast, which he found to be poor fur country, he and his men were nearly wiped out in a surprise attack by the Umpqua Indians in Oregon. Only Smith and two of his men survived. Making their way to the Columbia River, they were hospitably received by Dr. John McLoughlin, the Hudson's Bay Company's resident eminence at Fort Vancouver. (This lay across the Columbia River from what is now Portland, Oregon.)

After this experience, Smith sold out his interest in the firm of Smith, Jackson & Sublette and entered the Santa Fé trade out of Independence, Missouri. He was killed by the Comanche on his first trip to Santa Fé on the Cimarron Desert, in his thirty-second year.

Smith was the first American to reach California overland from the east, and the first of any nationality to traverse the approximate full length of the state. These accomplishments, added to his earlier participation in the discovery of South Pass (Wyoming)—the most feasible way for wagons to cross the Rocky Mountains—give him an honored place in the roster of American explorers of the Far West. He also gave his country its first accurate information about the whole Far West and Pacific region, which is an added laurel wreath.

After Smith came other Americans. James Ohio Pattie, mentioned earlier, entered California on a trapping junket from New Mexico with his father, Sylvester Pattie, and was jailed in San Diego, where his father perished. A smallpox epidemic ravaged California at this time, and Pattie later claimed to have earned his freedom and the undying gratitude of the *Californios* by vaccinating them by the thousands against the dread disease. Thereafter he departed California for good and all, and found a publisher for his reminiscences in Cincinnati. Hyperbolic though they were, and despite a hopelessly snarled chronology and geography, they played their part in quickening American interest in the sleepy land called California.

Ewing Young trapped out of New Mexico into California

85

in the late 1820's and early 1830's, giving his first lessons in wilderness skills to a runaway saddler's apprentice named Christopher Carson and nicknamed "Kit." The route used by these trappers out of New Mexico to the Gila River in Arizona became one of the principal overland trails to California during the Gold Rush.

In 1834 Joseph Reddeford Walker led a party of trappers west from the Rockies by way of the Humboldt River, which was destined to become the major overland sluiceway to California before, during, and after the Gold Rush. In his efforts to cross the Sierra, Walker became the first white man known to have looked down into Yosemite Valley, although he did not enter it. He also discovered Walker Pass in the Tehachapi Mountains. He and his party wintered at Monterey, where they were well received, or at least not molested. This may have been because their rifles represented more effective firepower than the entire Mexican military establishment in California could muster. Walker returned again to California during its golden heyday and was buried at Martinez, where his long trail finally reached its end.

In the 1830's, too, a group of American ex-trappers headed by "Peg Leg" Smith and a mulatto and a master of wilderness craft, James P. Beckwourth, combined with the Ute Indians under their great war leader Walkara to write some of the largest horse thefts known into the annals of California. Leaving the Ute homeland around present Spanish Fork, Utah, the raiders would traverse southern Nevada and the Mojave Desert to enter California by Cajón Pass. The *ranchos* along the San Gabriel and Santa Ana rivers were their targets, and they are said to have stolen hundreds of horses at a time in these forays, driving their booty as far east as Pueblo, Colorado, for sale.

Americans were not the only overland adventurers to enter California in this period. The Hudson's Bay Company began sending trapping expeditions down from the Columbia River into the Great Valley as early as 1829. Traveling southward, east of the Cascade Range peaks in Oregon, they entered Cali-

"We crossed the prairies, as of old/The Pilgrims crossed the sea. . . ."
The overland journey was as hard on oxen as it was on men, as shown in
the anonymous, undated sketch above. Many of the new pilgrims found
surcease at Peter Lassen's rancho in the Sacramento Valley, seen below
in an 1849 drawing of J. Goldsborough Bruff.

LASSEN'S RANCHO

fornia near Goose Lake, angling thence across the high pine barrens and lava flows to the Pit River, and into the Great Valley by a pass just east of present-day Redding, California. Trapping well down the valley, they left a record of their presence in French Camp, near Stockton, which commemorates the French-Canadians in their expeditions. That beaver were plentiful in the Great Valley is supported by the fact that one of the Hudson's Bay Company parties trapped one hundred beaver in one day at the Sutter Buttes. That they were formidable competitors for the fur riches of the Far West and California is supported by the wry American comment that H.B.C. stood for "Here Before Christ!"

It was the need for some kind of resident authority in the Great Valley, unsettled by either Spain or Mexico, to check these poaching intrusions by foreign trappers that caused another adventurer to earn the honor of erecting the first effective habitation there. This was the Swiss dreamer, Johann Augustus Sutter, whom we know today as John Sutter.

Sutter arrived in California from the Hawaiian Islands after a disastrous financial involvement in the Santa Fé trade. Rumor still emanates from his past that he was not a model of probity in handling funds entrusted to him by Swiss friends for investment in the United States. That he had a tremendous personality seems certain, and this may have been his major asset in obtaining from the Mexican governor of California the grant of an enormous tract of land at the confluence of the American and Sacramento rivers. Here in 1839 he began the erection of Sutter's Fort, which was to be the economic and military center of his dreamed-of personal empire and to which he gave the name of New Helvetia in honor of his homeland. Sutter's reach was always longer than his grasp was strong; his dreams were always too large for his capabilities; and he had an appalling appetite for credit at ruinous rates of interest. Nonetheless, no man was turned from his door hungry, and instead of checking the flow of immigration when it began, he encouraged it. Ironically, Sutter, whose sawmill spawned the Gold Rush, was ruined by it.

IMMIGRANTS MAY BE DISTINGUISHED FROM adventurers, such as the fur trappers, and from drifters, such as the deserters from foreign vessels, by the fact that they set forth from their homes with a compulsion to find new land and there settle down. Also, their orientation was primarily agricultural.

It should be remembered that the bulk of the American movement into the Far West in the period 1840–47 was bound for, and went to, Oregon, not California. Oregon in this period was a disputed region under "joint occupancy" by Great Britain and the United States. California, on the contrary, was the possession of a foreign power, Mexico. Another factor in the Oregon emphasis was that for many years it had benefited from Protestant missionary publicity in the eastern part of the United States—publicity which had combined the virtues of bringing light to the heathen and adding territory to the United States. Underlying these reasons was a definite feeling among Americans, regardless of sectional or other phobias, that "perfidious Albion" (England) should be prevented from in any way gaining a solid foothold on land that belonged to the United States by divine right.

The first party of avowed overland emigrants from the States to reach California got its principal impetus from glowing accounts of the climate and fertile soil, sent east by John Marsh—called "Doctor" on insufficient grounds. Marsh had a certificate of completion of a classical education from Harvard when he reached California after unfortunate personal experiences elsewhere. Finding a shortage, actually a vacuum, of medical men in California, he used his Harvard certificate to establish his claim to medical training and acquired a grant of land from the Mexican governor near Mount Diablo, in what is now the Walnut Creek–Lafayette–Concord area. His letters back to friends in Missouri, coupled with accounts of conditions in California by Antoine Robidoux, who had visited California as a trapper, triggered the so-called Bidwell-Bartleson Party's emigration from Missouri in the spring of 1841.

John Bidwell, a young man in his early twenties, became the mainstay of the group, even though he was not its elected trail captain. As far west as Fort Hall (Pocatello), Idaho, they followed the trappers' route, using South Pass to breach the Rocky Mountains. From Fort Hall to California they used some of the information derived from Joseph Walker's journey in 1834 but had God's own time of it, having to abandon their wagons en route. They crossed the Sierra in the vicinity of Sonora Pass, with Bidwell getting credit for being the first American to see the Big Trees *(Sequoia gigantea)* in the process, probably what is known today as the Calaveras Grove. In this party was the first American woman, Mrs. Benjamin Kelsey, to enter California overland, and her infant child has a comparable distinction. Bidwell was the only one of this party to make a truly distinguished career for himself in California, and his residence in Chico, which he founded, is now a historical monument administered by the state.

The first wagons to reach California came with the Stephens-Townsend-Murphy Party of 1844. Under the guidance of Caleb "Old" Greenwood, four wagons were forced up and over the sheer granite face of what was later called Donner Pass before the party bowed before the threat of too much winter too soon. The rest of the wagons, about thirteen, they left at the east end of what came to be called Donner Lake, under the care of a seventeen-year-old named Moses Schallenberger. This teen-ager guarded the wagons and their contents all winter, and all alone, which is no mean feat. The crude cabin that he occupied was used in 1846 by the tragic fragments of the emigrant party that left the name of Donner for all time on the central pass through the Sierra Nevada.

Cannibalism clings to the Donner Party's legacy and gains irony from the story that one Keseberg, said to have been the chief practitioner of this very ancient human survival act, later opened a restaurant in Sacramento. What is little known is that this party was so delayed before reaching the Sierra that an early severe snowfall caught them in the mountains. Their major delay occurred in the rugged Wasatch Mountains east of Salt Lake City, simply because they believed a guidebook written by a young man *who had not even traveled* the

The Pacific Coast was short on harbors and long on navigational pitfalls—as the master of the Glenesslin *found in 1913.*

San Francisco Bay was one rare haven for whalers and hide-and-tallow traders beleaguered by coastal storms and currents.

shortcut he recommended at the time his book was published in Cincinnati, Ohio, in 1845. This young man was Lansford W. Hastings, and his handbook to disaster for the Donner Party was *The Emigrants' Guide to California and Oregon.* By far the most appealing aspect of this tragedy of human disintegration is the heroism of such as Tamsen Donner, who stayed with her injured and much older husband knowing full well what her fate would be, and the heroic, literally super-human efforts of the successful relief parties sent out from Sutter's Fort to rescue the survivors.

Donner Pass, which was a terrible obstacle at best to wagons, and livestock, and their owners, gained an unsavory reputation as a result of the Donner tragedy. The main Gold Rush passes through the central Sierra were Johnson Pass, roughly where U.S. Highway 50 crosses today, and Henness Pass just to the north of today's Interstate Highway 80. It should be borne in mind that the Sierra Nevada passes get progressively higher as one goes south down the range. Thus, Carson, Ebbets, Sonora, and Tioga passes were not favored by wagon travelers. From Tioga to Tehachapi and Walker passes, the High Sierra was not breached by wheels, and is not today. Current demands to open this segment of the Sierra Nevada to motorized recreationists are being opposed right stoutly by conservationists.

It may be well to remember that wagons by and large can go only straight up or straight down. Their center of gravity is too high for contour following, and the physical labor involved in making a "dugway," which is a trench on the uphill side of slopes for wheels to use (thus lowering the center of gravity) was too exhausting and too time-consuming for people in a hurry to reach the Promised Land. Going up, they would double-, triple-, or quadruple-team each wagon. Coming down, they tied a tree behind the wagon for a drag brake, rough-locked the wheels by chaining them into immovability, and sometimes let the wagons down by snubbing a rope around a tree trunk and paying it out as needed, against too precipitous a descent.

In order to gain title to land in California after their arrival, the immigrants had to become Mexican citizens, and this seems to have been a matter of leaving their consciences somewhere east of the Sierra. Many of them did not go through this formality—remaining "enemy aliens," so to speak —but simply squatted on land that looked good to them and began subsistence farming. The beginning trickle of immigrants in the early 1840's and the independent attitude of many of them caused the Mexican government to fear that California would be the scene of another Texas-type usurpation of Mexican territory.

Another group of those who sought their Canaan in California deserves inclusion here. For one distinction, they came by sea, the only pre-Gold Rush party of settlers to do so; for another, they were all Latter Day Saints (Mormons) seeking religious freedom under the leadership of Samuel Brannan. They arrived in San Francisco by the ship *Brooklyn* from New York *after* California had been conquered by the United States, and their landing date is recorded variously between August 30 and September 5, 1846.

It is this arrival of Mormons, fleeing persecution and pillage in Illinois and elsewhere in the East, that has given rise to the claim that they conducted the first Protestant church service in California. Omitting any remembrance of Francis Drake's chaplain, the question here well may be whether the Church of Jesus Christ of Latter Day Saints accepts membership in the Protestant community.

This group, plus the "Mormon Battalion," which arrived in 1847 as part of the United States' military forces under Colonel Philip St. George Cooke, put a substantial number of Mormons in California before the Gold Rush. Mormons were among the work force building Sutter's sawmill in 1848; Mormon Island on the American River, until it was submerged beneath the waters of Folsom Dam, commemorated their presence in the earliest days of the rush; Sam Brannan, leader of the sea-traveling Mormons, is credited with making the sleepy, fog-washed, sand-drenched, flea-bitten hamlet of San

93

Francisco accept the fact of the discovery of *gold!* The question arises as to just how important a part the Mormons played in the Americanization of California that truly began with the Rush.

Sam Brannan was an ambitious man. So was Brigham Young, *the* leader of the Church. The two men split violently over their respective dreams and ambitions, and there is strong rumor that Brannan did not remit the tithes he collected in California in the name of his Church, to Brigham and that Church in Deseret (Utah). Brannan left the Church as a result of these differences and suspicions, and wrote a fantastic personal chapter of life in California before he died —a broken, semi-alcoholic dreamer.

The great majority of Mormons who came to California before the Gold Rush obeyed the dictates of Brigham Young and moved back to Utah while the Rush was at flood tide. This is a remarkable tribute to their religious fidelity. It also prevented the Mormons from exercising any sustained influence upon the early Americanization of California.

The major interrelationship between the Mormons and the Gold Rush seems to have been in the economic advantage the brethren in Utah derived from trading with travelers to California. It was substantial and contributed to the initial expansion of the Mormon establishment in the Great Basin.

Donner Lake, for some a scene of tragedy, depravity, and calm courage—today, a synonym for fun in the snow.

Halls of Montezuma: California Chapter

TWENTY YEARS AGO, it would have been quite proper to describe the territorial acquisition of the Far West south of 42° north latitude by the United States as a necessary and an inevitable expansion to fill the "divinely ordained" boundaries of the republic. But in the nation's mood today (agitated by the Viet Nam conflict and ethnic minority demands), the conquest of California—indeed, the whole Mexican War—is apt to be castigated as an exercise in aggressive imperialism.

This problem is compounded by the Bear Flag syndrome within California. What popular belief holds to be the "Bear Flag Republic" was never a government *de jure* or *de facto;* it existed between June 14 and July 7, 1846, primarily in the minds of the men involved, and they were only a handful. We are confronted here by the conflicting views that the Bear Flaggers—*"los Osos"* to the *Californios*—were either dedicated patriots, determined to raise the banner of individual freedom and political democracy above an alien and outlandish batch of Papists; or that they were a bunch of brandy-happy ex-trappers and recent in-migrants who sought absolution from the crime of horse theft by declaring themselves a republic of revolutionaries against despotism.

An added and a dangerous emotional snare is set by the figure of John Charles Frémont, misnamed "the Pathfinder," who was in actuality a "path follower." One view holds that Frémont was the hero who single-handedly conquered Cali-

97

John Charles Frémont, Captain of Topographical Engineers, pathmarker, and "conqueror" of Mexican California—a portrait probably taken in about 1850.

fornia by virtually cutting his way through a wall of human flesh, while trailing the robes of Caesar in the flowing blood. The other view holds him to be an insubordinate young army officer, who belongs among the gaudiest popinjays in American history.

The fact remains that Texas and California are linked indissolubly in the tangled skein of events leading up to the Mexican War. The protection of Texas against reconquest by Mexico is the ostensible trigger of these hostilities, while the necessity of obtaining the harbor of San Francisco, which to the commercial and political powers in the East meant California, seems to have been the finger on that trigger. President Andrew Jackson had sought to acquire California from Mexico by purchase as early as 1835, and the matter never was absent thereafter from the calculations of American statesmen and politicians and traders.

In addition, Mexico itself was an unstable, weak, and impoverished political entity. Such governments always have been a menace to their near neighbors, and Mexico's chaotic internal political structure gave the young United States due cause to fear that Mexico would fall easy prey to the designs of European powers such as England and France. This was compounded in the case of California by the fear, fed by rumors along the diplomatic grapevine, that Mexico would cede California to England in order to liquidate her indebtedness to the British. Such a happening would forever limit the United States to the land east of the Rocky Mountains; it would drastically affect the possibility of our ever obtaining Oregon; it would place an exponent of monarchial absolutism in a position to threaten, perhaps even more than by her presence in Canada, the liberties and political principles of the United States. Added to these was the widespread feeling among individual Americans that the Almighty had ordained it to be the mission of the United States to spread the glories of an enlightened political system wherever possible. These political and emotional forces coalesced into what became known most conveniently as "Manifest Destiny," a concept that provides a context for certain events in California history.

In 1842 Commodore Thomas ap Catesby Jones, a fiery American officer of Welsh extraction and long in the naval service of his country, commanded the U.S. Pacific Squadron, which was stationed at Callao (Lima), Peru. In September of that year, Jones received faulty intelligence that war had broken out between Mexico and the United States. This posed the threat that England's Pacific fleet would seize California forthwith. Jones sailed immediately for Monterey, sent his marines ashore without meeting resistance, and claimed California for his country. Afterward he discovered that there was no war. Somewhat embarrassed, he hauled down the American flag, restored the Mexican ensign to its place, and made profuse apologies all around. These apologies did not expunge the insult to Mexico's *dignidad nacional,* and Mexico City's newspapers made much of the barbarity of "ape" Catesby Jones. The resident *Californios,* however, did not seem to take the affair too seriously.

In 1843 Thomas Oliver Larkin, the principal American merchant in Monterey, was appointed his country's consul at that only official port of entry in the province. In 1845 he was appointed the confidential agent of President James K. Polk, who had been elected in 1844 on a platform dedicated to expanding America's territorial boundaries. In the latter capacity Larkin was instructed to promote a revolution within California that would create an independent republic favorable to the United States. In time this entity would be expected to petition for annexation to the United States, as had Texas under conditions which seem to have provided the pattern for the proposed gambit in California. Larkin found allies among prominent *Californios,* primarily in the north, and especially General Mariano Guadalupe Vallejo at Sonoma. Larkin's position as the leading merchant and dispenser of credit in northern California did not hamper his machinations. Frémont did.

As a lieutenant in the Corps of Topographical Engineers, then the Army's *corps d'elite,* Frémont had made two explor-

99

ing expeditions beyond the Rocky Mountains, which brought him the title of "Pathfinder." The fact is that ex-mountain men, such as Carson, Fitzpatrick, Maxwell, and Godey, had been the guides for Frémont's expeditions, and they *knew* at all times where they were and how to get from there to the next place. Frémont, however, does deserve laurels for his reports of these two expeditions, because these gave his country solid scientific data, by that day's standards, of the lands he had traversed. Frémont had been in California on the second of his wayfarings, in 1844, and had been hospitably received. Also, he had refrained from making an unmitigated nuisance of himself on this first visit.

In the early weeks of 1846, Frémont returned to California, crossing the Sierra at Carson Pass in the dead of winter, and coming down to sanctuary at Sutter's Fort. His official orders did not instruct him to visit California at this time, but Frémont was the son-in-law of one of the most powerful senators in Washington, Thomas Hart Benton of Missouri, and a large body of questionable evidence has been presented to support the claim that Frémont was acting on secret instructions, suggestions, or thinly veiled hints from his father-in-law.

Frémont squattered about California for several months, having a bloodless run-in with José Castro, the military commander at Monterey, and in the process knocking Larkin's secret negotiations in the head. This involved Frémont's construction of an alleged "fort" on Gabilan (Hawk) Peak, southeast of San Jose, and its abandonment. Frémont then moved slowly up the Great Valley toward Oregon, where he was supposed to have been pursuant to his general orders. In the vicinity of Klamath Falls, he was overtaken by a lieutenant of U.S. Marines, Archibald Gillespie, who was bearing dispatches to both Larkin and Frémont from Washington, dated in October, 1845—many, many months before the War with Mexico erupted. Gillespie also brought letters from Frémont's family, and these allegedly contained secret instructions in a family code upon which Frémont subsequently acted. Whether they did or not, Frémont turned back to California,

IOI

Mariano G. Vallejo, with daughters—his sympathy with American acquisition was rewarded by incarceration in Sutter's Fort.

making his camp at the Sutter Buttes; and the Bear Flag Revolt began to swirl about his presence.

American settlers in the Sacramento Valley, between Sutter's Fort and today's Hamilton City, in Glenn County, were fearful at this time that Mexican officials were going to expel them from California. Some of these were Mexican citizens only for purposes of land acquisition; others were recent arrivals who had not deigned to become more than squatters, after the American frontier tradition. When a herd of horses was dispatched from Sonoma to Monterey, under the escort of a Mexican officer and several *vaqueros*, it was imagined that this presaged an army with fire and sword to drive the Americans out. Therefore, a group of settlers led by a stuttering ex-trapper named Ezekiel Merritt determined to prevent this by capturing the horses. Among his party was Robert "Long Bob" Semple, whose height allegedly caused him to fasten his spurs to his calves, not his heels, that he might tickle his mount without undue contortions. They asked Frémont to join them and to take command in his capacity as an army officer. Frémont refused. The settlers went right ahead and captured the horses at Murphy's Ranch on the Consumnes River in the Sierra foothills. Flushed with this success, they then determined to capture Sonoma and again asked Frémont to lead them. They got another refusal.

Securing recruits from recently arrived immigrants (including William Todd, a nephew of Abraham Lincoln's wife, and William Brown Ide, a millwright who was suspected of Mormonism), they rode for Sonoma to rinse away the blot of horse theft in the ardent waters of patriotism. In the early morning of June 14, 1846, they demanded the surrender of Mariano Guadalupe Vallejo, whose title of "General" made him the ranking Mexican military force in that region. This was Vallejo's first intimation that war was loose in his land; after accepting this fact, he surrendered with great hospitality. The result of this hospitality was that Ide, a teetotaller, drew up a Proclamation of Independence (the only state document resulting from the capture of Sonoma); and a crudely fashioned flag—bearing the Lone Star from Texas and a grizzly bear, with the legend CALIFORNIA REPUBLIC—was hoisted above the captured citadel of despotism. The bear was so badly drawn that it looked like a pig to the *Californios*, but this has been rectified in the state flag that floats over California today. In consequence of the Bear Flaggers' success, Frémont brought his party of ex-trappers, Delaware Indians, and plain military men over from Sutter Buttes and assumed command of the forces of the new republic—*after* the fact, be it remembered. Frémont's true contribution to this imbroglio was psychological. He was an army officer, he had been junketing about California for months, he had left and then returned, and he had powerful connections in Washington. It was natural for the settlers to feel that there was more to Frémont's presence in California than scientific curiosity, and their course of action undoubtedly was influenced by some expectation that he would support them with his armed might if events caught the revolutionaries between a rock and a hard place.

While Frémont was riding up and down and around, major events were taking place outside California. War with Mexico actually came to pass along the lower Rio Grande, when a Mexican cavalry patrol defeated a similar American force allegedly trespassing on Mexican territory. Word of war filtered across Mexico to Mazatlán, where Commodore John D. Sloat had the U.S. Pacific Squadron at anchor. Sloat was a sluggish man, and cautious, but he finally set sail for Monterey. Arriving there, he took a few days more to make up his mind to act. Then, on July 7, 1846, the Stars and Stripes were raised above the ex-capital of Mexican California for all time. Frémont and his enlarged command rode down to Monterey to be mustered into Sloat's forces, and as the "California Battalion," they took part in the bloodless American conquest of California.

The small amount of real fighting that occurred in California came about after this initial seizure as a result of heavy-handed actions by American forces and officers, and it erupted

OVERLEAF: *A view of San Francisco and the Bay drawn by Daniel Coit shortly after American appropriation of California. The 1835 adobe of William A. Richardson is seen at the left.*

and had its main center in southern California. American occupation troops were expelled from Los Angeles in the skirmishing, and the one real battle of the entire Mexican War in California was fought at San Pasqual, some miles northeast of San Diego. Here the American "Army of the West," about two hundred men coming overland from New Mexico under Stephen Watts Kearny, was defeated by a force of *Californios*, whose superlative horsemanship made their lances and *riatas* most deadly weapons. Rallying from these setbacks, the American sea and land forces reconquered southern California with a minimum of bloodshed. Thereafter, the governance of the conquered land degenerated into an unseemly bickering between Kearny, Frémont, and Commodore Stockton (who had relieved Sloat), which resulted in Frémont being court-martialed on charges of insubordination. While the charges were not proven, Frémont resigned the service in a huff and Kearny's reputation has been diminished ever since by pro-Frémont partisans. So strong, however, was the popular image of Frémont as "Pathfinder" and "Conqueror of California" that it helped him to become one of the first two United States senators from California in 1850, a millionaire mine- and landowner at Mariposa, a candidate for President on the Republican ticket in 1856, and a major general in the Civil War.

California remained under a military government after the conquest, and in 1847 more emigrants from the States went to Oregon, more even to Utah, than to California. Of the less than two thousand Americans who did enter California in that year, the great majority were soldiers of the Third New York Regiment of Volunteers, a rowdy lot, and of the "Mormon Battalion," most unrowdy, both of which arrived too late for any fighting but served as occupation and garrison troops until their enlistments expired.

By the Treaty of Guadalupe Hidalgo, we paid Mexico $15,000,000 for the lands she ceded and assumed claims of American citizens against Mexico in the amount of $3,250,000. It seems worth noting here that payment by a conqueror for what it has acquired by force of arms is not common practice in international relations.

California eventually would have been given official status as an American territory, and would have followed the procedures pertaining to the transition from territory to state. How long it would have taken for these steps to have brought statehood must remain forever unknown. The Gold Rush settled the question with speed and finality.

Even more important than bringing California statehood, virtually by Caesarian section, the Gold Rush set in motion the process of sustained acceleration of growth based upon technology and population that has continued to this day. The bounteous natural resources of California were, and are, vital to this self-regenerating saga.

The Golden Stone in
the Pool of History

GOLD MADE THE GOLDEN TROUT the state fish and the golden poppy the state flower. Gold brought to California men to match the mountains where the gold was found, and brought them in such numbers as to transform San Francisco from a desultory haven for 812 persons to a frantic hive of 25,000 in two years; to lift California from less than 10,000 total population to 100,000 in the same two years, and to 264,435 by the state census of 1852.

Economically, gold gave California a self-contained source of capital that not only prevented it from sharing the common far western fate of exploitation by the financial east but enabled California to become an investor in, and exploiter of, the Far West in her own right. This does not mean that great hordes of prospectors struck it rich in Shirt Tail Gulch or Bogus Thunder or wherever, and thereafter invested their gains in ranches or other mines or real estate in Nevada or Oregon or Idaho or Arizona. Rather, it was the mercantile class, the men who mined the miners, who accumulated the initial investment capital and reinvested it elsewhere.

Socially, gold transformed California from a sleepy, isolated, pastoral land into a bustling, basically urban, very cosmopolitan, and socially fluid member of the world community.

Politically, gold enabled California to bypass the territorial period, simply by implicitly advising the Congress that if California were not admitted to the Union on her own terms, she was quite able, and more or less willing, to establish her-

"You can scarcely form any conception of what a dirty business this gold digging is," one miner wrote. The slow daguerreotype lens could not catch the moving water.

self as an independent entity until such time as the Union wanted her.

It is interesting to note here that the first Constitutional Convention at Monterey in September, 1849, drew up a state constitution, not a territorial document; that a full slate of state officers was elected; and that a state government was functioning some months *before* California was granted membership in the Union.

It should be noted also that this first constitution carried an antislavery section and that California was admitted as a "free" state, thus upsetting the balance of power between free and slave states in Congress. This action had a considerable effect upon fixing more rigidly than before the lines of sectional cleavage that culminated in the Civil War.

It is most germane to point out that the antislavery proviso in the first constitution did not really represent a moral indictment of slavery on the part of Californians, many of whom were from the Deep South. Negroes in California (there being about one thousand of them in the census of 1850, or about 1 percent of the total population) did not get any true semblance of civil rights, such as the franchise and the right to testify in court cases involving white Americans, until 1863, after the Republican Party had risen to political prominence in the state.

The antislavery section seems to have been inserted simply to prevent the use of slave labor, be it chattel Negro, or trinket-happy Indian, or *peon Latino,* in the mines. The first years of the Gold Rush were years of individuals seeking on an individual basis a fair share of "anybody's gold." It was, indeed, *anybody's gold,* for the land was not yet surveyed, nor had any arm of any government any means to enforce no-trespass laws on the public domain. In these first years, say 1848–50, any individual was entitled to as much gold as he could find anywhere by his own exertions; but it was not right, or fitting, or American to use slaves, or servants, or employees to gain an unfair advantage over one's fellow-seekers who did not have such extra arms and hands.

California remained the world's leading gold-producer for the balance of the century, giving the United States its first great source of precious metal for both coinage and currency support. Of world importance, gold from California was the first major infusion of new precious metal since the Spaniards first tapped the accumulated hoards of Aztec and Inca.

Perhaps five hundred million dollars flowed from California's mines in the years before the Civil War, and this almost exactly equals the amount invested in new industrial capacity in the eastern states over the same span. It is presumptuous to make a one-for-one relationship here, but California gold can be said to have played a substantial part in creating the industrial supremacy that was so vital to the Union's ultimate victory over the Confederacy. The lure of California and the nation's expanding economy also caused emigration from Europe to the United States to double between 1848 and 1851 and to maintain this new level for several years. In as much as the bulk of the newcomers settled in states that came to the Union's support, California may be said to have contributed another substantial element to the preservation of the Union.

ALL DOWN THE MILLENNIA before the Gold Rush, the forces of nature had been extracting gold from the quartz ledges in which it had been formed in the Sierra Nevada. Erosion had exposed the ledges; frost had split off chunks of gold-bearing rock; rains and snows had carried these into stream beds; and the force of falling water had carried them downstream for varying distances, pounding and crushing out the gold between the rolling native-rock boulders in the process. Gold is one of the heaviest of metals, a fact obvious to the forty-niner but unknown to most of today's urban residents. This fact is basic to the extractive processes, from miner's pan to modern concentrator, and played its part in the distribution of gold in the watercourses—the "free" gold that made the placers of the forty-niners.

The finest, or "flour," gold was found farthest down the streams, sometimes almost into the Great Valley. Then, working upstream, the golden placer grains got bigger—grain gold, pea gold, nut gold, nuggets, gobbets, and chunks. This progression gave rise to the belief that somewhere, high in the shimmering heights of the Sierra, there must be the one great "Mother Lode" whence all this golden treasure sprang.

In the spring of 1850, the rumor that someone had found "Gold Lake" high in the Sierra fastnesses—a lake whose sands were pure gold—unhinged some two thousand miners sufficiently that they spent fruitless weeks in seeking it. Today, the Lakes Basin Recreational Area in the Plumas National Forest (Sierra County) boasts a Gold Lake, among its numerous glacial tarns, in the same region that was traversed by those who sought the mythical lake a hundred years ago.

California's main gold belt extended from Mariposa in the south up the western slope of the Sierra to about Oroville, where the North Fork of the Feather River became regarded as its northern terminus. From this demarcation north into the southern Cascade Range, the volcanic activity discussed earlier had overlaid the late Tertiary (fifteen million years old) formations so deeply with lava that natural forces had not been able to perform the work of extraction and distribution as in the main California auriferous belt.

From the North Fork of the Feather River, the gold belt jumped northwestwardly across the Great Valley into western Tehama and Shasta counties, into Trinity County around Weaverville, and thence ranged northward toward and into southern Oregon's Klamath Mountains. This put western Siskiyou County also into the secondary gold belt. Isolated pockets of placer gold were found in southern California, a matter discussed later in this section, but these were of small import to the state, its people, or its growth.

Few important deposits of gold were found on the eastern slope of the Sierra within California's present boundaries, although the town of Bodie—now preserved in a state of arrested decay by the Division of Beaches and Parks—had a

A map of the northern mines, drawn by William Eddy, a working miner, in 1851.

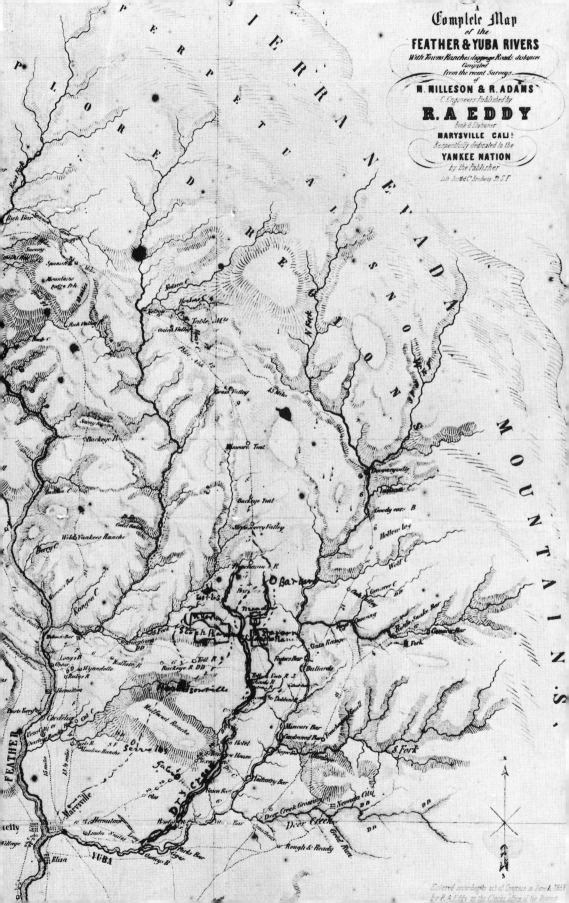

A
Complete Map
of the
FEATHER & YUBA RIVERS
With Towns Ranches diggings Roads distances
Compiled
from the recent Surveys
of
N. MILLESON & R. ADAMS
C. Engineers Published by
R. A. EDDY
Book & Stationer
MARYSVILLE CALI.
Respectfully dedicated to the
YANKEE NATION
by the Publisher

hectic life as a gold camp both promotional and productive. Indeed, the major mineral east of the Sierra summit was silver, a fact emphasized by the millions in silver bullion torn from the bowels of the Comstock Lode beneath Virginia City, Nevada, between 1860 and 1880.

The existence of gold in California was known at least in the Mexican period, for small shipments of placer gold were made to New England during the heyday of the hide-and-tallow trade. They seem to have been brought to the missions by the Indian converts, or by wild Indians from the Sierra for trading purposes. Such minor amounts, however, did not stimulate any gold-seeking expeditions of consequence—some say because the Franciscans had seen the evils wrought by gold upon the native population of Mexico and did not wish to see such havoc repeated in California.

The first, repeat *first*, veritable discovery of gold in California was made near present-day Newhall, where a roadside marker commemorates the event and slightly misplaces it. The date was March 9, 1842, and the discoverer was a *vaquero* named Francisco Lopez, who, according to legend, pulled up a bunch of wild onions to flavor his dried meat (jerky) and found gold flakes clinging to the shallow roots. Legend or not, the fact remains that shallow placers were worked in that area for several years, and relatively substantial amounts of gold extracted, some of which was shipped to the Philadelphia Mint by Abel Stearns. For reasons still unclear, the resident *Californios* seem to have ignored this gold strike. Certainly, none of the great *ranchero* families of the Southland—Pico Lugo, Yorba, Sepulveda, Dominguéz, del Valle—got excited about it. The majority of the working miners in these placers were from Sonora, Mexico, and when the shallow deposits were worked out, about 1845, they went home to Sonora. They returned by the thousands in 1848–49.

Even though this first discovery was vastly overshadowed by the discovery of January, 1848, it must be mentioned, simply to keep the more rabid Southern Californiacs from unseemly protest. At the 1948 centennial celebration of the gold discovery at Coloma, the late Phil Hanna, creator of *Westways* magazine for the Automobile Club of Southern California, spoke at some length on the manifest injustice then being perpetrated in depriving Southern California of the honor of having the first gold discovery in the state. A similar fate has befallen the find made by thirteen-year-old Billy Gorman on February 22, 1870, at Julian, in the mountains behind San Diego. The mine that came from Billy's find was named appropriately for George Washington, and the camp that resulted from the find is said to have produced some fifteen million dollars before it declined and the strike at Tombstone, Arizona, in 1880 siphoned off its population.

The discovery that triggered *the* Gold Rush was set in motion by John Sutter's need for lumber at his imperial seat of New Helvetia. His quest for a sawmill site convenient to his establishment at Sacramento had been carried on for several years before one was found in a bend of the South Fork of the American River at a spot the Indians called *Culloma* (perhaps *Culloomah* [beautiful vale]), which is today's Coloma, in El Dorado County. A cadaverous, introverted Yankee millwright and carpenter, James W. Marshall, was Sutter's partner and superintendent in building this mill— a vertical saw powered by a waterwheel that operated a Pittman rod off an eccentric on the wheel. In the "tailrace" of the mill (the channel that carries water away from the revolving wheel as its buckets discharge their contents), Sutter's workmen, Marshall being the first, discovered a "mettle" that looked to them like "goald." Debate still continues over whether the exact date of this discovery was January 19 or January 24, 1848. The commonly accepted date is the latter one, and to this writer the argument seems a little academic. The operative fact is the timing of the news affecting the rest of the world, which would not have been affected by the earlier date in any measurable way.

Even though the knowledge of gold's existence became widespread, several months elapsed before it had discernible impact upon California. Sam Brannan, not yet an apostate

Mormon, is said to have started all the excitement by riding through the sandy somnolence that was San Francisco, holding aloft a bottle filled with flakes and shouting, "Gold! Gold! Gold from the American River!" The fact that Brannan had just opened a store at Sutter's Fort may have stirred him into stimulating transient trade.

In the wake of Brannan's ride, the adult male population of California decamped in a body, it seems, for "the diggin's." The memoirs of a young army lieutenant then stationed in California, the immortal William Tecumseh Sherman of later Civil War fame, bear witness to the reduction of U.S. Army forces in California virtually to nothing by desertions of those who sought sudden fortune in the gold-rich streams of the Sierra Nevada.

Rumors of the gold find trickled eastward in the ensuing months but did not find wholehearted acceptance there. The same rumors rippled northward into Oregon, and westward across the Pacific to Hawaii and to Australia, and made their way southward to Mexico and on into Chile and Peru. Men from all these regions, unlike the skeptical Yankees, forthwith made haste to California, and the "forty-eighters," between six and ten thousand of them, came from these places, a very large proportion of them from Mexico. Many of the first-comers, especially the Oregonians, went home when the panning season ended with the advent of the winter rains.

Gold production in this first year has been estimated at ten million dollars, but the existence of gold in quantities beyond belief did not impress the residents back in the States until President Polk's message to the Congress on the State of the Union in December, 1848. His message contained official information from Colonel R. B. Mason, commanding what army he had left in California, that gold had been discovered, and that in quantity. Then the roof fell in, and the astonishing pattern of human movement to California was established, a pulsating migration that has continued throughout her history, as men have sought to better their condition in life beside the Golden Shore.

PERHAPS ONE HUNDRED THOUSAND AMERICANS comprised the starting "Argonauts of '49"; and barring such esoteric promotional schemes as a hot-air balloon line, they ventured by land and sea, and by a combination of these hazards. Leaky, worm-eaten old tubs were hastily refurbished, and tickets to disaster were sold to the frenzied throngs seeking sea passage to the Golden Shore. In the outfitting points along the Missouri River—Independence, Westport, St. Joseph, St. Louis—the prices of horses, mules, wagons, salt pork, flour, powder, and lead went out of sight. And wagons were rigged with sails to make a lumbering navigation of the Great American Desert.

The first of the Americans to reach California did so via Cape Horn, a passage of eighteen thousand miles that consumed six to eight months—with luck. In later years, both the *Flying Cloud* and the *Andrew Jackson* made eighty-nine-day passages from New York to San Francisco; but these were clipper ships, the finest flowering of American genius under sail, which were far, far different from the "butter tubs" that carried the forty-niners on the Cape Horn passage.

Crowded quarters, poor food, and the resultant scurvy and other disease took their toll on this artery, by which perhaps twenty thousand reached California in '49. By July 1, 1850, more than six hundred blue-water vessels, abandoned by their crews, lay rotting and forgotten in San Francisco Bay and its tributaries.

The quickest route, and the one that remained the fastest communications link until the transcontinental railroad was completed in 1869, was by sea and land via Panama. A journey by ship from eastern and Gulf ports to Aspinwall (Colon), then a tortuous overland trek across the Isthmus, then passage in an overloaded side-wheel steamer to San Francisco—it took from five to eight weeks at first. A variant of this route ran by way of Nicaragua. Chagres (yellow) fever, dysentery, malaria, and bandits killed many of those who used this route, but perhaps ten thousand of those who essayed it won through to California.

Merchants' Express Line of Clipper Ships
FOR
SAN FRANCISCO!

NONE BUT A 1 FAST SAILING CLIPPERS LOADED IN THIS LINE.

THE EXTREME CLIPPER SHIP
OCEAN EXPRESS
WATSON, COMMANDER,
AT PIER 9, EAST RIVER.

This splendid vessel is one of the fastest Clippers afloat, and a great favorite with all shippers. Her commander, Capt. WATSON, was formerly master of the celebrated Clipper "FLYING DRAGON," which made the passage in **97 days,** and of the ship POLYNESIA, which made the passage in **103 days.**

She comes to the berth one third loaded, and has very large engagements.

RANDOLPH M. COOLEY,
118 WATER ST., cor. Wall, Tontine Building.

Agents in San Francisco, DE WITT, KITTLE & CO.

These routes were used chiefly by those who resided near salt water. Argonauts from the Mississippi River Valley generally took the overland trails. There were several of these to California, but the one handling the bulk of the traffic was the old Emigrant Trail, the so-called Central Overland Route, which later was followed generally by the Union Pacific–Central Pacific rail linkage. The Central Overland required from sixty to ninety grinding days on horseback, or from three to five months of even more abrasive travel by wagon. Cholera swept the trail in '49, some five thousand graves bespeaking its ravages; and the young men of the Plains tribes acquired status and improved their skills by picking off stragglers and ill-guarded livestock. Approximately forty-five thousand people won through on the Central Overland, but even these did not do so unscathed. Over the forty death-dry Nevada miles between the Sink of Humboldt River and the snow-fed, life-giving waters of the Truckee, one observer who survived its crossing counted 362 abandoned wagons, 350 dead horses, 280 dead oxen, and 120 dead mules along this *via dolorosa*. In addition, these miles were littered with abandoned household treasures; one mound by the wayside was composed of six hundred pounds of jettisoned bacon sides.

We do not know the total human losses on the routes to California in '49. Those who used the variant overland trails brought the estimated total arrivals to upwards of ninety thousand. (Perhaps one-fifth of this number perished within six months of their arrival on the Golden Shore.) These were young, virile, lusty and aggressive, and they represented in many ways the cream of young American manhood of the time. There was a high proportion of literate men, of educated and professional men, among them, and this gave a distinctive flavor to California's first tidal influx of Americans from the older states.

They brought their homegrown political allegiances with them, Whig and Democrat, and it was never settled beyond a reasonable doubt which persuasion held the hardest drinkers. Whig or Democrat, they held firmly to the fixed belief that

119

They came by land and by sea, and by whatever conveyance would carry them (although few flying fish were available). The fastest way of all was by the sleek and beautiful clipper.

every man had an equal right to an equal chance to his fair share of fortune; and it should be remembered well that this was the very first time in America's history that Dame Fortune had extended to the individual the prospect of sudden riches, of gold for the grasping, without let or hindrance or seemingly much effort. Whig or Democrat, they were fundamentally and irrevocably Protestant, cherishing an active mistrust of Popery in every form; and they brought with them an animosity towards Spain and her descendants that went back in time to the Spanish Armada.

They held that God's bounty belonged to native-born Americans, and white at that, and this was reflected in the laws they passed levying a special tax upon "foreign" miners in California. The gold-seekers brought with them the frontier's tradition of free land for the squatting and an ignorance of the property rights of the *Californios* and such as John Sutter—rights which had been acquired pursuant to the laws of Spain and Mexico, and rights that the United States had pledged its honor to uphold in the Treaty of Guadalupe Hidalgo. As a result, they overran lands granted under the preceding governments. Poor, portly John Sutter, the open-handed dreamer, once the self-styled Baron of New Helvetia, was destroyed financially by their locust-like invasion of his broad acres near Sacramento.

When the Argonauts reached California, they quickly expanded the known extent of the "diggin's" from its first center at Coloma. In this expansion, some of them satisfied their avarice with rich discoveries. To meet their needs, and the needs of the teeming thousands of less fortunate seekers, became the destiny of San Francisco.

The heart of the city first beat frantically along the curving little beach of Yerba Buena Cove, which was the city's principal landing spot. Its northern extremity was today's "foot of Broadway," currently the center of an exposure of female flesh; its southern extremity was Rincon Point, where the western buttresses of the Bay Bridge stand today. The waters of the cove lapped against the line of the present Montgomery

Captains lost their crews, merchants their clerks, and French
bourgeois *their servants—all to the lorelei of gold.*

  For a time, a state of greedy hysteria reigned on the East Coast—a
state of mind lampooned by a number of New York's snide lithographers.

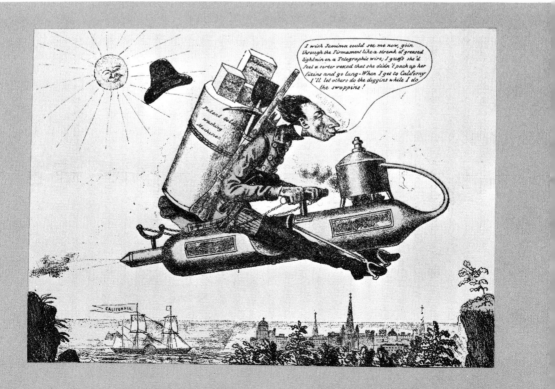

Street at the foot of the California Street hill. Thus, the financial heart of today's San Francisco, from Montgomery Street to the Embarcadero, is built on "fill" from the then near-by small sand hills and other, less prosaic materials.

Deserted sailing ships were burned to the water's edge and then scuttled to make more fill. Commodities that arrived to find a glutted market also were consigned to the bottom of the Bay; stoves, bales of cloth, hogsheads of tobacco, barrels of flour, and assorted jars, boxes, bundles, and parcels of almost anything you care to name became part of modern San Francisco's underpinning.

One of the deserted ships became California's first state prison, before more formal quarters were constructed at San Quentin. Other vessels were driven up onto the beach of the cove to serve as warehouses, hotels, and restaurants. In these usages, the hard fact is reillumined that gold-crazed California's umbilical link with the outside world was the sea, even as it had been in Hispanic days.

Among the more exotic shipments said to have reached San Francisco in '49 was a bevy of *señoritas* from Mazatlán to bring solace and excitement to the Argonauts. Another was a shipment of several hundred cats to combat the hordes of rats, brown, black, gray—all large, all hungry, and all incredibly agile—that infested San Francisco. They were a more obvious pest, although no more voracious, than the sand fleas for which the city was notorious.

San Franciscans who had more than one shirt sent their laundry to Honolulu in the beginning. Some, it is said, sent it clear to Canton, China. Perhaps the first "service" industry in San Francisco was the laundry business; and its first practitioners were brawny Irishwomen, who resented, often forcibly, the later intrusion of the Chinese "washhouses."

THE LURE OF GOLD for the peoples of all the world is shown clearly in the first accurate federal census for California, that of 1860. In this year, the state's total population was

Building and selling and hustling after the main chance: San Francisco's Sacramento Street in about 1851.

379,800 persons, of whom 4,086 were American Negroes; almost 40 percent of this total were foreign born from: China, 34,935; Ireland, 33,147; Germany, 21,646; the British Isles, 15,897; Latin America, 9,150; France, 8,462; Canada, 5,438; and Italy, 2,805. The cultural diversity these seekers brought to California has given the state a distinctive flavor ever since.

The native-born *Californios,* perhaps ten thousand in 1849, were relatively unaffected by the first flush years of the Gold Rush, although many of them profited from the demand for beef cattle that the Rush engendered. For one thing, their land holdings were not in the gold regions of the state; for another, very few of the *Californios* actively participated in the Rush after the earliest months of 1849. By and large, the area of major *Californio* influence remained un-Americanized until after the Civil War. This was Southern California, especially Los Angeles, which became a place of refuge for those who felt that continued residence in San Francisco or the mines would subject them to a fatal attack of "hemp fever." For twenty years after the Rush began, Los Angeles was as tough a little town as California history affords, and it tallied forty legal hangings and thirty-seven impromptu ones in this period—to say nothing of the ones who got away.

The resident Indians suffered most from the Gold Rush, simply because their ancestral homelands either were on the roads to or contained, the "diggin's." There never was what properly could be called an Indian War in California, despite rampant local legends to the contrary, until the reduction of the Modoc in the Lava Beds of northeastern California in the 1870's. Neither was there an organized campaign of genocide against the Indians, despite allegations to the contrary from modern observers conditioned by the horrors of Buchenwald and Auschwitz. Wherever the Indians were in the way, they were removed; and certainly there was violence incident to the clashes between Stone Age and Industrial Revolution. The disruption of the Indians' environment, coupled with the introduction of diseases such as measles against which there was no hereditary immunity, and the introduction of alcohol, for which the Indians had no tolerance to equal their affinity, did more to reduce the Indian population than any other factors. Only in the deserts of Southern California, and along the eastern slope of the Sierra, and in the far northern Sierra and southern Cascade ranges, did the aborigines escape the initial culture-shock of the Gold Rush. To a lesser degree, they escaped it in the Coast Range intervales of Lake, Mendocino, and Humboldt counties. It will be remembered that these areas were not within the gold belt described earlier.

Negroes, as noted earlier, made up about 1 percent of the total population in both 1850 and 1860. These in the main were freed Negroes, and there is little evidence of any significant number of slaves coming to California in the Rush. It was not until World War II that Negroes made an appreciable segment of the total state population, according to federal census reports.

The major foreign element in the first two years of the Rush were Latin-Americans, most of whom came from the north Mexican state of Sonora, which fact is preserved in the California foothill town of that name today. The bulk of these proficient *placeros* was concentrated in the so-called "Southern Mines," from Sonora to Mariposa. So numerous were they that the first anti-foreign legislation in California, the Foreign Miners License Law, was passed in 1850 with them in mind. It imposed a special monthly tax on non-native Americans, and was designed actually to reduce competition for the gold from this source. The law also applied to French and Italian and other foreign-born, although British and British colonials seemingly were exempt from it; later the statute was reinstituted to apply to the Chinese. By the end of 1851 most of the Sonorians, Chileans, and Peruvians had returned to their homelands.

It is commonly accepted in California folklore, and even in all too many history texts, that the corporate ancestor of the Southern Pacific Railroad imported the Chinese for construction purposes. It is demonstrably true that the original Central Pacific Railroad did import vast numbers of Chinese

"Abundance of gold does not always beget . . . a grasping and avaricious spirit. The cosmopolitan cast of society in California, resulting from the commingling of so many races and the primitive mode of life, gave a character of good-fellowship to all its members."

in the latter 1860's to do construction work that the white Californians did not want to do. However, a few Chinese had arrived in San Francisco before 1849; by 1852 there were at least twenty thousand of them, mostly from Canton, and mostly clustered in San Francisco and the valley supply towns. In these communities they filled the need for domestic and other labor that had been created and sustained by the exodus to the mines. That they were hospitably received at first is indicated by the fact that a Chinese contingent was invited to participate in the Fourth of July parade in San Francisco in 1852.

It was not until the Chinese began to compete in the mines, and to do so as the chances for quick fortune faded, that their persecution began. This was aggravated by the economic williwaws of the 1850's and 1870's, when the Chinese became branded as horrible, alien, and outlandish creatures who were taking the bread from the mouths of honest American working-men and their families. This made the basis for the state's long friction with the federal government over restrictive immigration legislation directed against all Asiatics, and it is considered by this writer to have laid the psychological foundation for the emotional hysteria that sanctioned the internment of the Japanese during World War II. Ironically enough, the earliest agitation against the Chinese was sparked in part by other immigrant groups, the Irish being prominent among them.

The Gold Rush came at an opportune time to solve some of Europe's human problems. Ireland had been in the grip of a potato famine for some years in the late 1840's, and it was better to emigrate than to starve beyond the pale of an English landlord's mercy. The Irish element in San Francisco did the brute labor of the port, and their wives did the city's washing and domestic chores before the Chinese came. The Irish quickly became important in the city's politics and have remained so to this day, as the roster of candidates in any municipal election attests.

France had internal problems, too, in this period, and the

French government went so far as to establish a state lottery in which the chief prizes were free passages to California. The Gallic presence in California was expressed quickly in a French-language newspaper, and the great tradition of fine cuisine in San Francisco had its roots in this element. The French, as noted, encountered anti-foreign sentiment in the mines, and a pitched battle between American and French gold seekers was fought near Mokelumne Hill, on the Mother Lode.

Germany experienced an abortive revolt in 1848. Many of its leaders and partisans fled to the United States, including California, where a German-language newspaper sprang up in San Francisco. The bulk of the German segment seems to have eschewed the mines in favor of urban trades, small businesses and professions. One of the first savings banks in San Francisco was organized by a group of Germanic immigrants, and Anaheim was founded as a cooperative colony by a band of German farmers in 1857.

Trace elements of many another ethnic group can be found in the Rush. Hawaiians, being magnificent seamen, had been in California ever since the hide-and-tallow trade. The cadre of Sutter's initial working force at Sutter's Fort had come from the Islands. Place names, such as Kanaka Bar, reflect the Hawaiians' presence in the mines, and, strangely enough, the name of Owyhee County in southwestern Idaho derives from their homeland islands.

The Australians who came to California in the Rush, a national rather than an ethnic minority, constituted an important influence in their own country's later development after their return. What they had seen and learned in California prompted the Aussie "diggers" to look for gold in their own backyard, and their strikes at Ballarat and Bendigo triggered a minor Gold Rush to Australia, which helped to lift it out of its penal colony heritage.

The strong Italian flavor that still exists in parts of San Francisco appears to have been a post–Gold Rush development. So, too, the Portuguese element at Half Moon Bay; the

Henry Austin, M.D.
John Bates
Chs. G. Moxley
J. Goldsborough Bruff. Capt.
Washington City Company
July 26. 1849.

"A long dreary road of more than 2,000 miles lies before you. You that start across the plains . . . will find your ambition and courage fail; and yet. . . ." Above, a camp below Independence Rock, on which travelers have etched their names. Below, crossing the Platte River.

Finnish enclave at Fort Bragg; the Armenian group at Fresno; and the Italian-Swiss grape growers in Sonoma County.

The Japanese influx began in the middle 1890's, encouraged by the need for "stoop labor" in the developing sugar beet industry. In this century, the Filipino element in the Salinas Valley was another response to the demand for agricultural labor, this time in strawberries and lettuce. There is a Sikh (Indian) enclave at Yuba City–Marysville that stems from the same need. The raw labor force additions from Mexico during and after World War I already have been noted.

All these groups, as well as the steady torrent of in-migrants from within the United States, simply highlight California's constant need for labor and her capacity to absorb it because of a continually expanding economy. How true this will be in the future—or is even today—for unskilled labor is thrown into serious question by the Watts riots and similar troubles.

California's growth in every sense has brought her to the impasse of labor versus automation a great deal sooner than a somewhat less violent and certainly a more sustained acceleration would have done.

Popular fancy, as well as many a media presentation, commonly depicts the Gold Rush as a saturnalia of unbridled licentious lust—for gold, for women, or whatever. It warn't necessarily so! At least, not during the first flush times— say, from 1848 into 1850, perhaps even into the mining season of 1851. Personal opinion extends the halcyon days into the latter period; equally competent opinion limits it to 1850.

Whatever its length, this period was the Golden Age of good fellowship in the mines, foreigners excluded. There were isolated murders, plus brawls, fights, horsewhippings, and the like, but in the main, the diaries and letters from the mines at this time reflect a camaraderie that seems unbelievable today. Men could leave their pans of nuggets and dust unattended in their crude brush-and-canvas shelters without fear of loss. The same applied to their tools, which were vital to the task of gold-getting, and to their supply of foodstuffs. Men helped one another, shared with another, in the golden haze of plenty-of-gold-for-all.

Even after the division of the state into counties, each with its duly established and elected officialdom, the men in the mines handled their own problems in a crude but effective working democracy. And it was not a democracy based upon brute force or physical prowess, foreigners again excluded. All the miners (and they were a transient lot) that were assembled at any camp or river bar or gulch comprised the Miners Association of that place at any given time. They drew up their own code of laws applicable to the particular locale; regulated the size of claims, thus equalizing opportunity for all; passed laws regarding the use of water; and, in general, made a constantly shifting congeries of self-governing entities. Heinous crimes were punished either by banishment from camp or by flogging, in the tradition of Captain Bligh. Occasionally, there was a hanging, after a jury trial, and less frequently there was a lynching. The record made a remarkable demonstration of self-discipline by men who were under the cruellest of compulsions, that of material gain for the seizing.

This almost idyllic time drew to a close as the easy-to-get placer gold petered out. Its demise was hastened, in my opinion, by the civic housecleaning in San Francisco effected by the First Committee of Vigilance in 1851, which inspired an unsavory exodus to the interior mines. Thereafter, the inland incidence of what we now call crimes of violence increased. The actions of the Committees of Vigilance of 1851 and 1856 in San Francisco, incidentally, may be considered as essential surgery to restore the health of the body politic, a view long held; or they may be considered prototypes of Fascist totalitarianism, a contemporary view among more gentle souls, and among those who refuse to believe that anything vile can be spawned in an urban setting.

In the realm of outlaws, a matter dear to the media mythologists, California can present three—Joaquin Murrieta, Black Bart, and Tiburcio Vasquez—who have been fixed right firmly in the public consciousness.

Joaquin Murrieta, today is as much figment as fact. His story, and it has been repeated *ad nauseam,* was born in the 1852 writings of a half-Cherokee newspaper editor at Marysville, John Rollin "Yellow Bird" Ridge. That there was an actual fleshly body with the name of Joaquin Murrieta is indisputable; that he did all the things Ridge attributed to him is highly questionable. In fact, he seems to have gotten the credit for a number of hair-raising stunts perpetrated by other Hispanic gentry such as Joaquin Carillo, Joaquin Valenzuela, Joaquin Ocomorena, and Joaquin Gonzalez—all of whom had a deficient sense of property rights. This may explain why the legislature offered a reward for the capture of "Joaquin," patronym unspecified. A company of California Rangers was organized under Harry Love, the so-called "Black Knight of Zayante," and in due time a severed head preserved in alcohol was exhibited as the veritable visage of the "Robin Hood of El Dorado." The hard core of the Joaquin legend seems to be in the creation of a folk hero, and his virtual enshrinement in the Hispanic lore of California may indicate his role in assuaging their sense of dispossession and persecution by the Anglo-Americans.

Black Bart—who signed himself "The P O 8," in an execrable pun—was one Charles E. Bolton, or Boles, who holds the distinction of staging the first successful stagecoach robbery in the state, and this not until the early 1870's. He was a mild-mannered little man of incredible endurance, who lived most of the time in San Francisco, enjoying its amenities, and only took to the road when his purse was becoming bare. He told his friends in the city, including members of its police force, that his absences were occasioned by having to look after his "mining properties" in the mountains. Over a span of years, he robbed about twenty-six stages; never killing anyone, never wounding anyone, never retaining ladies' purses, and

"For the mutual protection of life and property. . . ."
A certificate of membership in the Vigilance Committee of 1856.

always using an unloaded shotgun as his means of moral suasion. Legend holds that in each looted treasure box, he left a derisive bit of doggerel, or "P O 8-try" (poetry). Wells Fargo, which bore the brunt of his extractions, has but two of these verses, and his reputation as a practicing poet seems to have been exaggerated. The following sample may support this premise:

> "I've labored long and hard for bread
> For honor and for riches
> But on my corns too long you've trod
> You fine-haired sons of bitches."

Black Bart finally was apprehended because he dropped a handkerchief bearing a San Francisco laundry's mark. He had stopped his last stage with the time-honored shout of "Throw down the box!" when he was shot in the rump by the rifle of a youngish rabbit-hunter who was near by. A hoary legend holds that Bart was released from prison on his promise not to commit any more crimes, including the writing of verse!

Tiburcio Vasquez ranged California in the 1870's and 1880's, from San Benito to Fresno to Los Angeles and the Mojave Desert. That he was able to do this in a day of intra-state telegraph and railroad communications is a tribute to his horsemanship, to his daring, and to the Hispanic Californians who befriended him, partly out of fear, partly as a despoiler of *los gringos*. Vasquez was an outlaw, nothing more or less, and a cutthroat as well. His enshrinement is of a piece with the maudlin process that has made a social activist out of the buck-toothed, murderous little thug we call "Billy the Kid."

Many of the men who won through to California in the Rush were veterans of the Mexican War; many more of them would fight in the Civil War that grew out of the one great failure to date in the essential democratic process of compromise. No matter what material goods they had to abandon along the trail to the Golden Shore, their cultural baggage

Protectors of life and property: Vigilance
Committee "Sharpshooters," 1856.

*"There are rare chances here of seeing human nature
in one of its most dark and exciting phases."*

held intact a sense of personal honor that could be satisfied in but one way: "Pistols for two and coffee for one"!

The men who framed the state's first constitution recognized this habit in their fellows by inserting an anti-dueling provision in that document. It was honored more in the breach than the observance, and between 1850 and 1860 California counted more fatal duels than any other state in the Union. Among these was the notable encounter on September 13, 1859, between the Chief Justice of the California Supreme Court, David S. Terry, and U.S. Senator David C. Broderick, in which the latter was mortally wounded. This has been said to constitute the "fourth most noted duel in the United States." More importantly, Broderick's death gutted the Democratic Party in California, inasmuch as the quarrel had its origins in a brass-knuckled battle for that party's control; its outcome was of no little assistance in bringing the Republicans to a position of dominance within the state.

E ACH SUCCESSIVE AMERICAN FRONTIER in our westering surge was marked by a slow evolution from raw wilderness to stable society, a process that was accelerated tremendously in California. On our other frontiers, the transition required a generation or more; in California it took perhaps five years.

The heyday of the happy individual gold-seeker—when the surface gold could be harvested with pan, pick, and shovel—dawned in 1848 and flourished at least through 1850. Then, after loose gold had been depleted from the stream beds and gulches, it became necessary for the miners to band together in associative groups, or partnerships, to accomplish the physical tasks necessary to obtain the less accessible gold. This period began in 1851, and by 1853 the search for gold had entered the corporate stage because of the amounts of capital required to engage in relatively sophisticated types of mining. Thus, the three stages in the transition, in terms of the individual, were: (a) self-employed placer miner; (b) member of an associative group; (c) wage-earning employee of a corporation. In 1852, gold production approximated eighty million dollars, which marks the peak of the placer period in stages (a) and (b) above. Thereafter, production declined steadily to about seventeen million dollars annually and stabilized at this figure for the remainder of the century, as mining itself became stabilized in stage (c).

The advent of the third stage began the stabilization of the Mother Lode communities. The mining camps that had vast gravel beds to be sluiced away by the hydraulic technique, those that had quartz ledges to be exploited by shafts and hoists and mills—these were the ones that endured, the ones that brought schools and churches and other appurtenances of social community to themselves and the area around them. The purely placer camps became trodden dust, of each one of which it can be said, " 'Twas lively while she lasted." Many of these today are not even ghost towns.

Between stages (b) and (c) above, the slow erosion of population in the Mother Lode counties began. This was not swift enough to prevent the location of the state capital at Sacramento in 1854, after some political peregrinations between San Jose, Vallejo, and Benicia over the preceding four years. The gold counties wanted the seat of government where they could reach it more easily than by traveling to tidewater; perhaps, too, they wanted it away from the cosmopolitan corruptions of San Francisco. Whatever the reason, they had the political muscle to gain their point; in 1854, for example, El Dorado County boasted four state senators, out of sixteen total; and eight assemblymen, out of thirty-six total. The city and county of San Francisco in the same year had but one more legislative member, an assemblyman, than did El Dorado County. It should be remembered here, particularly in view of the recent furore over reapportioning the legislature, that between 1850 and 1926 California elected both houses of the legislature on a population basis, not by the so-called "federal" system.

Mining as a corporate enterprise: Above, the milling works
of the Quartz Mining Company, Grass Valley. Below, placer
operations on the Middle Fork of the Feather River.

The continued flow of people out of the gold counties gave an impetus to agricultural settlement and community development in the Great Valley. The major internal market for the valley's crops was the urban nucleus of the San Francisco Bay area, and the port of San Francisco was the valley's major means of access to world markets. The financial and commercial dominance of the state by San Francisco would remain unchallenged until the emergence of Los Angeles in the next century. Similarly, the political dominance of the state would be exercised practically continuously by its northern urban areas—San Francisco Bay, Sacramento, Stockton—until the balance of population shifted to Southern California during and after World War II.

It is the speed of the transition from self-employed placer miner to wage-earning corporate employee, coupled with the growth of the urban areas in the north, that enables us to say that California was the first urbanized state in the whole Far West. A great measure of social stratification and class consciousness would have come to California with this rapid transition and the population shift it promoted had it not been for the Comstock Lode. Erupting out of the almost lunar landscape of western Nevada, the Comstock gave California an infusion of new capital and an impetus to all forms of production that kept the fluidity of its social structure alive.

Technological changes wrought by gold came more slowly than social changes, simply because the basic techniques of initial mining endeavors in California were as old, at least, as the Phoenicians. By and large, the refinements of these techniques in California were only adaptive and expansive. Further refined on the Comstock Lode, they spread throughout the whole mining frontier of the Far West, which is to say, roughly, the vast expanse between the summits of the Rocky Mountains and the Sierra Nevada–Cascade Range. Needless to say, California capital was instrumental in developing these other mining operations.

Very few Americans with any experience in gold-mining came to California in the Rush. Cherokees and whites from

139

OVERLEAF: *The great Sacramento flood of 1850.*

VIEW OF SACRAM

AS IT APPEARED DURING THE GREAT INUNDATION

The City is situated on a Plain, on the east Bank of the Sacramento River about 145 miles from San Francisco
from the Mountains was about 20 feet. The small Island covered with tents at the head of J. St. on the left is called by the In
during the Flood   In the distance at the head of J. St. will be seen Sutters Fort about 2½ miles from the Levee   In the ex
mostly covered with Snow the year round and present a most striking and beautiful appearance when view'd from the City
was ... during the summer 1849 at a Cost of $73,000. The Sutter Hotel the large frame building facing the Levee on the est

NTO CITY.

ANUARY 1850.

se of the River during the Flood occasioned by heavy rains and the melting of Snow
Sacum a Knoll of ground made by the Indians and the only dry spot visible for miles
distance will be seen the Sierra Nevada Mountains or the Gold Region whose tops are
e City Hotel, the large Frame building facing on the Levee or River on the left of J. St.
ght was built during the fall of 1849. Cost $ 50,000.

We cheerfully concur in recommending the above Picture
and accurate Drawing of the City of Sacramento as
during the Flood of January 1850.

Capt.

Mayor of

Editor of the
Sacramento City.

Georgia, where a minor gold rush had developed in the 1830's, were the only native Americans with any proficiency in the skills of placer mining. Other Argonauts from the Michigan Peninsula brought with them the skills they had acquired in the mining excitement that began there in 1846. The most experienced body of gold-miners were the Sonorians from Mexico, who were adept at "dry washing" auriferous sands in a shallow, circular wooden bowl *(la batea)* very similar to the pan used in wet washing. The *batea,* too, was rotated in a circular motion, but instead of washing away the lighter material with water, the Sonorian blew it out very carefully. Much fine gold was lost by this process. Another dry-washing technique of the Sonorians was to toss gold-bearing gravel on a blanket, just as in winnowing wheat in olden days, letting the wind blow the lighter dirts away and then carefully hand-sorting what was left to get the gold. Again, this was a wasteful and time-consuming process.

Water was the *sine qua non* for those who groveled in the golden gravels of the Mother Lode, and the pattern of California's climate, with its marked dry and wet seasons, greatly limited the continuity of placer mining at first. It was confined of necessity to those periods when there was enough, *but not too much,* water in the streams—say April to July, and again between mid-September and the heavy rains of winter in late November. These time spans, of course, varied with each year and with the specific locale in the Mother Lode, because of the "micro-climates" of this region.

James Marshall and his helpers at Sutter's ill-starred sawmill extracted their first gold by the simple expedient of prizing it, with a knife blade, out of the crevices in the native rock where it had been deposited and held fast by its weight. The belief that this was a common practice in California became so widespread that people arrived with specially made tongs, very like ice-bucket tongs today, to extract their share; some even brought padded stools upon which to sit in comfort while they did so.

The basic placering instrument at first was the "miner's

pan," which can still be purchased today in many an inland hardware store. A common frying pan would serve, and do double duty when the day's work of getting gold was done. The favorite spots were gravel bars and terraces beside running water. The pan was filled with gravel, sand, and water, and rotated between the hands to spill out these elements gradually and gently until nothing was left but the heaviest particles, including the gold, if there was any.

As the readily accessible treasure troves were depleted, it became necessary to build dams to divert the stream flow through canals (dug by hand) in order to get down to the bedrock where the gold concentration was always heaviest, or believed to be. (As early as 1918, marine diving suits were used to reach bedrock beneath deep pools on the Middle Fork of Feather River, and today's enthusiasts use scuba-gear and suction equipment for the same purpose.) These efforts took more capital than one man could muster; they required more muscle and sweat than any one man possessed. Hence, these ventures became associative ones.

Concomitantly, the miner's pan was replaced by a more efficient instrument, the cradle. This was shaped just as its name implies, with an inclined floor, crossed with cleats to act as riffles to catch the gold. Dirt was shoveled in at the upper end, and water was poured in, too, while the miner rocked the cradle and speeded the extraction process. A very strong or a most determined man could work a cradle alone; two men were better and processed more dirt per day. The cradle was so short that much of the finer gold was lost in the process.

The cradle evolved into the "Long Tom," or sluice box. It consisted of three-sided sections, dovetailed into one another to get whatever length was necessary to prevent undue loss of fine gold. The length of the sluice box was crossed with cleats, as in the cradle, and a refinement was to coat the bottom of the sections with mercury, which has an affinity for gold. The recovery rate was much improved by this method, and the mercury amalgam was distilled in iron retorts to get the gold. The mercury was recovered for re-use by means of a vapor condenser. Here again, the sluice-box technique was too much for one man to build and operate properly.

There was never any single, great "Mother Lode" in the Sierra, but many, many lodes, or veins. One man could sink a shaft on one of these veins by himself, but once he dug deeper than the length of a long-handled shovel plus his own height, the task of getting the rock out of the hole became tedious. Even two or three or four men could go down only so far with windlass and bucket before the necessity of mechanical hoisting energy and equipment became mandatory. Also, crushing quartz rock by hand was a laborious way of getting the ore ready to be washed by pan, cradle, or sluice box. Lode or shaft mining, as it is often called, thus became a partnership venture from its beginnings, and evolved into a corporate one.

The Empire Mine in Grass Valley began as a group effort about 1850 and produced more than $80,000,000 in its century of operations. Its shaft eventually probed 7,000 feet below its mountain surface and bottomed 1,500 feet *below* sea level. In Amador County, where about one-half of all the vein gold mined in California has been produced, the Argonaut Mine yielded more than $25,000,000 between its beginnings in the latter 1850's and 1942; its shaft had a vertical depth of 5,570 feet. Forty-seven men perished underground when fire swept the Argonaut's workings in 1922. In this same county, the Kennedy Mine produced some $45,000,000 in its lifetime out of a shaft that went down 6,000 feet. Wooden bucket-wheels, forty-eight feet in diameter, lifted the tailings (waste) from its mill into flumes that carried them away to ever-increasing spreading grounds.

Lode or shaft mining was a tremendous impetus to the state's young explosives industry, which thus meshed with its and the state's needs. The California Powder Works began operations near Santa Cruz as early as 1865 and produced the state's first smokeless powder. Two years later, the Atlas

Powder Company (now Hercules) produced the state's first dynamite. Its rights to use the patents of a Swedish inventor enabled it to produce Dr. Nobel's Patent Blasting Oil (nitro-glycerine) just in time to give mining and the Central Pacific Railroad a mighty hand against the granite of the Sierra Nevada.

Drilling machinery using steam and compressed air was infinitely quicker than hand sledge and drill steel for putting in the holes to hold the powder. Better rock-crushing machinery, such as the steel-shod stamp, the agitating table, and other extractive equipment were just as necessary to quartz mining as hoisting and blasting equipment. These demands both nourished California's heavy industry and were supplied by it.

Gold-bearing gravels were sometimes found in great bodies well away from any living water with which to wash them by any of the usual processes. The finder of such "dry diggin's" originally had the back-breaking task of shoveling his dirt into a leather bucket or a canvas sack and carrying it on his back or in a barrow, if he could afford one, to the nearest stream. This was hard work and slow. It was more practicable to bring the water to the gravel. This solution, however, conflicted with the basic English common-law doctrine of "riparian rights" to water, which prohibited the diversion of water from a stream unless it was returned undiminished, save for domestic consumption. To meet their needs, the miners evolved their own law of waters, which became known as the doctrine of "appropriation and beneficial use." While Spanish law had permitted the appropriation and diversion of waters to non-riparian lands, this does not appear to have been the ancestor of mining-camp laws on the same subject.

The new doctrine permitted water to be diverted from its normal course to be used beneficially elsewhere, without necessarily having to be returned to the stream of origin. This solved the problem of profitably working many dry diggings and laid the basis for California's present water laws, without which diversion for irrigation would be impossible. It also laid the foundation for hydraulic mining, California's first great innovative contribution to mining technology.

All up and down the Sierra's western slope, particularly along its northern reaches, lay tremendous bodies of gold-bearing gravels that were too low grade to be worked profitably except in great volume. The miners therefore utilized the force of falling water to cut down whole hillsides, hundreds of feet high, and send the liquid muck (called "slickens") through sluice boxes that reached thousands of feet in length. The water was played against the bluff or hillside through gigantic nozzles (called "monitors"), often more than six feet long, that threw as much as a nine-inch stream up to four hundred feet under tremendous pressure. These gigantic undertakings left dramatic remains—tall spires and minarets and fluted columns—of which the most startling examples are to be seen at Cherokee, Butte County, and near North Bloomfield, Nevada County.

Water from the higher reaches of the Sierra Nevada was what made possible these monster operations; some 425 of them were operating at the peak of the hydraulic industry in the latter 1870's, and they consumed seventy-two million gallons of water per day. Storage dams were developed in the high country to provide water for year-round operations, and this water was delivered to the monitors by an extensive network of canals, flumes, ditches, and pipes. The Middle Yuba and Eureka Lake Company alone had more than seven hundred miles of delivery system. Water sales to others were often more profitable to this company than its own gold recovery. Two years after Alexander Graham Bell received his first patent, another gigantic water-supply firm, the South Yuba Canal Company, strung 184 miles of telephone line to maintain contact with its water sources and delivery systems; this is said to have been the world's first long-distance network. Today many foothill towns owe their water supply to the original hydraulic developments. One of the most prominent of these is at Paradise, Butte County.

In just one year's operations, the hydraulic mines of the

Until hydraulic mining was banned in 1884, enormous jets of water sluiced out the gold, silted up the Sacramento River, and left the land maimed and rutted, as shown in the photograph below.

northern Sierra dumped forty-six million cubic yards of slick-ens into the streams that fed the Sacramento River. This was the equivalent of a solid mass one-mile long by one-mile wide by forty-five feet high. By 1878 hydraulic debris had raised the bed of the Yuba River more than thirty feet, and the city of Marysville found itself *beneath* the level of the river and dependent upon levees for protection. The problem was aggravated downstream as the bed of the Sacramento River was continually built up by the influx of slickens, with result-ant flooding of agricultural acreage. The farmers built their levees higher; the hydraulic monitors relentlessly washed down more of the Sierra foothills; more flooding ensued.

This brought about a bitter conflict that pitted farmer against miner, and violence flared before it finally was settled by legislation and court action in 1883–84. A requirement of the settlement, that hydraulic operations construct their own catchment areas to prevent ensilting of the Sacramento and other watercourses, proved so costly that hydraulic mining came to an end. It is said that some four hundred million dollars could be recovered from the North San Juan Ridge (Nevada County) if hydraulic mining could be resumed.

Dredging was the last phase in the technological evolution of California mining, and made the state's second major inno-vative contribution to mining processes. The dredges were used mainly in the lower foothills and along the rim of the Great Valley, as they required reasonably level terrain to gar-ner the "flour" gold in the gravelly soil. Once more, volume was the key to profits. As dredge capacity increased, it became possible to work ground that returned as little as forty-three cents per cubic yard.

A dredge was a boat hull floating in a man-made little lake. It held machinery that caused a boom-supported, revolving bucket-chain to lift up the gravel and dump it onto a revolv-ing cylindrical screen where water washed the finer materials down onto mechanically agitated riffle tables coated with mer-cury. The vast quantity of waste was ejected in windrows behind the dredge, filling in the lake behind as the dredge

They dreamed, travelled, and sweated for gold.
Some won, some lost, and most made wages for grub.
OVERLEAF: *San Francisco, the city that dreams imagined, and gold built.*

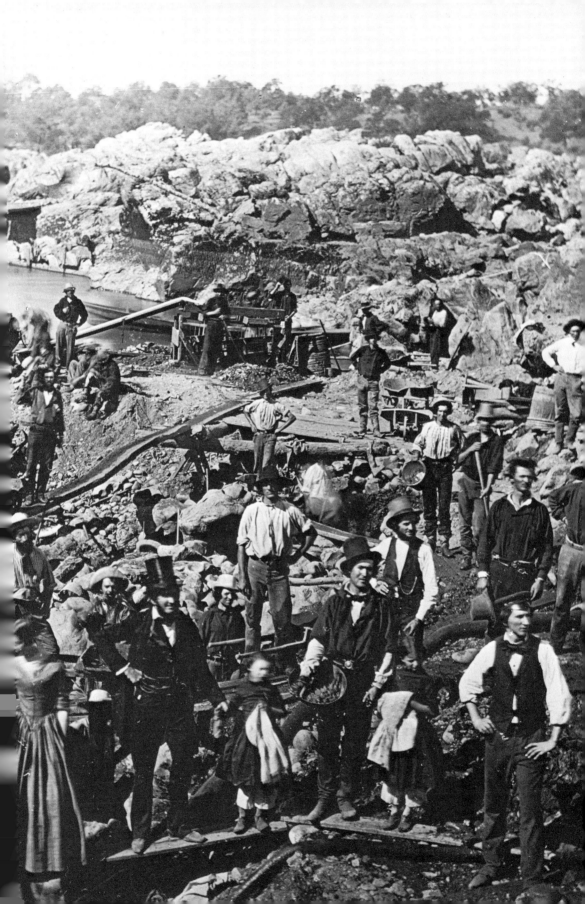

gnawed its way forward with its revolving buckets. Rock windrows are a common sight throughout the Sierra foothills, and it is noteworthy that debris from dredging operations was the major source of material for the gigantic, earth-fill Oroville Dam, which has begun to impound water for future delivery to Southern California as this book is being written.

Today's Natomas Corporation and Yuba Consolidated Industries both began as gold-dredging operations. Dredges made in California found use all over the world, for tin as well as for gold, and three specially designed dredges were airlifted into the New Guinea highlands in the 1930's for Bulolo Goldfields, Ltd. The last of these monsters to work in California is coming to the end of its operations today near Marysville.

The flush years of the Rush saw California without any adequate medium of exchange. The first state constitution prohibited banks from issuing currency, and a branch of the United States Mint was not established in San Francisco until 1854. Even though coins from all over the world circulated freely, coinage was so scarce that a man with minted Mexican dollars could swap them for dust or nuggets at eight dollars an ounce. Scales for weighing gold were not as common in the Rush as is often imagined today, save at express company offices, banks, and the larger mercantile firms. A "pinch" of dust, the amount that could be lifted between thumb and forefinger, was commonly accepted as an ounce, worth sixteen dollars at par. (Thus, the saying "How much can you raise in a pinch?" acquired its meaning.) Gold from different sections of mining country brought different prices per ounce; that from the "southern mines" around Sonora and Columbia being more valuable than that from the "northern mines" around the Yuba and Feather rivers' drainage. Unscrupulous fellows were given to mixing a judicious quantity of copper or brass filings with their dust to increase its weight and offset low values received in exchanging it for coinage or goods. An unfortunate inability to distinguish between the gold from the different regions of California is said to have played a part in the col-

One gold rush paid off—so why not another, and another, and another?
Goldseekers board a steamer bound for Alaska in 1897.

lapse of the banking firm of Page, Bacon & Company, triggering the financial panic of 1855 in San Francisco.

To meet the state's need for coinage, private firms built around assay offices that had smelting or refining facilities minted their own coins—illegal under the federal Constitution but allowed by necessity. Coins struck off by these private mints, especially the fifty-dollar octagonal gold slugs, are rare collector's items today; the author has fondled two of these, each valued at $1,275 in today's fiat currency. Even after a branch of the federal Mint was established in San Francisco in 1854, private assay offices continued to transform raw gold into bars for their customers at charges lower than those levied by the Mint for the same service.

VERY FEW OF THOSE WHO PARTICIPATED in the buoyant, boyish Jasonic quest for the Golden Fleece that was the Gold Rush made fortunes from it. A day's work waist deep in the rushing icy waters of a Sierra stream might average out at sixteen to twenty dollars. With eggs at one dollar each, flour at three to five dollars per pound; boots and blankets at forty dollars per pair, and whiskey in proportion—this did not leave much room for saving, even by doing one's own cooking. The *big* finds—the nameless Chinese who once scratched out a nugget worth $5,000 near Bed Bug; the single lump worth $43,534 that was found near Carson Hill—were just like today's jackpot winners at Reno or Las Vegas. We refuse to remember, or even to thing about, the small winners and the inevitable losers. Yet, for the men who made the Rush, it was the great adventure of their lives, and the memories of it warmed their hearts until they died.

The Gold Rush laid the foundations for California's industrial manufacturing, for its banking and transportation systems, for its commercial activities. It gave a tremendous impetus to agriculture, and it shed a golden haze across California that affected the minds and hearts of people all around the world, and still does. It was the catalytic agent between land, man, and growth in California.

155

"I would not for ten thousand dollars have stayed at Madison and lost what I have seen. . . ."

Green Gold:
Eternal Asset?

TRULY CAN IT BE SAID that Colonial America was trees; a dense hardwood forest that covered the eastern one-third of the nation, except on the rolling grassland prairies of western Indiana and Illinois. The English colonists learned, from the Swedes and Finns along the Delaware River, how to build log cabins. Lumber became the first export commodity of England's colonies, and the axe and the saw were as indispensable as the long rifle in the westward movement between the Atlantic seaboard and the Mississippi River.

Beyond the rolling river, west of eastern Kansas, the environment changed to semiarid, then arid, as the land lifted slowly towards the snow-crowned crests of the Rocky Mountains. Only in the higher elevations abutting the Continental Divide, only along the beds of streams whose waters were "too thin to plow and too thick to drink" were there "timber islands" to provide the settler with the building materials that he knew and needed. Between the Rockies and the Sierra–Cascade summits, the timber situation was even worse, thanks to the climatic changes wrought by the upheavals of geologic time. Thus, the formation of the California landscape gives us another example of Nature's generosity in its magnificent timber stands.

These include the cathedral-column redwood, the world's tallest living plant, the *palo alto* of the Spaniards, one specimen of which has been measured as soaring skywards more

"And the forests shall be leveled. . . ." An ox-team hauls timber out of the northern California mountains.

than 369 feet; and the "Big Tree" of the Sierra, the world's largest living plant. In the White Mountains across Owens Valley from the forbidding granite scarp of the Sierra, the world's oldest living thing, the bristlecone pine, clings tenaciously to life as it has for more than five thousand years. Together with these superlatives, California's timber largesse includes oaks and pines and firs and cedars—all useful to man's past and present needs, and vital to California's future. This natural resource demanded a superior technology to permit its development in the service of the state, the nation, and the world.

With the exception of the canoe-building peoples of the Santa Barbara Channel and along the Klamath River system, if one Indian used up one tree in one lifetime, he was guilty of conspicuous waste. The California Indians made no use of timber, except for the windfalls or branches they gathered for firewood and shelter framework. The Spanish and the *Californios* under Mexico's regime took but little more advantage of this tremendous natural resource.

Beams for the missions, for the presidios, and for dwellings were hacked painfully from the coastal timber stands, but the basic building material of Hispanic California (1769–1846) was the sun-dried *adobe* brick. The crude, two-wheeled cart *(la carreta)* that was the bulk transportation vehicle of Hispanic California had a framework of poles, covered with hides, and its wheels were sections of tree trunk. Doors, window frames, tables, benches, and chairs were virtually unknown in California until the advent of "foreigners"—Russian, English, and American—introduced the first crude tools and techniques of lumber-processing.

The Russians at Fort Ross appear to have been the first to make commercial use of the towering redwood *(Sequoia sempervirens)*, one specimen of which today can yield enough lumber to construct twelve two-bedroom houses. At the time of their first utilization, the redwood groves spread along the coast from Crescent City to the Santa Lucia Mountains below Carmel, and reached inland with the coastal climate belt along the San Francisco Peninsula, the Marin and Sonoma hills, and in the Coast Range folds behind Berkeley and Oakland. By 1827, it is believed, the Russians were whipsawing and splitting redwood planks and timbers that were sold in the Hawaiian Islands. They also are reported to have manufactured prefabricated houses by erecting them at Fort Ross, then marking and numbering the pieces, and knocking them apart for export.

In the 1830's, Thomas Larkin, the United States Consul at Monterey, began developing an export trade in redwood, using the whipsaw and splitting techniques (remember that redwood follows its grain for seemingly incredible lengths). His source of supply was the redwood groves of Santa Cruz County, and his markets were in Southern California, Mazatlán, and Hawaii. In this same period, an Englishman known as "Bill the Sawyer" began whipsawing and splitting redwood near today's exurban community of Woodside.

Who established the first powered sawmill is a matter still of some conjecture. A water-powered sawmill is known to have been erected by Juan Bautista Roger Cooper along the Russian River in either 1834 or 1837. Another is believed to have been built near Zayante, Santa Cruz County, in 1840 (some say 1842) by Peter Lassen, the perdurable Danish blacksmith who left his name on a volcanic peak, a county, a national park and a national forest, all in northeastern California. In this same period an ex-trapper turned *ranchero,* George Yount, erected a water-powered sawmill on the slopes of Mount St. Helena; and a few years later, Edward T. Bale gave three thousand acres of land to Ralph Kilburn in payment for a sawmill Kilburn had built near Calistoga. The first sawmill to use steam is believed to have been brought from Baltimore in 1843 by sea captain Stephen Smith, who erected it on Salmon Creek, near Bodega Bay. John Sutter's need for lumber was a factor in his purchase of Fort Ross, and his continuing quest for lumber, of course, led to the discovery of gold—which destroyed him.

Lumber became the first natural resource to be exploited

after gold, although it also can be said that it was exploited concurrently with gold. It can be said further that, without the extravagant supply of timber in close proximity to the gold belt, the production of gold would have been far smaller.

At the time the Rush began, the virgin stands of coniferous timber grew much lower down the western slope of the Sierra than it does today. The best of these stands (best because they were the most easily worked into planks and beams and timbers) were the two great pines: the three-needled yellow pine *(Pinus ponderosa)* and the five-needled sugar pine *(Pinus lambertiana).* The availability of these species in quantity throughout the Mother Lode provided the raw materials for cradles and sluice boxes, for water flumes and diversion dams, and for the timbers and planks so vital to both the shaft- and hydraulic-mining processes. For building and for fuel as well, the Mother Lode's timber resources were indispensable.

Sawpits were the first means of converting timber to lumber for the mines. A hole was dug and heavy timbers, or small tree trunks, were laid across it, onto which a log was rolled. Then one man got on top of the log and another underneath, in the pit, and they used a crosscut saw to inch their way slowly through the log, making planks. The bottom man, of course, got the sawdust down his neck, but he also might find gold in the pit while waiting for a new log to be rolled into place. The sawpits were soon followed by water-powered, then by steam-powered, mills. The first were the same as Sutter's mill: a crosscut saw, set in vertical guides, and pushed up and down by a Pittman rod working off an eccentric on the water-wheel, or later off the action of the steam cylinder piston rod. Ironically enough, had Sutter retained title to his sawmill, he might have salvaged a financial gain from the disaster that the Gold Rush brought him. Lumber from these early Sierra mills brought one dollar per linear foot, regardless of width, and a common price in 1851 was around $650 per thousand board feet.

Although lumber from the Sierra Nevada stands was vital to the mines and camps of the Mother Lode, the terrain of

161

The Big River, *one of the many small, two-masted lumber schooners that operated out of the "doghole" ports of the Mendocino Coast.*

the foothills and the Great Valley precluded its utilization elsewhere until the subsidiaries of the Central Pacific Railroad began to traverse the valley floor in the 1870's. The roads down into the Great Valley and on the valley floor itself were classed as "impassable, not even jackassable" most of the winter months, and were hub-deep in dust come summer. Thus, hauling costs were prohibitive. And the courses of the rivers plunging down from the Sierra imposed additional transportation obstacles.

Men from New England, where log-driving on the rivers was basic to lumbering operations, tried to float or raft logs and timbers down the California rivers with a notable lack of success. As might well have been said by these hopeful "river pigs": "Of all the variable things in Creation, the most uncertain are the actions of a jury, the workings of a woman's mind, and the conditions of California's rivers. The crookedness you see ain't but half the crookedness there is." Too, the basic weather pattern in California left the streams with insufficient water in the summer months to make the rivers suitable for consistent log or lumber transportation. And winter logging was not practiced in California as it was in New England and the Great Lakes region, again because of the weather pattern.

California's first urban needs for lumber were met in part by importations around Cape Horn from New England, and even by camphorwood planks from China. Prefabricated houses, both of lumber and of iron, were shipped to San Francisco in the 1849–51 period. The main source of supply was the redwood stands of the coastal mountains, where the sea provided a ready and usable route to market. Six so-called sawmills were operating in the Santa Cruz Mountains by the closing months of 1849; two years later there were fifteen in the Woodside area, and Redwood City acquired its name because it was the shipping point for their production. Across the Bay, along the *contra costa*, the lumbering settlement of Clinton became the nucleus of today's Oakland. San Francisco was swept by fire six times during the first two years of

Men, steam, and timber: two views of the 1880's.

the Rush, and each time it was rebuilt largely with redwood lumber. The importance of accessible redwood stands, and of the sea access route to market, is demonstrated by the fact that 90 percent of the lumber consumed in Sacramento in 1858 came from the Redwood Coast and from the Puget Sound and Columbia River timber stands.

The interaction of the Puget Sound and Columbia River regions with California should not be overlooked. It was particularly important to the growth of Los Angeles and the resultant sustained demand for lumber. The basic timber of these two regions was, and is, Douglas fir, which possesses far more structural strength than redwood or pine—a characteristic vital to construction. Too, these regions had the great advantage of sea transportation the length of the Pacific Coast, which required no other investment than a vessel and the crew's wages. Later on, when the seaports of San Francisco and Los Angeles were joined by rail with the Great Basin and southwestern states, Douglas fir from the Pacific Northwest became important in the development of towns, mines, and industries in these inland regions.

California was more than a market for the Pacific Northwest's lumber. From its gold, it furnished much of the initial investment capital to develop the lumbering industry in that region, and it played a major role for many years in distributing the production of this industry to other parts of the Far West.

The need for ships to transport lumber stimulated shipbuilding in both California and the Pacific Northwest; this in turn led to a unique contribution to naval architecture, the so-called "steam schooner." With engines and boilers located aft, like a miniature tanker, these vessels were admirably suited to carrying cargoes of long timbers and were very "handy," in maritime parlance, when it came to navigating into and out of the dangerous "dog-hole" ports of the Mendocino and Humboldt coasts. This lumber trade evolved techniques of loading lumber that provide a classic demonstration of the uses of industrial technology.

Inasmuch as a through rail connection between San Francisco and Eureka on Humboldt Bay did not materialize until 1915, the importance of sea transportation to both the redwood lumber industry and the urban growth of California was tremendous.

Before the Sierra timber stands became a major factor in California's internal development, they were vital to the successful development of the Comstock Lode. The eastern slope of the Sierra and the contiguous territory in Nevada is timber-deficient, because of the "rain shadow" effect discussed earlier. The Comstock Lode—literally the bowels of Mount Davidson—could not have been worked safely or profitably without ample supplies of timber to shore up its miles of tunnels and stopes and winzes and shafts, the last of which became among the deepest in the world. The steam-powered hoisting machinery, the ore reduction plants along the Carson River, the construction and domestic needs of Virginia City and Gold Hill and Carson City—all were dependent upon forest products. After the eastern slope of the Sierra had been denuded, these needs were met by timber from the Lake Tahoe basin. The eastern rim of the basin around Glenbrook was cut out first; then log rafts were towed across the lake from the western shore to meet the insatiable demand of the Comstock for lumber in all its forms and uses. The logs were sawed at Glenbrook; then the lumber was hauled up to the lip of the mountains by rail and sent *whooshing* down the slope to the Carson Valley in V-shaped flumes made of lumber.

Transplanting the V-flume technique to the western slope of the Sierra solved one of the major problems that heretofore had prevented true commercial utilization of that region's magnificent timber stands, the problem of prohibitive hauling costs from mountain sawmill to valley floor. Another problem, that of getting Sierra lumber to the state's and the world's markets, was solved concurrently by the coming of the railroad to the Great Valley. The V-flume and the railroad made Sierra lumber a dependable commodity at a competitive price and greatly stimulated the development of inland California.

This impact was felt first in the Sacramento Valley communities of Chico, Red Bluff, and Redding, and then worked southward along the central and southern Sierra slopes.

The southern Sierra holds another phenomenon of California's forest bounty, the Big Trees *(Sequoia gigantea)*. While never as commercially important as their coastal cousin the redwood, or the pines and other species of the Sierra, the Big Trees certainly are among the most awesome aesthetic experience Nature provides to keep egocentric man properly humble. The preservation of some stands of Big Trees and some groves of redwoods is a victory of conservationists.

It cannot be denied that during the Gold Rush and for many years thereafter, the lumbering industry was incredibly wasteful. The soaring trunks went one hundred feet to the first limb, where the knots began, but the initial rule of thumb was "take three logs and leave her." More lumber than was used was left to rot on the forest floor in these early years of primitive harvesting. Forest fires were left to burn unchecked, except when they threatened the sawmills and other appurtenances of the industry. The record of dedicated conservationists and public-minded forest products firms in curbing this waste is an inspiriting chapter in the state's history. It is a chapter which requires constant writing and rewriting.

It was concern for the natural beauties of the Tahoe basin that sparked the first efforts at legislation to protect its timber resources in 1883. These efforts gained momentum in 1885, when Governor Stoneman of California established the first State Board of Forestry in the United States. The agency seems to have succumbed to economic and political pressures in 1893, when the legislation that established it was repealed, leaving a gap in official conservation concern that was partially filled by private groups.

Among these early groups, the Sacramento Valley Development Association and the Water and Forest Association of San Francisco both pointed out the relationship between sustained forest cover and the water-retaining capacity of the

Building, building, building . . . "Green Gold" went into the making of a hundred spanking new towns and subdivisions of the 1880's.

And rebuilding . . . San Francisco's Van Ness Avenue after the fire of 1906.

Sierra Nevada, upon which California's life depended then and depends today. The Sempervirens Club of San Francisco, whose primary purpose was to "Save the Redwoods," also preached the gospel of forest conservation for material benefits as well as for spiritual values. Such local efforts benefited tremendously from the presidency of Theodore Roosevelt and the work of his chief forester, Gifford Pinchot, who gave national impetus and prestige to the entire conservation movement.

The Roosevelt-Pinchot era was accompanied in California by the election of a new governor, Dr. George C. Pardee of Oakland, whose inaugural address of January 7, 1903, contained a long passage devoted to forest conservation. During his administration, a State Board of Forestry was again created, with E. T. Allen as State Forester, and the first redwood grove to be preserved, Big Basin near Santa Cruz, was set aside as the first state park. Pardee has been called with reason "the father of conservation in California."

During the Civil War, an interesting facet of California's forest bounty was developed when supplies of turpentine, resins, and other so-called "naval stores," which had come from South Carolina, were cut off. Turpentine was the basic ingredient for a lamp fuel called "camphene," made by distilling turpentine over fresh lime. Camphene at this time was the leading urban illuminant, surpassing tallow candles and whale-oil lamps, so the need for turpentine was quickly felt.

To meet it, the stands of yellow pine *(P. ponderosa)* in the Sierra were tapped, and turpentine distilleries and collection depots became concentrated along the higher foothills of Butte County, where the community of Dogtown (Magalia) became the industry's center. Production bounties offered by the state legislature stimulated the infant industry's growth. But with the ending of the Civil War, supplies from South Carolina reentered the market, and by 1866–67 the local turpentine industry came to an economic end.

It left an interesting legacy to the Internal Combustion Engine Age, because during the turpentine "rush" some dis-

A working scene on the Klamath River, ca. 1895.

To augment the production of California's burgeoning timber industry, great log rafts were towed down from the green hills of the Northwest.

tressing accidents had resulted from turpentine stills exploding. These finally were traced to their having been charged with pitch from Jeffrey pines *(Pinus jeffreyi)*. The trouble with this pitch was simply that it contained a high amount of hydrocarbons, a chemical matter foreign to other species of pine.

In 1926 largely owing to the improvement of the gasoline engine and its application to air transport, the need for better fuels arose and with it the need for a standard of measure to determine their octane rating. The peculiarly consistent and measurable hydrocarbons from the Jeffrey pine, obtained by tapping a stand of this species in Lassen National Forest, proved most valuable as the required measuring agent.

The effects of the lumbering industry continuously widened throughout California's development after the Gold Rush. Early manufacturing was given a great impetus by the lumbering industry's needs for machinery and equipment. Transportation both affected the industry and benefited from it, in construction and in traffic. Agriculture found a market in the provender needs of lumbering and provided a market for that industry's products in such things as citrus-fruit containers, dried-fruit boxes, grape stakes for vineyards, and fencing. The components of urban growth—domestic, industrial, and service industry construction—long affected, and were affected by, the lumbering industry.

The plentitude of lumber, coupled with the salubrious climate, made it feasible to adapt the "bungalow" style of dwelling from Asia for use in Southern California. A variant of this style, dubbed "Bay Area Redwood Shingle," became fashionable in the San Francisco region. As with the "San Diego Moorish" style, the sustained influx of cultural mores and technological advances dissipated these rudimentary gropings toward a distinctive regional, or typically "California," architecture, especially in residences. Lumber's plentitude, too, permitted the lavishly ornamented residences, all fretsaw and scrollwork, of the nabobs atop Nob Hill in San Francisco. The best surviving example of what can be termed

A wilderness conquered: for more than a century, California's awesome redwoods, the largest living things on earth, have been a mainstay of the state's timber resources. Above, a moment of fancy caught in about 1890. Below, the stunning reality of today.

"carpenter Gothic" is the Carson House in Eureka, and it will well repay your visit.

California's lumbering industry today is firmly rooted in the state's 17,300,000 acres of commercial timberlands—private, state, and federal. It continues to be a vital part of the state's economic base and provides *the* economic heartbeat to many northern coastal and mountain counties with its enormous range of uses and products—newsprint, kraft-board, paper plates, egg cartons, toys, furniture, pressed paneling, disposable hospital sheets, and even disposable wearing apparel.

Intelligent forest conservation provides the only surety that this aspect of California's economic base will endure. And intelligent forest conservation means something more than an emotional reaction that any and every tree stump is an unpardonable affront. The tree that is harvested under sound forest management practices is embarked upon a new and useful life in the service of mankind. Then it must be replaced by another. Few citizens are aware that trees are the only natural resource that can be replenished, even increased, by man's ingenuity and intelligence. Few citizens are aware that without the products, influences, and services of the forests, the people of California could not maintain their present standard of living, let alone meet the challenges of the future in this regard. It is well to note, and to note well, that without the forest cover on the Sierra Nevada, its capacity to receive, to store and to release water would be so diminished as to place a sure check upon California's future growth.

Equally important—perhaps even more important as the urbanization of California continues its acceleration — are other values that result from sound forest management practices by governmental agencies and by private industry. "I will lift up mine eyes unto the hills" is a familiar saying; and rest, relaxation, and spiritual replenishment for the city dweller are provided by the timberlands of the state.

Good citizenship, enlightened self-interest, and simple love of the land demand that every Californian seek and support a sustained program of sound forest conservation. And this requires that each individual accept *personal responsibility* for forest conservation, instead of leaving the entire burden upon the bowed shoulders of Smokey the Bear.

Agriculture:
An Immigrant Saga

FROM CULTIVATION'S BEGINNINGS two centuries ago to today's "factories in the fields," California's soils and climates have welcomed seeds and seedlings, cuttings and rootstock from all the world. Against this backdrop, the story of California agriculture is a two-part saga of transition: first, the transformation from subsistence farming during the Hispanic period to one of the world's great grain-producing regions within twenty years after the Gold Rush; and second, the change from basic cereal grains to the intensive and diversified cultivation of high-value row and orchard crops.

Certain factors are common to both stages; (a) relatively large-scale operations, such as today warrant the term "agri-business"; (b) the need for quantities of supplemental labor at harvesttime—first human, now increasingly mechanical, and (c) an export market, both inside and outside the United States.

Stage One above may be illustrated clearly in several ways. The first of these is the shift in the numbers of Californians engaged in mining and agriculture respectively between 1850 and 1870.

YEAR	MINING	AGRICULTURE
1850	57,800	fewer than 2,000
1860	82,600	35,800
1870	36,340	47,900

The mechanics of agri-industry: a steam harvester in the San Joaquin Valley, ca. 1890.

This human shift was accompanied by an economic shift, in that the value of agricultural production by 1870 exceeded the value of gold production in the state's economic mix. The political implications of this shift may be touched upon by noting that the original vast extent of Mariposa County, as defined in 1850 when Gold was King, later enabled the agricultural counties of Fresno, Kings, Madera, Merced, and Tulare to be carved from it when agriculture replaced gold as the dominant economic force.

Stage Two in California agriculture stems directly from the expansion and improvement of irrigation, which, by and large, was possible only because of the huge water-storage capacity of the Sierra Nevada. The expansion of irrigation, as we have noted earlier, had its legal roots in the water doctrine of "appropriation and beneficial use" developed by the miners during the Gold Rush, because the ancient English common-law doctrine of riparian rights to water precluded its use for irrigation. As early as 1862 the legislature granted ditch and canal companies the right to condemn private land for right-of-way purposes. In 1887 the base of today's irrigation was laid down by the Wright Act, which gave legal status to mutual, cooperative irrigation districts in taking advantage of the "appropriative" doctrine.

Among their many solid accomplishments, the Franciscans must be credited with practicing the first irrigation in California. Some twenty miles of ditches made Mission San Gabriel one of the most productive of them all, although extensive irrigation works were also constructed at other missions, San Diego and San Buenaventura prominent among them. The *Zanja Madre* that gave Los Angeles its first water supply was three feet wide by four feet deep, and the *zanjero* (water-master) was more important than the *alcalde* (Mayor) in the town's affairs. Despite their pioneering role, it does not seem historically sound to date irrigation, as we know it today, from the Franciscans. Though there is some evidence that the *rancheros* of Southern California in part restored and used some of the missions' irrigation works, it appears to me that any extensive practice of irrigation was nonexistent after the breakup of the mission system by secularization. Irrigation was equally foreign to the experience and practices of the Americans who made the Rush, with one notable exception.

In 1851 an outpost of Brigham Young's "Great Basin Kingdom" was established at what is now San Bernardino by the purchase of 35,509 acres from the Lugo family for slightly more than two dollars per acre. By 1855 this outpost boasted a Mormon population of 1,400 and had 4,000 acres under irrigation, thus deserving the accolade of being the first widespread practice of irrigation in California's American period. When the settlement was abandoned in 1857 because of the so-called "Mormon War" in Utah, these irrigation works passed to the purchasers of the Mormon holdings. By 1879, more than 110,000 acres were under irrigation in Southern California, and the importance of this technique to the rise of grape and citrus-fruit production in that region cannot be overestimated.

As noted earlier, the Indians of California harvested Nature's bounty by hunting and gathering; but they were not agriculturists, save for the Yuma and Mojave peoples along the Colorado River, who practiced flood-plain cultivation to produce crops of melons, corn, and squash, which had been the foundations of the much earlier Mayan and Aztec agricultural civilizations in Mexico and Central America.

The Spanish introduced agriculture to California, and the Franciscans again deserve the credit for providing the transmission belt. At the missions that were strung like beads along the coastal strip of California, the *padres* introduced the basic cereal grains, the basic vegetables, and the basic deciduous fruits of their civilization. They also introduced the first grapes, the first citrus fruits, and the soft-shell English walnut, which had its origins in Persia. They also cultivated hemp for shipment to the rope walks of Mexico.

Corn was ground on primitive grinding stones, adopted by the Spanish from the Indians, to make the raw material for *tortillas;* and other grains were ground into flour in the same

fashion. In the case of wheat or barley or oats, the grain was separated from the straw by piling the cut grain on a corral floor (usually of hard-packed earth) and then turning a band of horses into the corral. Driven around and around atop the mass, the horses trod out the grain from the straw; winnowing was done by Indians, and the precious kernels were collected and stored for use.

During the Mexican period, 1822–46, after the breakup of the missions, agriculture declined to the status of subsistence farming at each *rancho*. The life and economy of the *ranchos* revolved around their herds of beef cattle, while sheep were usually limited to flocks just large enough to provide wool for homespun cloth and to afford a change from the almost constant beef diet. Many *ranchos* had orchards of deciduous fruits and the "Mission" orange, and most had vineyards of Mission grapes for making wine and brandy. Ignacio del Valle of *Rancho Camulos* (Ventura County), where Helen Hunt Jackson gained much of her data for *Ramona*, was noted far and wide for the products of his trees and vines—fresh, dried, and liquid.

The Gold Rush spawned a demand for meat that between 1850 and 1853 drew perhaps sixty thousand head of cattle from Texas to the mines, where they sold at prices from fifty to one hundred and fifty dollars each. In this same period, an undetermined number of what were advertised in California as "American bullocks" made their plodding way from the Mississippi River Valley to the slaughter pens of the Mother Lode camps. The Gold Rush also brought what truly can be called their "golden years" to the *rancheros*. Whereas in the 1830's an animal had been worth $1.25, the price of its hide, it brought forty times that amount, and more, in the mining camps.

Great herds of cattle were trailed up from Southern California to the diggings, and the *rancheros* rode sedately homeward with bulging saddlebags of raw gold. This welcome prosperity was reflected in the horse hardware of one of the Lugo *gente*, which was said to be worth more than five

179

Bringing water to the land—the Central Valley's San Luis Canal, 103 miles long, 200 feet wide, and 36 feet deep.

thousand dollars; and by the great coach, ornamented in silver, in which the De la Guerras were wont to journey from their town house in Santa Barbara to visit their far-flung holdings, more than three hundred thousand acres, accompanied by outriders dressed in velvet livery. When beef production in Northern California began to catch up with the demand, about 1856, the hard times of the Southern California *rancheros* began.

During the first flamboyant years of the Rush, California agriculture was so deficient that flour was imported from Oregon and Chile and became the great speculative commodity in the frenzied mercantile life of San Francisco. Wheat did not do well along the coastal plains because the moist air promoted "rust." Barley was the basic coastal grain crop, but even its tolerance for moisture often required that *vaqueros* be sent riding through the fields at sunup, with a *riata* stretched between them to sweep fog droplets from the ripening heads. It was not until grain farming worked its way into the hotter, drier reaches of the Great Valley that California attained ample wheat production.

The state neared self-sufficiency in this basic source of foodstuffs about 1856; by 1860 it was growing more wheat—some six million bushels—than the combined production of all the other far western states. It was not until the Civil War's disruption of world commerce had ended that the great grain days in California got underway. In 1868 the state produced twenty million bushels of wheat, about one-third of which was exported to Australia and England, and in 1873 California was the largest wheat-producing state in the nation. It held this rank again in 1877 and was rarely below second place until the 1890's when Australia, Canada, and the Argentine poured their crops onto the world's markets, and California growers quickly converted their acreage to less competitive crops, more intensively cultivated. It should be noted that California's major export market for wheat was always the world at large, because she could not compete in the eastern urban markets with wheat from the Great Plains.

The climate of the Great Valley was admirably suited for wheat cultivation. Hot, dry summers permitted the grain to ripen evenly, and to be stored in the open for weeks before shipment without fear of spoilage. It was a hard wheat, well suited for withstanding the rigors of ocean transportation and for milling; it became known as "California White Velvet" on the world's principal wheat market at Liverpool, England.

Wheat and flour both were exported from California, through Port Costa, Vallejo, Crockett, Benicia, Oakland, and San Francisco itself, to the world beyond the Golden Gate. At the peak of the wheat trade, Port Costa, where the inland waterways met the Bay, shipped approximately one million tons of wheat and flour annually. Some said it was the largest grain port in the world; certainly it was the largest on the whole Pacific Coast between Bering Strait and Cape Horn. Its glory days declined as the price of California wheat at tidewater sagged from $1.48 per hundredweight in 1888 to but $0.90 in 1894. It should be noted that many a California community had its own flouring mill, of which the Starr Mills at Vallejo was one of the largest for both export and local use.

These were the days of the "bonanza grain farms" in the Great Valley—days when Hugh Glenn of Colusa County could envision producing one million bushels of wheat in one year from his own land. The great reapers were drawn by as many as thirty mules each, moving like an army through the square miles of waving wheat. Threshing crews worked from sunup to dark, their cooks even longer; and the mountains of chaff rose high enough, it seemed, to tower above the Sutter Buttes. On both the Sacramento and San Joaquin rivers, barges or shallow-draft, "dew-skimming" steamers took the golden grain down the rivers to the Bay, which led to the world beyond.

Because most of California's wheat was winter planted, the millions of migratory waterfowl in the Great Valley liked nothing better than to feed on the succulent green shoots when they popped above the ground. Men were hired as gooseherders, using eight-gauge shotguns to protect the crop from the gabbling, honking, quacking foragers. Even today, men use airplanes, and flares, and smoke bombs to keep the now-protected waterfowl from damaging the valley's crops.

Vineyards that descended from those introduced to California by the Franciscans gave Los Angeles County a production of five hundred thousand gallons of wine in 1858. It was from grapes of the Mission variety that Luis Vignes, pioneer Southern California vintner, produced his celebrated "Sparkling California" to challenge the supremacy of champagne among the state's elite. The foundations of California's world-famous wine industry were laid down by a Hungarian nobleman who backed the wrong side in a revolution at home and found it advisable to emigrate. He was Count Agostin Haraszthy—flamboyant, visionary, talented beyond most men when it came to grapes and wines. He settled first near Crystal Springs in San Mateo County but found the climate more to his liking in Sonoma County and removed his operations there. The Buena Vista Winery he founded is said to be the oldest continuous wine operation in the state. In 1862 Haraszthy was authorized by the legislature to represent the state on a collecting tour of Europe's most famous wine regions. The legislature, however, did not see fit to appropriate any funds for his traveling expenses, and Haraszthy made his great contribution to the state at his own expense. He returned with one hundred thousand cuttings and rooted vines of literally hundreds of varieties of Europe's best grapes, and saw many of these become adapted to California before his mysterious and unsolved disappearance in Nicaragua in 1869.

The interior coastal valleys of California—Napa, Sonoma, Livermore, Santa Clara—were most admirably suited to wine-grape cultivation. In fact, these are among the most favored wine-grape regions in the world, their soils and climate making for less variation in vintages from year to year than their European counterparts; and the varietal wines which each section produces best have carried California's name afar. Under the pressure of today's urban sprawl, especially in the Napa, Santa Clara, and Sonoma valleys, such famous

As early as the 1880's, California's wheat supplied much of the western world with its daily bread. Above, hay scows down from the Sacramento delta await unloading. Below, a harvesting crew and rig somewhere in the rich Central Valley.

names as Almadén and Paul Masson have brought thousands of new acres into wine-grape cultivation in the San Benito–Paicines–Tres Piños region.

While the varietal wines are the most famous of California's grape products, the larger dollar value over the years has come from lesser-known wine grapes and from raisin grapes in the Great Valley and Southern California. Leland Stanford once had the largest brandy distillery in the world on one of his ranches at Vina, Tehama County, which became part of his bequests to found the university that bears his son's name. Raisins from California have become world famous under the Sun Maid brand name, and it was the raisin industry, by and large, that carried California's viticulturists and viniculturists through the traumatic experience of Prohibition.

Citrus fruits, even more than grapes, have spread California's name and fame afar. One of these wrought a drastic change in the dietary habits of the nation, under the lash of finding an outlet for the productive capacity of Southern California's peculiarly suitable climate and soils. "California for health, Oranges for wealth" became the promotional cry of the Southland at the turn of the century, and orange juice for breakfast became a part of the American way of life because of popular response to this siren song.

The so-called "mission" orange introduced by the Franciscans was thick-skinned, pithy, stuffed with seeds, and often sour. Despite these drawbacks (by modern standards), William Wolfskill, an ex-trapper who had settled in Southern California, planted about twenty-five hundred mission orange trees where Los Angeles' Union Station welcomes its few trains today, and became the state's first commercial and profit-making citrus orchardist. Wolfskill also is credited with making the first shipment of California oranges to the East, in 1876, a coup made possible by the advent of rail transportation into Southern California that year.

Given the mission variety's liabilities, it seems most likely that oranges would have remained a *curiosa California*, had it not been for the U.S. Department of Agriculture. In 1873 this agency received a few seedlings of the sweet and seedless "Washington navel" orange from Bahia, Brazil, whence it apparently had been transplanted from China by parties unknown. Some of these precious seedlings were sent to Florida, where they expired. Fortunately for California, those that were consigned to it became entrusted to Luther C. and Eliza Tibbetts, residing at Riverside. Their efforts in propagating the new variety made Washington navel oranges the true Golden Apples of the Hesperides for California.

The expansion of orange groves was rapid and steady thereafter, as attested by the fact that from less than 30,000 trees in 1870, California boasted more than 1,000,000 navel orange trees in 1890, and more than 5,000,000 in 1900. Most of the individual groves were small, about ten acres; and the problems of production, marketing, pest control, and frost protection led to the formation of growers' cooperatives, for which Sunkist may stand as exemplar. This method of association-handling of individual problems proved so successful—the first enduringly successful agricultural cooperative of any magnitude in the nation—that its pattern has been followed by growers of other farm commodities, such as walnuts, almonds, raisins, rice, and eggs.

Even though the word "navel" was for many years too *risqué* for advertising exposure, the promotional campaigns conducted by the citrus cooperatives played an important part in publicizing California throughout the rest of the nation. This contributed both directly and indirectly to the popular, albeit mythical, image of the state in other less favored climes. Certainly, their role in inculcating the belief that Southern California was the "Italy of America" and the "Riviera of the Pacific" is undebatable.

While the Washington navel made the foundation of today's citrus industry, this base was broadened immensely by the introduction of the Valencia orange from England in 1876. A summer-ripening variety, it was adaptable to the foggy coastal climate, which the winter-ripening navel was not.

The citrus base established by oranges was expanded by

the rise of lemon acreage, stimulated both by a disastrous freeze in the Florida groves in the winter of 1894–95, which set lemon orcharding there back for many decades, and by development of the "Eureka" lemon, which is free of thorns. The Limoneira Ranch near Santa Paula, Ventura County, is the largest lemon grove in the world today, and its production contributes to California's second-place rank in world lemon production, just behind Italy. Grapefruit entered the citrus picture when the Imperial and Coachella valleys were opened to cultivation by Colorado River water after the turn of the century, and both mandarin oranges and tangerines are comparative late-comers to California's arsenal of citrus fruits.

Today, urban sprawl in Southern California and the prevalence of smog have forced a most substantial proportion of its once vast citrus acreage into the San Joaquin Valley, where climatic and other growing conditions are less favorable. Citrus acreage in Santa Barbara County also has increased in importance, although the citrus future of this region is questionable, due to accelerated urban expansion there. The oft-heard dirge that citrus is dead in California is belied by the fact that some twenty million acres of new citrus plantings have been made since 1953–54; the state's total acreage in citrus fruits still is below its peak, but production per acre is higher. In dollar value, citrus fruits still rank high among California's crops, and their margin of profit, enhanced by frozen concentrate products, still depends upon an export market, primarily within the United States.

California's agricultural productivity is the result of its transportation facilities and its agricultural diversity; this diversity in turn stems from the variety of favorable soils and climates—plus always *irrigation*—that the state affords. Asparagus in the peat islands of the Sacramento Delta; avocados along the favored slopes of Southern California; early melons and lettuce in the Imperial and Coachella valleys; dates at Indio; Christmas strawberries from Thermal; artichokes in the fog-belts of Santa Cruz County and up the Pajaro Valley and along the Skyline Drive south of San Fran-

Men who use the land must use other men to harvest the fruits of investment: A Mexican migrant worker of the 1930's.

cisco; a veritable torrent of lettuce from a steady procession of maturing crops up the climate zones of the Salinas Valley, plus strawberries and carrots as well; the nation's "Peach Bowl" in the Sutter Basin; pears and apricots and nectarines and peaches elsewhere in the Great Valley; apples at Sebastopol; the nation's largest production of short-grain rice in Sutter, Butte, Glenn, and Colusa counties (with specially designed and cooperatively owned vessels transporting it to overseas markets); almonds and walnuts galore; tomatoes, a tremendous crop (five million *tons* in 1968) that gives Stockton and other interior processing centers the rich smell of catsup for weeks at a time during their harvesting; and cotton in the San Joaquin Valley providing the raw material for Japanese textile mills. Cotton—fiber and cottonseed together—is the largest cash money crop raised in California, accounting for more than $200,000,000 in 1967. The advantage of longer staple and better spinning quality that California cotton has enjoyed over cotton produced elsewhere in the United States now is threatened by artificial fibers, polyester chief among them. Added to these must be the celebrated "Spice Islands" herbs and condiments, many of which are grown on the firm's own acreage near Dixon, California. Possibly the most exotic crop of all is the cut-flower and flower seed crop, as well as agricultural crop seed production.

To these exotic crops (exotic in the sense that their market consumption seems based upon an affluent society in the main) one must add such staples as hay and grain, potatoes and sugar beets. Each one of these takes full advantage of California's diversity of soils and climates.

Population growth and affluence, not climate or soil, has spawned the state's production of mushrooms, which must be cultivated in buildings where such things as humidity, temperature, and air movement can be controlled most carefully. Estimates of the state's current mushroom production approach ten million pounds annually. Slightly more than one-half this total is consumed fresh, while the remainder goes into cans, and at times fresh mushrooms are air-freighted

Water and technology: enormous sprinklers at work in Kern County.

Pears, peaches, oranges, apricots, kumquats, and plums—almost anything that can be grown anywhere on earth can presumably be grown in California.

from Pennsylvania to meet the California demand.

The net result of this diversified productivity is to make California the *leading agricultural state* in the nation, in terms of raw farm production. The *annual* value of this raw production *exceeds* the total value of *all the gold* mined in the state since 1848, and approximates $4,000,000,000.

This raw worth, plus the nine million dollars added by the manufacturing and distributing processes, coupled with the payrolls and taxes paid by these processors, make agriculture a major bastion of the state's prosperity and growth. It also gives California a direct and vital interest in worldwide markets and international tariff agreements.

California's agricultural growth, in conjunction with its larger-than-average-size farms and relatively higher labor costs, has had direct and important effects upon agricultural machinery production. The Holt "caterpillar" tractor was a California-born extension of the steam traction engine, which had supplanted the thirty-mule teams for harvesting. The "Stockton gang plow" was evolved to meet the need for more efficient turnover of more acreage for planting. Today, the need to replace hand labor with machinery at harvesttime has given us the cotton picker and machines on self-propelled tracks that pick tomatoes, carrots, and lettuce. In some instances, sorting, washing, and packing for market are all done on the same machine. Mechanical almond-knockers and walnut-tree-shakers are in use, together with mechanical sweepers to collect the nuts. Recent experiments with machines that shake peach and other fruit trees for harvest have been proven reasonably successful, thus obviating laborious, ladder-climbing handwork. And the successful use of machines to harvest the raisin and bulk wine crops is imminent.

In many of these instances, the development of machinery has gone hand in hand with the development of new strains of crops. A prime example of this is the tomato plant that ripens its whole bearing at once, or close enough to it that the machine simply plucks the whole plant and lets the crew on board do the rest. In the development of both machines and

"*California, Arizona, I make all your crops,*
Then it's north up to Oregon to gather your hops;
Dig beets from your ground, cut the grapes from your vines
To set on your table your light sparkling wine."

new crop strains, research work done at the University of California at Davis has been invaluable—the most dramatic illustration of which is the current research into the development of square tomatoes!

It should be noted that rice-growing is one of the most mechanized operations in all agriculture. Seeding, fertilizing, and pest control are done by air, harvesting by self-propelled machines on very broad treads. The paddy layout also is accomplished by machinery, as is the drying of the harvested crop. The only handwork in rice cultivation in California is in irrigation control.

The development and expansion of rice-growing in California played a major part in the successful introduction of the ring-neck pheasant into the state. The irrigation checks and canal banks provided the essential *covert* for what has become the state's most popular upland game bird. The sale of hunting rights on rice lands provides supplemental income for many rice growers, and at least one of these is now experimenting with his fallow paddies to raise catfish for the Los Angeles market.

The place of rice in California's agricultural mosaic brings up the fact that the modern development of deep-water ports at Stockton and Sacramento is linked directly to the industry and diversity of the Great Valley, which these cities serve, today as in the past, as distributing centers. The natural waterways reaching inland from San Francisco Bay have made it possible for the best California malting barley to be shipped from Stockton or Sacramento to Scotland and be returned directly to those ports in the form immortalized by the late creator of "Musterr Glencannon," Guy Gilpatric, as "Duggan's Dew of Kirkintilloch" whiskey.

No outline of California's agricultural growth would be complete without a note on what may be termed without apology "agri-silliness." The mythical properties of the state's climate have led to ill-starred schemes for the raising of such crops as coffee, bananas, lichee nuts, and the like. One of the most errant of such schemes was that of planting and cultivating mulberry trees to make the base for a local silkworm, hence silk, industry. Of more national concern was the plan of producing rubber from the Mexican *guayule* shrub, which began during the rubber shortages caused by World War I. After many years of searching and experimentation, a combination of suitable soil and climate for *guayule* cultivation was found in the Salinas Valley. Some fifteen thousand acres were planted to *guayule* there between 1926 and 1931, and a processing plant was constructed, but the development of cheap synthetic rubber doomed this venture to failure.

What began as a "five acres and independence" type of California promotion—a type not unknown in the state today—involved what inadvertently became a great contribution to California's landscape, the pungent eucalyptus tree. The first seeds were imported from Australia in the 1850's, and the first seedlings were raised for sale by the Golden Gate Nursery in San Francisco as early as 1858–59. Elwood Cooper near Santa Barbara was active in their propagation for sale in the early 1870's. This fast-growing tree was thought to be the answer to Southern California's serious shortage of forests, a natural shortage compounded by consumption for fuel. An almost statewide boom erupted around the turn of the century when the Santa Fe Railroad planted three million eucalyptus seedlings for cross-tie production. Glib-tongued promoters used this example to sell the idea that a few acres of eucalyptus would go on yielding and yielding and yielding, sending up new shoots from each stump in succession, and that the railroads alone guaranteed a market. It did not materialize (the Santa Fe turning their eucalyptus plantation into the residential community of Rancho Santa Fe), but the stately, bark-tendril-draped trees have made a lovely, and distinctive, and aromatic part of the California landscape ever since.

Agriculture's transition is epitomized by the change in dairying since 1850, when butter was packed in snow for shipment across the Sierra from the Mormon settlement in the Carson Valley to California. In our time, for example, gigantic milk tank trucks roll out of Modesto early each morning to

193

OVERLEAF: *A view of Southern California, two generations removed.*

meet the needs of Los Angeles and its satellite communities.

In our time, too, Bossy spends her life on concrete or asphalt; she is fed a scientifically balanced and mechanically mixed and weighed allotment of feed; her milk output is tabulated daily by a computer; and when it falls below the profit point, Bossy winds up as hamburger in a "Sno White" drive-in. And the barefoot boy who used to bring the family cow home at milking time each night now earns a degree in dairy science, or business management, or both.

The same change is reflected in the old-time family flock of hens, which today is an antiseptic and cage-bound battery of laying pullets. Their brothers become broilers under similar conditions, without ever touching the ground or chasing a hen. Similar conditions govern the production of thousands of gobbling turkeys around the year in California.

As was noted earlier, the Gold Rush created a demand for meat in California that the herds of the *rancheros* could not fill, and the state has been an importer of meat-on-the-hoof ever since. Approximately five million head of cattle, sheep, and hogs were imported in 1967 from states as far away as Texas, Louisiana, Nebraska, and Missouri. Thus today, as in the past, much of California's agricultural production is used to put weight on imported livestock. Bakersfield early became the "feeder cattle" capital for the livestock producers of the Southwest and remained so for many years.

Cattle and sheep provide a direct link with the nostalgically romantic days of the *rancheros*. The transition from those days of hide-and-tallow slaughtering, of open range and daring *vaqueros*, to today's automated and computerized feedlots— such as the one at Bakersfield that has a capacity of thirty thousand head—is as dramatic as the changes in crop production and dairying. The old days are preserved—or prostituted, as you prefer—in the professional sport known variously as "rodeo" or "stampede" or "Frontier Days."

Such words as "buckaroo" from *vaquero*, "hackamore" from *jaquima*, "hoosegow" from *juzgado*, "chaps" from *chaparejos* reveal the Hispanic influence upon the modern language of the fence-mending, feed-weighing, Jeep-riding cowboy. And Hispanic horse hardware, such as the center-fire saddle, the spade bit, the rawhide *riata*, spread from California into Nevada and western Arizona, into eastern Oregon and Idaho, as California ranchers and cattle-buyers extended their interests into those regions.

Economic problems that beset the *rancheros* following the decline of cattle prices in 1856, which was a year of deficient rainfall as well, were compounded by others that could be attributed only to the Will of God. These natural catastrophes affected all of rural California, and all of those who lived by the land and its bounty.

Beginning in the Christmas season of 1861, California was swept by a procession of moisture-laden Pacific storms that continued virtually without cessation for thirty days. Los Angeles saw the sun but once, and that briefly, during this period. The Great Valley became in effect a great inland sea and so remained for seemingly interminable weeks. When the sun returned, the grass and weeds grew luxuriantly; the surviving herds grew sleek and fat, and the glutted cattle market sagged even lower.

More importantly, no beneficial rains blessed California's farms and pastures for more than thirty months after the deluge ended. More than seventy-five thousand head of cattle perished in Monterey County and almost two hundred thousand head in Santa Barbara County; the losses in crops and farm livestock were never calculated. For *rancheros* and plain farmers alike, this destroying drouth burned away land and hope and the psychological bulwark these two had provided. This dry spell, the worst in California's recorded history, had a shattering impact on the independent farmer and contributed to the growth of tremendous agricultural-pastoral enterprises, several of which have endured, albeit on a reduced scale, to this day.

Among these is that founded by Henry Miller, an immigrant German butcher boy, who had reached San Francisco in 1853 and subsequently laid the foundations of the state's meat-packing industry at "Butchertown" (South San Francisco). To meet San Francisco's expanding needs for meat, Miller plowed his profits into buying ranches and raw land around Hollister and the San Joaquin Valley and turning them into livestock-producing units. He bought other acreages for the production of hay and grain for feeding purposes, was an extensive user and developer of irrigation systems, and is credited with being the first large-scale grower and user of alfalfa in the state. He also is credited with amassing three fortunes: one for himself, one for his associates, and one for his lawyers. The legend holds that at the peak of his almost imperial holdings, Henry Miller could ride from Mexico to Oregon and sleep every night on his own land. Not quite true, but pretty close to it, as his holdings in Nevada and eastern Oregon were vast. The family firm, Miller & Lux, Inc., with offices in San Francisco, still controls considerable acreage in the San Joaquin Valley, operated largely as diversified agricultural lands.

Lloyd Tevis and James Ben Ali Haggin (the latter once a semisacred name around Stockton), obtained their initial capital as moneylenders and private bankers in San Francisco during the Gold Rush. They ventured risk capital in the Comstock Lode and saw it returned manyfold. They then began to acquire vast landholdings in the upper San Joaquin Valley, centering around Bakersfield, and created a grasslands empire of more than 1,400,000 acres in Arizona and New Mexico. The latter was, and is, operated for cow-and-calf ("feeder" cattle) production. They combined their agricultural production in California with their livestock production in the Southwest, via railroad linkage on both the Southern Pacific and Santa Fe lines, to make Bakersfield important in meeting the ever-growing market for meat in ever-growing Los Angeles. Their corporate descendant, Kern County Land Company, is one of the state's largest cattle feeders and farming operators today.

Edward Fitzgerald Beale was a certified hero of the California phase of the Mexican War, and a man who treated the California Indians humanely. The other side of his coin is depicted by the legend that President Abraham Lincoln refused to reappoint him as U.S. Surveyor-General for California because "Beale became Monarch of all he surveyed." What he began is known today as the Tejón Ranch Company, now owned by the Chandler family of Southern California, who also own the *Los Angeles Times*. This firm controls a tremendous acreage in the Tehachapi Range, extending south and east from the present swooping route of Interstate Highway 5 through those mountains.

The native Hispanic cattle, introduced to California with the Portolá expedition, were inbred descendants of the original importations from Spain, the first of which reached Mexico about 1520. Long of horn and colored even as was Joseph's cloak, they were cat-hammed, wasp-gutted, and deer-legged, with shoulders that could split a hailstone. They also managed, even as their Texas counterparts, to walk incredible distances to market; and they were fierce enough to contend against varmints on the unfenced range, be they coyote or mountain lion or grizzly bear. Improvement of this native stock by the use of imported bulls from Europe and the East (Durhams at first, then Herefords) was due to a demand for better beef and for greater efficiency in converting grass to meat. This pattern of upgrading, of meeting increased operating costs with better meat-producing animals per pound of feed, is reflected today in such strains as the Santa Gertrudis from Texas, and the Charolais from France.

The Hispanic sheep was the Spanish merino, and in California before the Gold Rush it was an inbred, long-legged, scanty-fleeced animal called *churro*. The improvement of sheep seems to have started before that of beef cattle. In 1851, the partnership of Flint, Hollister & Bixby left St. Louis with some six thousand head of American sheep, a basically French merino strain; they reached Southern California some twenty months later at a cost of more than half their flock. The movement of sheep from the Mississippi River Valley to California in the 1850's appears to have been of some magnitude, but it is a largely unrecorded and certainly an untold story in the

"Better than the Utopia of the ancients is this Utopia of the Pacific;
better than the Gardens of Hesperides, with their golden fruits, the
gardens of this sunset land...." Above, the gardens of the past.
Below, the gardens of the present and the future.

livestock annals of California. It did work a substantial improvement in the quality of California's flocks within ten years.

There was a major movement of sheep from Arizona and New Mexico into Southern California in the 1850's, perhaps aggregating five hundred thousand head; and after the California sheep had been upgraded, as noted above, rams and breeding-ewes were sent back into the Southwest to improve the flocks in that region. Sheep from Northern California stocked the ranges of eastern Oregon and Idaho beginning in the middle 1860's, and there are numerous instances of bands of sheep from California trailing as far east as Wyoming and Colorado, sometimes requiring two years for the journey. The sheep industry in Montana gained its start by importing sheep from California about 1869.

Until well into our present century, an almost biblical scene was enacted yearly in California by herds of wandering woolies. Flocks in Southern California, each about twenty-five hundred sheep, with a herder and his dogs, moved north across the Mojave Desert in the spring, as soon as the first vegetation was up and while the scattered waterholes still held moisture from the winter rains. Moving up the Owens Valley, they grazed along the eastern slope of the Sierra until the snow melted in the passes. Then they worked up and over the Sierra's spine and down the western slope into the upper San Joaquin Valley, whence those that were not sold for meat or breeding replacements turned southward across the Tehachapi into Southern California. The seasonal migration came to an end with limitations upon the number of animals that could be grazed upon the national forests and other public lands.

These so-called "tramp" bands of sheep provoked animosity among settled, tax-paying residents of the lands they traversed. Even so, it is hard to find anything in California's past comparable to the bloody range wars between sheepmen and cattlemen that pocked the history of Arizona, Colorado, and Wyoming.

The sheep industry is primarily responsible for the Basque element in California's ethnic mix, for these were and are sheepmen par excellence. They are a most important factor in the state's contemporary sheep industry, and Sheepherder Bread becomes a favorite of recreation seekers in the Bishop–Lone Pine area. It may even surpass San Francisco's famous sourdough variety in flavorful durability.

Horses were introduced to California by the Spanish, and were of the mixed Arab-Barb strains that were predominant in northern Mexico. These were riding types, light horses; and there is no evidence that California had any kind of draft horse during the Hispanic period. For one thing, they had no need for them; oxen were the main tractive power. For another, they had no harness; and the only wheel they employed, lacking tools and technique for making any other, was a slice of tree trunk used for their two-wheeled *carretas*. Juan Bautista Alvarado, while *el gobernador* of California in 1838, is said to have been given a proper carriage, brought all the way from Boston, by a shipmaster desirous of cementing friendly relations. Alvarado had two mounted *vaqueros* affix their *riatas* to the carriage shafts and pull the vehicle, while he sat serenely inside. This vehicle later was owned by José Arnaz, who planted the apple orchard that still purveys cider and fruit in season to motorists between Ventura and the Ojai Valley.

The burro, too, was a Spanish introduction, as was the hybrid we call the mule. It is believed that the ancestors of the famous Missouri mule reached the "Show Me" state from California or New Mexico in the course of the Santa Fé trade. The feral stripes on the burro's back often form a crude cross at the shoulders, and Hispanic folklore holds that this dates from the time when a burro carried Our Savior's mother on her way to Bethlehem.

The native California horses were quite suitable for the first stagecoach lines, once they had been educated to look through a collar, but they lacked the heft and stamina for tractive power. The improvement of horseflesh by imported

Citrus groves in Orange County. Today, more than 375 acres of such land disappear daily beneath a smother of blacktop and concrete.

draft-type stallions became a necessity. Horses and mules were *the* motive power in California's development during its first seventy-odd years as a state. They drew the city's delivery wagons and its first municipal transit cars; they powered the great grain harvesters and did the heavy work of plowing and cultivating. They were essential to the high-sided freight wagons that dominated much of California's inland transport even after the railroad spanned the length of the state. Horses, and mules, and burros (the prospector's *confidante* and the sheepherder's friend) gave man in California a controllable source of energy until they were replaced by the internal combustion engine in all its manifold mutations. The twenty-mule teams of Death Valley probably symbolize this fact in the public consciousness.

It is hard to find a draft horse anywhere in California today. But horses do play an important part in the leisure time of our affluent society. No civic parade is complete without its mounted units, and the state's numerous trail-ride groups—of which *Los Rancheros de los Visitadores* at Santa Barbara is the most famous—could not function without horses. Neither could the producers of Westerns for cinema and television audiences. These are play-world horses, but they should not be overlooked, especially in view of the tax revenues derived from horse racing.

The two-part saga of California's agricultural transition already confronts a third phase that may be of far greater import than its predecessors. The bulk of the state's annual agricultural production, which currently has a raw worth approximating four million dollars, comes from the eight million irrigated acres of the state's total of ten million acres classed as cropland. The remaining acreage in this total that is susceptible to irrigation is not nearly so desirable as those acres already consumed by urban sprawl. And this urban sprawl continues to consume prime farmland at the rate of thousands of acres per month.

The seriousness of the trend has been recognized by passage of the Williamson Act. This provides for the assessment of farm lands on the basis of income, rather than upon industrial or subdivision values, providing that the owner agrees to retain such lands in farm use for ten years.

Optimists hold the view that water provided by the Feather River Project and other aspects of the California Water Plan will bring many thousands of currently unfarmed acres along the west side of the upper San Joaquin Valley under cultivation. Many years and large sums of money will be required to make these salt-laden lands susceptible to growing the high value crops that their invested capital will demand.

Until this happens, maintaining agricultural production from a diminishing acreage may be accomplished in part by more extensive use of the hydroponic technique (in which plants are grown in liquid nutrients, not soil), of which one large-scale installation devoted to tomatoes now is underway in the Napa Valley. Another palliative is to be found in the expansion of a new technique called "high density seeding," which amounts to putting crop rows closer together and putting more seed per acre in the ground; from 12,000 seeds per acre for tomatoes to 20,000 and more per acre. This technique stems from the prior perfection of chemical weedkillers, a product of the state's petrochemical industry; the utilization of sprinkler, rather than flood irrigation, and improved crop strains developed by the state's agricultural institutions.

Despite these hopes for a future clouded by rising population and the spectre of world hunger, California today cannot escape the steady loss of farm acreage and farm families to urban takeover. Within this context, it is sobering to realize that one of the principal thoughts in Chairman Mao's "little red book" stresses the necessity of capturing the villages and the countryside before the final, and presumably victorious revolutionary assault against the cities. If California's cities reverse this premise by capturing the villages and the countryside, what then for California?

The Web of Industry

RICH AS SHE WAS in other natural resources, California lacked practicable amounts of the two essential ingredients of the Industrial Revolution—coal and iron. She still does. The state did not have an integrated steel operation (from raw materials to fabricated products) until the Kaiser interests constructed the Fontana complex during World War II. Although this plant uses iron ore from within the state at Eagle Mountain, coal must come from Utah and New Mexico. In this reference, the manner in which the Santa Fe Railway runs its specially designed and operated 84-car coal trains from York Canyon, above Santa Fe, New Mexico, to Fontana is a triumph of modern railroading.

Despite these lacks, California quickly established a basic heavy industry because she had to. The impetus of the Gold Rush, and of the continuing population explosion it set in motion, triggered an exploitation of natural resources that could move in only one direction.

Iron pigs (ingots) from the East and from England and Europe made ballast for the tall-masted Cape Horners, sometimes whole cargoes. A bigger problem in respect to bulk was obtaining the coal to convert these ingots into usable products.

Coal was imported from Nanaimo, British Columbia; from Australia; from the eastern seaboard; and from Scotland, Cornwall, and Wales. The best coking and forge coal, essential to iron foundry and blacksmith alike, long sold for $40

The Mechanics Monument, Market Street, San Francisco—
a tribute by Douglas Tilden to Peter Donohue and the men
who forged the beginnings of California industry.

per ton in cargo lots, alongside San Francisco's wharves. Inland transportation costs increased this price to $53 at San Jose, and to a whopping $110 in Marysville. Increase in cost at inland points gave San Francisco an industrial supremacy it held for many years. Heavy industry in Los Angeles was hampered by its distance from the seaport of San Pedro until the advent of petroleum, and this effect was compounded farther inland in Southern California.

Some coal was mined within the state, principally at the predominantly Welsh hamlets of Nortonville and Somerville on the slopes of Mount Diablo, Contra Costa County. The shipping port for this coal was the town that began as New York-of-the-Pacific and became in turn Black Diamond and today's Pittsburg. More coal was mined at Corral Hollow, near Tracy, where the Tesla Mine sent coal to San Francisco by river barge in the 1890's. Local production never seems to have exceeded about 2 percent of the state's requirements, which totalled 1,650,000 tons imported by sea in 1888, plus the undetermined tonnage brought in overland by the Southern Pacific and Santa Fe lines both for commercial consignees and to fuel their motive power.

The state's ability to import the required tonnages of both iron and coal to meet the steadily growing needs of its economy was aided immeasurably by the export trade in grain. Coal, iron, and wheat are all bulk commodities, which generally speaking require the lowest possible freight rate. With a two-way cargo virtually assured by the exportable surplus of wheat in California, ships brought coal and iron from the world's seaports and lifted outward cargoes of the golden grain from California's fields. This trade continued after the so-called transcontinental railroad was completed in 1869 simply because of the lower rates ships provided to and from the world's markets.

The first effective component of heavy industry in California known to this writer was the Union Iron Works, in San Francisco, established by the three Donahue brothers from Scotland. Peter Donahue was twenty-seven when he left

Glasgow for the Gold Rush; his brother James soon followed. They opened a blacksmith shop in an *adobe* on Montgomery Street, at the foot of Telegraph Hill, where they were joined by a third brother, Michael. The three men's skills were wonderfully complementary: Peter was a machinist; James, a boilermaker; Michael, a moulder, or pattern maker. San Francisco's numerous fires provided scrap metal, which they melted down to get the iron they needed to make cooking and heating stoves, their first major product. By 1851 they had prospered sufficiently to move to larger quarters at First and Mission streets in San Francisco, doing business there as the Union Iron & Brass Foundry. There they made the first quartz mill and the first railroad locomotive produced in California.

Other forge and foundry firms arose in San Francisco—Pacific, Vulcan, Sutter, Fulton, to name a few—and similar firms arose, to a lesser degree, in the principal valley supply towns of Stockton, Sacramento, and Marysville, which were the *entrepôts* respectively to the southern, central and northern mines. The Mechanic's Monument on Market Street in San Francisco, erected by the Donahues' descendants to honor their forebears, is in effect a memorial to the whole industry.

This was the Age of Steam, and the devices that both generated and controlled its power were made of iron. Boilers for river steamers and offshore vessels, boilers to generate steam for mine hoists and mills, boilers to power sawmills and flouring mills, boilers to power the main shafts that drove the belts that turned the tools in factories making shoes, and woolens, and furniture, and horseshoes, and wagons—all these were made in San Francisco. Steam engines were needed to use the steam these boilers generated, and these engines, too, were made in San Francisco. Miles and miles of heavy-gauge iron pipe, carefully hand-riveted with a double seam in eighteen-inch sections, were needed to deliver water to the hydraulic monitors that blasted whole hillsides of gold-bearing gravel into liquid muck.

Shipyards near Vallejo in 1870.

Refining plant of the Arctic Oil Works in San Francisco, where whale oil was processed and shipped to the markets of the world.

In 1881 John Dolbeer, founder of the great redwood lumbering firm of Dolbeer & Carson at Eureka, invented the "Dolbeer donkey," which brought steam to the brute-force task of handling the insensate mass of a redwood log. This "donkey" was a vertical boiler, burning wood and spewing sparks like a roman candle; it turned a vertical capstan, or "gypsy," around which several turns of rope afforded the friction necessary to haul in logs from the woods along greased chutes. Rope soon gave way to wire cable, and steam greatly accelerated the productive capacity of the lumber business.

From the know-how and facilities created by mining and lumbering, Andrew Hallidie was enabled to adapt his system of endless cables powered from a central plant to operate the cable cars that surmounted San Francisco's hills, and remain one of that city's great tourist attractions.

Rails and rolling stock for both state and municipal transit systems eventually came out of this heavy industrial capacity. In time, the Southern Pacific established its largest shops at Sacramento (using coal from its own fields in Washington) and gave that inland town a firm industrial payroll to complement its governmental employment.

San Francisco's needs for skilled labor in the forge and foundry business, as well as in other trades and crafts, were met at first by disappointed gold-seekers, for there were men of every skill and profession among the Argonauts of '49. This background of industrial labor established San Francisco's position as a strong union town, a position that has endured ever since.

The demands of inland waterway navigation and coastwise and transpacific trade gave the state a shipbuilding industry from the time of the Gold Rush. The availability of lumber for hulls, decking, and superstructures was another natural advantage. San Francisco's strategic position and the deep-water reaches of the Bay, coupled with the necessities of national defense as the United States became a Pacific power, led to the establishment of the Mare Island Naval Shipyard in 1854 and the Hunter's Point drydock in later years. In

1859 Mare Island built the first warship constructed on the Pacific Coast, the *Saginaw*, and today it is the only Pacific Coast yard capable of constructing nuclear submarines.

California's shipbuilding saga reached its peak in the tremendous production records set during World War II. The Permanente yard at Richmond and Calship at Wilmington accounted for 45 percent of all the Liberty-type vessels built in the United States. The nation's record for Liberty ship construction was set by the Permanente yard in building the *Robert E. Peary* from keelson to completion in just eight days.

Wartime needs for manpower in heavy industry, especially in shipbuilding, brought California a tremendous number of young immigrants; Vallejo, for example, jumped from a population of twenty thousand in 1941 to one hundred thousand in 1943. This influx completed the political transition already in progress from a preponderantly Republican electorate to one preponderantly Democratic by registration. It was the wartime influx, too, that brought the state its first appreciable Negro segment of population.

Another early and important California industry was its fisheries. This industry had its true beginnings offshore when the American whale fleet, primarily out of New England ports, had to flee the whaling grounds of the Atlantic during the War of 1812. The enormous "pods," literally herds of California gray whale, attracted whalers to the California coast. La Perouse, the French navigator who visited Monterey in 1786, probably witnessed an annual migration from their breeding grounds in Scammon's Lagoon, Baja California, when he wrote, "It is impossible to conceive the number of whales that surround the ship." For many years before the Civil War, a whaling fleet left San Francisco every summer for the Arctic whaling grounds, thus heralding the later salmon fleet of the Alaska Packers and directly stimulating American interest in the acquisition of Alaska. The annual migration route along the California coast also made it profitable for land-based whaling stations to arise during the American period.

Stations were located at Ballast Point, near San Diego; at Portuguese Bend, near today's Marineland-of-the-Pacific; at San Simeon, beneath the ostentatious display of Hearst's Castle; at Moss Landing and Davenport at Monterey Bay; at Point Reyes–Bolinas and at today's exotic enclave known as Sausalito. At one time during the 1840's, sidewalks and patios at Monterey were paved with whale vertebrae. The extensive onslaught against the gray whale—the female of which yields twenty gallons of milk at a time to give her calf a rate of growth approximating two hundred pounds per day—led to conservation measures, beginning about 1900, and today more than six thousand gray whale have been tallied on their immemorial migration. The Del Monte Fishing Company of San Francisco (not to be confused with the food-processing firm of similar name) today takes about one hundred of these mammals each year for conversion into livestock and pet foods, fertilizers, and the like.

The Hispanic peoples of California do not appear to have been notable fish-eaters, perhaps because they would have to get down off their horses in order to fish; but the later population of San Francisco, owing to the Irish and Italian influxes, has provided a market for table fish since the Gold Rush. One of California's greatest delicacies moved the tragic poet George Sterling to a famous outburst:

> "Some folks boast of quail on toast
> Because they think it's tony;
> But my tomcat gets nice and fat
> On hunks of abalone!"

As this is written, another of California's great seafood delicacies, crab, is expected to be taken in the amount of 19,000,000 pounds in 1968. This will be about twice the average annual take, a reflection of what crabbers have come to accept: that there are fat years and lean in crabbing.

The lean years have descended upon Monterey's "Cannery Row," the scene of some of John Steinbeck's most famous and

appealing tales. That port's sardine industry once took up-wards of one billion pounds of sardines annually for process-ing into food, fertilizers, and feed supplements. A shift in the ocean's sardine population in 1952-53 virtually eliminated this industry, and today's annual catch approximates but three million pounds. Cannery Row now processes tourists, not sardines.

There was a time when the coastal streams of California were clogged with hordes of salmon seeking their ancestral spawning grounds and salmon contributed heavily to San Francisco's economy. This once mighty asset has largely suc-cumbed, however, to a chain of diminutions that began with the hydraulic "slickens" and was compounded by industrial water pollution and exploitative commercial fishing. After the local supply was diminished, ships of the Alaska Packers Cor-poration for many years sailed out of the Bay for the northern fisheries.

Frenzied fish-seekers throng to Southern California's beaches in a frantic parody of commercial fishing during cer-tain high tides each spring when the tiny grunion comes ashore to spawn. By law, the grunion must be taken by hand, an act that gains a certain frenzied quality because the female grunion comes in on a wave, flirts a hole in the sand with her tail, deposits her eggs, and is gone—in thirty seconds! The grunioneers are either quick or fishless.

The sea offshore occasionally affects Southern California in a less appealing way. So-called "red tides" cover the beaches with a layer of the microscopic sea life known as "plankton"; it decays, the prevailing winds blow the aroma inland, and Los Angeles has "smish," which is smog with a fish flavor. More importantly, the wide-ranging tuna clippers, which can stay at sea two months and cruise clear to the Peruvian coast, land about three hundred million pounds of tuna at Terminal Island each year. Los Angeles is the nation's leading fishing port, landing more tonnage annually than do Boston and Gloucester, Massachusetts, combined.

Commercial and sport fishing only scratch the surface of

Importing an ingredient of the Industrial Age: coal is unloaded on the San Francisco docks, 1887.

the sea, which is still more mysterious than outer space. Whether one is "hanging ten" at Malibu or wet-suiting after abalone, the sea has an intimate relationship with all those who seek it for profit or pleasure. In the past, the kelp beds off California's coast have been harvested for iodine and stomach emollients. This was a primitive forerunner of what today's scientists foresee as "aquaculture"—the farming of the sea, which is self-renewing by natural forces, and the mining of this same sea for its vital minerals. There is a determined school of thought that holds that the true frontier of the future is the vast circulatory system of the sea, whence came all life. California's 1,264 miles of coastline lend added meaning to the future importance of "aquaculture" and facilitate marine research by such institutions as Stanford University, the University of California at San Diego, and University of the Pacific. Such a combination of natural assets with the reservoir of scientific and technological knowledge in California's institutions has explosive potentialities for the future, and this field of endeavor currently is attracting hundreds of hopeful small and large companies to explore its possibilities.

Solar energy was used in the beginnings of California's dried-fruit industry, with wooden trays by the thousands covered with raisins, apple slices, and split halves of peaches, apricots, and pears drying in the constant sun of the state's long harvest season. Patient Chinese were the mainstay of this work, and enough of the sulphur used in the curing process clung to the finished product to give the consumer a taste of one aspect of the Hereafter. Steam drying plants sprang up during the 1870's, but the sun remained important until after World War I. Today, such processes as vacuum-drying, dehydration, and quick-freezing make an industry all their own in California's complex of agricultural processing.

As we have said, the industrial growth of Los Angeles was hampered by the higher costs of imported coal in that city. Another deterrent was the South's lack of the hydroelectric power, which Northern California enjoyed in abundance, thanks again to geology, geography, and climate. The Sierra

Displaying a startling touch of the Mediterranean, lateen-rigged Italian fishing boats were the workhorses of the industry. At right, a Sausalito dock scene, ca. 1880.

rivers had cut their gorges fast and deep, falling up to 130 feet to the mile, whereas rivers such as the Hudson in geologically older lands fall but 14 feet, and the great muddy torrent of the Missouri falls only 17 feet.

The energy of falling water was first used to turn water-wheels, such as that in John Sutter's sawmill. Most of the early flouring mills and other industrial developments in the towns of the Great Valley and the Mother Lode also used falling water for power. The alternative source of domestic and industrial energy in these communities was firewood, which was plentiful and cheaply obtained, albeit its BTU efficiency was not outstanding. The first locomotives in California, the "muzzle loaders," burned cordwood; and even with spark-arresters on their balloon- or diamond-shaped stacks, they were rolling fire hazards to forest and grainfield alike.

Even when it came to firewood, Los Angeles suffered from a supply inadequate for the phenomenal growth that began in the middle 1880's. The natural supply never compared with that of the Sierra or the oak parks of the Great Valley, or the timber stands along the central and northern coasts. Charcoal-burners and woodchoppers for the domestic market had made such inroads upon this scanty natural resource that in 1880 stove wood was commanding fifteen dollars a cord in Los Angeles, a price that was exorbitant to the average householder.

The state's first use of waterpower to generate electricity appears to have occurred in Northern California on April 10, 1879, when the Excelsior Water Company used a cumbersome water wheel to generate enough "juice" to light three 3,000-candlepower lights, which enabled them to work their hydraulic operations by night and by day, thus doubling their "cleanup" from the riffle boxes.

This crude beginning was given a tremendous assist by an invention of Lester Allen Pelton, a millwright and carpenter in Camptonville on the Mother Lode. His compact turbine-type wheel with a double row of buckets and a "splitter" to get two jets of water from the same orifice, was first perfected to power the sewing machine of Mrs. Margaret Graves, Pelton's landlady. When he patented his invention on October 26, 1880, it marked a major breakthrough in the efficient utilization of falling water as an energy source. A statue commemorating Pelton's discovery stands today at Camptonville.

This invention was first used to develop energy for the mining operations along the North San Juan Ridge. When the South Yuba Water Company lost its hydraulic mining customers, owing to restrictive legislation, it used Pelton's wheel to generate electricity. By August 4, 1887, the firm was illuminating streetlights in Nevada City, and just twenty-three days later, it had streetlamps in Grass Valley with a total of fourteen miles of transmission lines. The use of hydropower in California has increased immeasurably since these beginnings, and improvements in Pelton's wheel continue to convert falling water's force into one of the state's essential servants.

The title of the state's "hardest working river" is claimed by the Southern California Edison Company for the South Fork of the San Joaquin River, where its eight plants use and reuse the river's flow to generate 690,000 kilowatts daily for transmission to Southern California. A counterclaim is asserted by the Pacific Gas & Electric Company on behalf of the North Fork of the Feather River, where its multiple plants make a "staircase of power" that develops 786,860 kilowatts for Central and Northern California. To place these capacities in perspective, it is noted that a three-bedroom home, with an all-electric kitchen and appliances, requires 5.5 kilowatts daily for functional livability.

While Northern California was blessed with falling water in abundance, the first hydropowered dynamo was apparently in Southern California. It is said to have been installed by George Chaffey, pioneer irrigation engineer and promoter, in San Antonio Canyon, near Etiwanda, whence he ran a transmission line to Pomona. Nevertheless, this plant and the few that followed it below the Tehachapi Range were not adequate to their section's needs.

At the very heart of Los Angeles' ability to enter the state's industrial complex was the discovery of petroleum in Southern California in such quantity as to make it a much cheaper and more readily available source of energy than any other. In fact, petroleum provided the whole state with its first self-contained source of fossil fuel (coal deposits being almost negligible) and gave a tremendous impetus to the industrial growth of California in the twentieth century. The importance of the petroleum story merits a separate chapter later.

We must note that the state lacks a self-contained source of uranium or other fissionable materials. However, the energy potential per ounce of such materials makes them far less costly to import than coal, with which the state's true industrial complex began.

The enormous sprawl of Los Angeles Harbor illustrates a major dynamic of California's modern history: the quicksilver shift of industrial and financial power to the south.

Of Wheels Ashore
and Wheels Afloat

CALIFORNIA'S SIZE AND SHAPE would have precluded the development of its diversified assets without adequate transportation. Indeed, it can be said that each of the great surges in the state's growth has been both stimulated and accompanied by the expansion and improvement of transportation facilities. These facilities have been both internal and external, and both got their start from the impact and influence of gold.

California's Hispanic years did not produce a road worth the name between San Diego and Napa-Sonoma. A few cart tracks around the missions, presidios, and pueblos, served for such hauling as their needs required; similar cart tracks from coastal *ranchos* to the nearest beach served to convey hides and tallow to the waiting ships. For all its years Hispanic California was a land where transportation meant an animal's back or human feet, and it was thus that travel largely used *El Camino Real,* later dubbed the "Mission Trail" and now followed generally by U.S. Highway 101.

The Gold Rush generated a need for transportation; not more and better transportation, just *transportation!* Consider how different the gold-accelerated years would have been if San Francisco Bay had not existed, and if the only other safe, natural harbors on the coast, Eureka and San Diego, had been the main portals of ingress to the gold-bearing interior.

San Francisco Bay gave safe harbor to blue-water ships from all the world and in any number imaginable. The inland

Turn-of-the-century excursionists on the
Mount Lowe Incline Railway near Pasadena.

reaches of that bay, via Carquinez Strait, gave access to the waters of the Sacramento and San Joaquin rivers. A look at a relief map will demonstrate most vividly the immense value of this inland waterway system. Today, the incessant diminution of the Bay by fill for industrial and subdivision purposes has progressed almost too far. Unchecked encroachment upon its water mass bids fair to destroy its aesthetic and climatic values, and leave it little more than a commercial sluiceway between interior and open sea.

Sailing launches were the first and fastest means of Gold Rush communication along these inland waterways. A tiny, Russian-built steamer, the *Sitka,* is said to have made a round trip between the Bay and Sacramento City in the summer of 1849. Shortly thereafter, a side-wheel steamer, the *Senator,* came around Cape Horn to put steam on the inland waterways to stay. She is said to have netted her owners the tidy sum of $600,000 during her first year of operation. She was followed by others, and the river steamers evolved into luxurious craft, built in San Francisco, that would have done credit to the more celebrated paddle-wheel packets of the Mississippi River.

Stockton, Sacramento, and Marysville were the main interior towns, and they were sired by easy water access to San Francisco Bay out of their proximity to the Mother Lode mines. Of these three, Sacramento was the most important from the start, and it has remained the hub of interior transportation in the Great Valley.

Red Bluff was the head of navigation on the Sacramento River, which dictated its growth as the transshipment point between steamer and wagon train and muleback for the mines and settlements of Trinity and Shasta and Siskiyou counties. When the railroad reached Redding in 1872, that city became the transshipping point for many more years. Red Bluff, however, remained the head of navigation, since the gorge of Iron Canyon, just above the town, precluded successful upriver commercial navigation.

On the Feather River, Oroville was the ostensible limit of

navigation, but this position was jeopardized by the commercial rivalry of Marysville downstream, manifest in the building of bridges above Marysville that were too low to permit steamer passage. It can be said that river traffic was never an important factor in the development of Oroville or the region it supplied.

Sustained commercial navigation of the San Joaquin River above Stockton is hard to document; even harder to determine is the commercial value of river transportation to the upriver lands. Of some significance to the upper San Joaquin Valley was the fact that Tulare Lake, now reclaimed, was navigable in wet years by shallow-draft stern-wheelers.

From the valley *entrepôts,* independent little stage lines and freight services fanned out into the gullies, gulches, river bars, and ridge-spine camps of the Mother Lode. The celebrated Concord coach, one of the finest products of American craftsmanship, which took its name from the Abbott, Downing & Company factory at Concord, New Hampshire, reached its peak of utility in response to the demand from California. By 1854 the multitudinous stage lines had been consolidated into the California Stage Company, and shortly thereafter a similar consolidation, the California Steam Navigation Company, came to dominate traffic on the inland waterway system.

Three-dog teams, hitched fan-fashion to a sleigh, were used in winter on the higher mountain runs, particularly between Oroville and Quincy; and horse snowshoes were developed for the stage teams and pack strings that braved winter travel at the higher elevations. As late as 1937 John Ahlgreen, a Finn, and Hooligan Johnson, an Indian, were still using horse snowshoes on animals carrying mail and supplies over Salmon Summit (between Etna, in Siskiyou County, and Forks of Salmon, in Trinity County). These snowshoes were also used on horses harvesting asparagus on the peat lands of the Sacramento Delta until the "caterpillar" tractor was perfected.

There does not appear to have been any consolidation—monopoly, if you prefer—of freighting operations such as developed in staging and steamboating. The high-sided, high-

225

The definitive California stagecoach scene, ca. 1885.

The Ferries & Cliff Steam Line of San Francisco, 1905.

wheeled freight wagons, owned individually in the main, were the bulk carriers for foodstuffs and machinery needed in the major foothill communities. The point at which they could go no farther became the head of "Whoa-Haw" navigation, and long strings of pack mules took up the transportation burden into truly isolated sections.

During the first years of the Rush, the miners' human desire to hear from home and to write to the homefolks led to the custom by which individuals, armed with lists of miners' names, would make the journey to San Francisco, there to collect mail for all from the one and only area post office. These they took back to the mines and delivered, charging as high at two dollars per letter and five dollars per newspaper for their services. This evolved into the performance of shopping chores for men too busy to leave the "diggin's," and to the carrying of gold dust down for deposit with some reputable merchant who had a good, stout safe. One of these carriers, Alexander Todd, is said to have transported more than a quarter of a million dollars in dust for his customers, using a small butter keg for his portmanteau. Out of these beginnings evolved the express business, which came to be dominated by Wells Fargo & Company after the financial panic of 1855 had ruined its principal competitor, Adams & Company.

By 1851 the gold country, which was then the economic heart of California—the heart with the most human heartbeats—had been tied together by a combination of inland waterways and wheeled-vehicle and animal transportation. Through San Francisco Bay, it had access to the world.

Transportation was somewhat different along the coast and in Southern California, probably because there were not the golden gravels to pay for it and to attract the population that required it. The importance of coastwise shipping to the redwood lumber industry and to the early growth of San Francisco has been noted. This avenue remained Southern California's chief communication link with San Francisco and the state capital at Sacramento until 1876, when the San Joaquin line of the Southern Pacific Railroad holed through the Saugus

Tunnel and linked the two sections by rail.

The sea continued even longer to provide an economic life-line for Santa Barbara and San Diego. The Coast Stage Line was established by Flint, Bixby & Company in the middle 1850's, but this was uncertain and far too expensive for anything heavier than mail, express, and those passengers in an uncommon hurry and who possessed a durable physique. The sea was Santa Barbara's artery of communication, for the first thirty-five years after the Rush; San Diego relied on it even longer. It continued to be of importance to the coastal settlements and ranches well past World War I, as the steam schooners that carried lumber down the coast to meet urban building needs returned northward with cargoes of grain, sheep, hogs, and sometimes cattle, as well as honey, butter, and cheese.

It should be remembered that Southern California was economically dependent upon San Francisco virtually until the turn of the twentieth century. Its markets and its sources of capital were in Northern California.

Construction on California's first railroad began from Sacramento in February, 1855, and reached its eastern terminus at Folsom, twenty-two miles distant, on February 22, 1856. The road's basic equipment came around Cape Horn at a cost exceeding seven hundred thousand dollars, all of which was raised within the state, thanks to the surplus capital accumulation made possible by the Gold Rush. The San Francisco & San Jose Rail Road began construction in October, 1860, but was not opened for service to San Jose until January 16, 1864. This enabled San Francisco's wealthy to begin the urbanization of the Peninsula and provided the first segment of the Southern Pacific's coast line, which was finally completed to Santa Barbara in 1902. A rail link between San Pedro and Los Angeles was opened in the early 1860's, but San Diego had to wait for its rail connection with the outside world until 1885, when the California Southern extended its lines to meet those of its parent corporation, the Santa Fe, at San Bernardino.

The development of the Great Valley, the unlocking of its

A sternwheeler—one of many that once provided the main line of communication between Sacramento and San Francisco—clears the San Francisco pier bound for Sacramento in 1887.

full agricultural potential, and the utilization of the timber treasures in the adjacent mountains began in the decade of the 1870's with railroad construction its entire length by subsidiaries of the Central Pacific.

Construction of the California & Oregon Railroad north from Roseville, up the east side of the Sacramento Valley, reached Chico via Marysville on July 2, 1870, crossed the Sacramento River at Los Molinos to reach Red Bluff in 1871, and inch on to Redding in 1872. Redding was its "end of track" for many years before construction was resumed up the Sacramento River canyon, climbing out of that meandering chasm in the shadow of Mount Shasta on its way to surmount the Siskiyou Mountains and enter Oregon.

Construction of the Southern Pacific Railroad—the name later applied to the whole rail network that developed from the original Central Pacific—began from Tracy in 1869. Its tracks forged slowly up the east side of the San Joaquin Valley, a choice probably stemming from the unproductive nature of that valley's west side, which is in the rain shadow of the Coast Range. A later rail line up the west side of the valley is said to have been a result of Henry Miller's development of irrigation in that section. The greatest engineering feat of the original line was the "loop" by which it surmounted the Tehachapi Mountains; its worst problem was tunneling through the San Fernando Mountains to gain access to the Los Angeles Lowlands.

This tunnel was "holed through" in 1876, giving Los Angeles its first rail link with Northern California and the nation at large. Its initial impact has been noted previously in Wolfskill's celebrated first shipment of citrus fruit to the East via rail. The Southern Pacific's line was continued eastward via San Gorgonio Pass, and reached the Colorado River at Yuma in 1877, thus blocking the "Espee's" ill-starred rival, the Texas & Pacific Railway, from gaining access to Southern California. In 1883 another extension of this line was built from Mojave, where it plunged off the southern slope of the Tehachapi Mountains, to Needles, Arizona, thereby blocking the Atchison, Topeka and Santa Fe from access to California until negotiations between the two roads smoothed the Santa Fe's entry into Southern California.

In 1887 a Southern Pacific branch line from Saugus via Ventura reached Santa Barbara, giving it a rail link with the outside world and starting its long career as a winter haven for monied easterners. The coast line of the Espee, which had been completed from San Francisco to Santa Barbara in 1902, was not extended into Los Angeles (via the Chatsworth Tunnel under the Santa Susana Mountains) until 1904.

It cannot be denied that the Espee's intrastate rail construction was vital to the state's growth and development. It also cannot be denied that for almost forty years, the Espee ruled the state as it saw fit, that it was economically oppressive and politically undemocratic. Frank Norris's great, naturalistic and turgidly Gothic novel, *The Octopus,* etched in excruciating detail the stranglehold of the railroad upon the state.

The story of internal transportation would not be complete without mentioning the famous San Francisco Bay ferries, of still sweet memories to this writer's generation. Of equal nostalgia, although more noisome in memory's circuitry, are the "Big Red Cars" of the Pacific Electric, which made one of the most efficient interurban transportation systems ever known. It was the Pacific Electric, operating 3,700 trains a day over 1,200 miles of track, that enabled the urban sprawl of Los Angeles to begin its sprawling, giving rise to the saying that "Los Angeles is about thirty-seven suburbs in search of a city hall." Both the Bay ferries and the Pacific Electric were essential to the growth and development of the urban centers that they served.

A similar, although less substantial role was played in the urban complex of San Francisco by the Key Route electric interurban system, which competed for many years with the Southern Pacific's ferry-interurban complex in expanding the Oakland-Berkeley portion of the Bay Area. In all truth, this intercity network gave the "mysterious East Bay," as Herb Caen dubs it, a functional entity of its own that aided its

231

OVERLEAF: *A 1916 view of Richardson's Bay from Sausalito, north of San Francisco.*

transition from a purely "bedroom" function for San Francisco.

An extension of the electric railways from Oakland to Sacramento by the Oakland, Antioch & Eastern, and thence to Chico by the Sacramento Northern, gave residents of the upper Sacramento Valley better connections with the capital city and with the Bay Area than they enjoy today. (So it is remembered from personal experiences both in the 1920's and the present.)

Like the Pacific Electric in Southern California, the electric transit systems in the north were killed by the internal combustion engine. Currently we seem to be strangling ourselves in the coils of concrete freeways; and those concomitants of the Internal Combustion Age, air pollution and parking space, are forcing us back into systems of mass transit remarkably similar to those that our passion for personal indulgence in transportation convenience destroyed. One who has ridden both the Big Red Cars and the rocketing, third-rail coaches of the Sacramento Northern will bear witness that they had more to offer in comfort, almost in elapsed transit time, than do the "Blue Pooch" buses or the "feeder" airlines of today.

Today, Roseville in Northern California contains the largest railroad assembly yard west of the Mississippi River, where trains are made up and disassembled by electronic aids. It serves the operational needs of the "friendly" Southern Pacific at the strategic spot where its main east-west and north-south lines intersect.

Northern California's internal transportation complex was enhanced in 1915 by completion of the Northwestern Pacific Railroad from Marin County to the Redwood Coast at Eureka. The line gave that region its first overland link with San Francisco and opened the interior of Mendocino and Humboldt counties to profitable settlement by agriculturists, lumbermen, and livestock raisers.

The roster of so-called "short-line" railroads within California is extensive. Perhaps the best known were the line that linked Nevada City and Grass Valley with the Espee's main line over the Sierra; the Sierra Railway to Oakdale and Sonora, which has been used in many motion pictures; and the "Slim Princess" line in Owens Valley.

Logging railroads were essential to the lumbering industry, and their story is a conglomerate of multitudinous details that are of interest only to specialists in railroad lore. One of these logging lines, the California Western, survives today as a tourist attraction, as well as lumber-hauler, operating special steam trains over its forty-mile length between Fort Bragg and Willits, in Mendocino County.

One of the greatest of the human sagas of California's internal transportation is that of "Snowshoe" Thompson, an immigrant from Norway, who wrote an incredible chapter in the annals of winter travel. He was not yet thirty in 1856 when he fashioned his famous "snow skates" (skis) from valley oak. Each one was ten feet long, with an eight-inch upward curve at the toe, and tapered from a six-inch width at the toe to four inches at the heel; their maximum thickness was two inches at the toe strap (the only binding), and the pair weighed twenty-five pounds. Using these ponderous planks and a balance pole, which he rode astride as a brake on downhill reaches, Snowshoe Thompson carried the mail over the winter-locked Sierra between Placerville and Genoa, Nevada, for almost fifteen winters.

On his first trip, carrying an eighty-pound mail sack, he made the eastward crossing in four days. He then reduced his average time for the 110-mile journey to three days eastbound and only two days westbound, where the long downhill slope of the Sierra was in his favor. Traveling alone, subsisting on dried beef and hard biscuits, he was *the* communications link when winter settled its grip upon the upper heights of the Range of Light. He saved James Sisson's life by making the round trip from Genoa to Placerville in less than five days to get medicine that was needed for Sisson's gangrenous leg. In 1858 the first font of type for the *Territorial Enterprise*, Nevada's first newspaper, went over the Sierra on his sturdy back and equally sturdy skis.

Thompson charged nothing for his services, including carrying the mails; and when he sought compensation from the government in his declining years, his requests became so ensnarled in bureaucratic knots that nothing tangible transpired. On his death, May 15, 1876, he was buried in the little cemetery at Genoa, and crossed skis were carved into his gravestone. In the mountain light as evening falls, they speak eloquently of at least one man who met California's need for men to match her mountains.

The essence of a booming Los Angeles is captured in this Spring Street scene of 1907, complete with streetcars, tin lizzies, and the 43rd annual session of the U. O. A. Druids.

Uniting California
to the Nation

By 1856 AT THE LATEST, Northern California had a transportation network that was adequate to its internal needs, and it must be remembered that at that time, Northern California was all the California that mattered. Its demands for safe, dependable, efficient linkage with the rest of the nation were some years in being filled.

Even as the offshore winds and currents had dominated Hispanic California's lifeline with the outside world, so was the sea basic to California's development until the misnamed transcontinental railroad was completed. Thereafter, the sea remained the one commercial artery that the Southern Pacific could not control, although at times it exercised leverage on ocean freight rates, simply because the Cape Horn passage was open to the ships of all the world.

It should be noted that the Gold Rush–born sea-land route via Panama, always superior to that across Nicaragua, was improved markedly after the flush years of the rush by the completion of the Panama Railroad from Colon to Balboa in 1855, which not only shortened transit time across the Isthmus but lessened exposure to disease along the way.

The Panama Railroad was built by American capital. It was built simply because the volume of traffic to and from growing California would make it profitable. It represented California's ability to demand and to get faster connections with the rest of the nation, and it had its logical culmination in

"We may now look forward with confidence to the day when the Pacific will be bound to the Atlantic by iron bonds. . . ."

1903 with the beneficial little revolution, probably inspired by Theodore Roosevelt, that created the Republic of Panama and gave the United States the Canal Zone within which to construct a trans-isthmian canal.

Severance of the overland link between California and Sonora at the Yuma Crossing drastically affected Spain's ability to expand her initial beachhead in California. Lack of an overland link with Mexico affected California's position within, and relations with, that republic thereafter. California's demands for a safe, fast, dependable overland link with its sister states to the east arose in the heat of the Gold Rush and were not abated until the Union Pacific–Central Pacific rails were joined in 1869. Down this twenty-year interim, the struggle to unite California with the rest of the nation by an overland route produced some epics of wheeled and horse-flesh transportation. It also gave the California story a unique aspect in the importation of camels.

It is very hard for members of today's jet-age society to understand that distance was just as much of a problem to the people and the technology of the mid-nineteenth century as it is to the launching-pad crews at Cape Kennedy today. A jet aircraft today covers the same distance in one hour that an oxteam headed west covered in two months. Seventy-miles-per-hour on a freeway today equals a week's travel by over-land oxteam. The point is that *the jet plane of the nineteenth century was the railroad train.*

At the time of the Gold Rush, not a single railroad line had crossed the Mississippi River! The golden lure of California and the demands of its tremendous population (relatively speaking) gave a violent impetus to the westward thrust of the rail network. Notwithstanding, railroad construction beyond the Mississippi River was delayed by sectional schism in Congress between proslavery and antislavery forces.

East of the Mississippi River, the railroads had followed settlement. Beyond the Mississippi, west of eastern Kansas, the railroads faced a barren waste, still shown on some maps of that time as the "Great American Desert," without revenue-producing settlements or crops until they reached the Mormon sanctuary in Utah. From Utah to the golden shore of California, there was another, perhaps even less inhabited and more inhospitable waste, which culminated in the massive barrier of the Sierra Nevada. Because railroad construction across this region promised to be and to remain an unprofitable venture for many years, it did not attract private capital.

The federal government's assistance was essential to make initial construction possible. However, any legislation favoring the so-called "central" route, which followed the old Emigrant Trail by the Platte River and across South Pass, was blocked by the southern members of Congress, who were afraid that such a route would redound to the economic and political interests of the antislavery North. Conversely, any legislation supporting construction of a railroad to California from Memphis, or Fort Smith, Arkansas, or Shreveport, Louisiana, met the same opposition from northern members of Congress because such, in their view, would abet the power of the South's "slaveocracy."

While federal assistance to railroad construction was denied by Congress because of sectional conflicts of interest and the emotionally inflammable moral controversy over slavery, California's demands continued to be voiced in strident tones. These were met, at least in part, by several enterprises, most of which were financed directly or indirectly by the federal government.

In 1857 the government sponsored the importation of camels (dromedaries, in reality) from Asia Minor, to see whether they could overcome the transportation hazards of the Great American Desert. These beasties were located at Indianola, Texas, where what today would be called a Basic Camel Training School was established to teach American soldiers and civilian packers the mysteries of the odorous creatures. Under Edward Fitzgerald Beale, they made a successful journey from Indianola to El Paso, thence to Albuquerque, and across Arizona to Los Angeles.

OVERLEAF: *The Sacramento shops of the Central Pacific Railroad in 1869.*

They could travel twice as far, and four times as fast, on a given amount of water as mules, and they gained weight on natural forage that gave a burro acute indigestion. They also scared hell out of the Indians along the way. Despite these manifold virtues, camels simply were not accepted because of their smell, their malevolent dispositions, and their tendency to frighten all other types of livestock they encountered. They were later used intermittently in Southern California to carry mail and supplies to isolated army posts along the Colorado River, and Beale is said to have broken a pair of them to pull his buckboard from Rancho El Tejón into Los Angeles. In the end, the government auctioned them off at a public sale at Benicia Arsenal in Northern California, and they wound up in Nevada, where their purchaser used them fitfully to haul salt and cordwood to the smelters of Carson Valley below the Comstock Lode atop Mount Davidson.

Concurrently, a San Francisco importer, Otto Esche, brought in some genuine, double-humped Bactrian camels from Mongolia. He planned to use these in an all-year, all-weather mail and express service to Utah. Again, the nature of the beasts defeated their utilization as planned, and these Bactrian camels also were retired to Nevada.

The chief result of the camel experiments, it seems, was to give a gushing fount of folklore to the Far West. Among them is the legend of the great red-roan bull camel that roamed the southern Nevada deserts with a skeleton lashed to its back—a version, perhaps, of the "Flying Dutchman." As late as 1946 a story emanated from Tonopah, Nevada, about a wild-horse hunter who claimed to have caught an animal that was half-horse and half-camel. Near Quartzite, Arizona, is a monument to "Hyjolly," born Hadji Ali, one of the imported Syrian cameleers, who became a prospector after the experiment failed.

The camel experiments, both private and governmental, must not obscure less exotic but more substantial efforts to meet California's demands for linkage with the States.

In May, 1851, George Chorpenning set out from Sacramento with a pack string of mules to carry the mail to Salt Lake City. He reached his destination five weeks later, more than two of which were consumed battling across the snow-locked Sierra. Chorpenning tried again in February, 1852, and this time spent two months on the trail, and had to walk the last two hundred miles into Salt Lake City. The winter hazards of the Sierra caused the governmental subsidy for mail carriage to be diverted to the so-called "Mormon Trail" during the winters of 1854–58. Mails from Northern California went to San Pedro by steamer, and thence by way of San Bernardino, Cajón Pass, and the deserts of southern Nevada to Salt Lake City.

An attempt to by-pass the mountain hazards of the central route resulted in a government contract being given in 1857 to what still is known familiarly as the "Jackass Mail." This line ran from San Antonio, Texas, via El Paso and Tucson, through the heart of *Apachería,* to San Diego—a route aptly described as extending "from nowhere through nothing to no place." While it lasted, twenty-seven days was the scheduled running time over this line.

The most successful of the early overland links was the justly famous Butterfield Overland Mail, which used 100 Concord coaches, 1,000 horses, 500 mules, and 800 men to traverse the 2,795 miles (some say 2,812 miles) between its terminals at Tipton, Missouri, and San Francisco. The scheduled contract time for this journey was twenty-five days. Butterfield coaches ran without overnight stops, changing teams at way points, which meant that the passenger had to possess a most durable *derriere* to make the journey. They also had to have two hundred dollars gold for the one-way fare, for which forty pounds of luggage were carried free, and they were advised to equip themselves with a good Sharp's rifle and one hundred rounds of ammunition.

The Butterfield line used the railroad between St. Louis and Tipton, Missouri, whence the stages swung southwestward via Fort Smith, Arkansas; Sherman and El Paso, Texas; to Las Cruces, New Mexico; Tucson, Arizona; the Yuma Crossing, and Los Angeles. From Los Angeles, they followed the route of *El Camino Viejo* across the Mojave Desert and the Tehachapi Mountains to Visalia and Firebaugh's Ferry in the San Joaquin Valley, whence they crossed the Coast Range via Pacheco Pass to Gilroy and rolled up the valley to San Francisco. Much of their route within California is approximated by Interstate Highway 5.

The first westbound Butterfield mail left St. Louis on September 16, 1858, and arrived in San Francisco on October 10, 1858, for an elapsed time of twenty-three days and twenty-three hours. So far as has been ascertained, the Butterfield always ran within its specified contract time, and by 1860 it was carrying more overland mail to and from California than went by way of Panama. With the outbreak of the Civil War, the Butterfield equipment was transferred to the central route, to avoid benefiting the Confederacy. It was over this route that Ben Holladay, the stagecoach magnate of the Far West, made the fastest long-distance stage run known: from Folsom, California, to Atchison, Kansas, in twelve days and two hours, at a considerable cost in horseflesh over the 2,030-mile journey.

California's demands for even speedier overland transportation gained new urgency from the exigencies of the Civil War, among them a fear that the state might be swayed toward espousing the cause of the Confederacy, or at best remaining neutral. A vicious fight for government contracts developed between various overland freighting firms. The result of the combined pressures was the creation of the glamorous Pony Express.

Several points should be borne in mind about "the Pony." Among these is that the first pony express on the Pacific Coast pitted the two express company titans, Wells Fargo and Adams & Company, in a head-and-head contest to deliver President Fillmore's State of the Union message from Sacramento to Portland, Oregon. Adams & Company triumphed; the year was 1854. Another point is that another pony express involved several transportation firms in a contest to deliver

"*Short line to and from the East—All year route—Pullman Sleeping Cars!!*" *An 1884 ticket office of the Atlantic and Pacific Railroad.*

A Southern Pacific Emigrant Train enroute to California in 1883 pauses in Mill City, Nevada.

President Buchanan's State of the Union message from St. Louis to San Francisco in 1858.

Yet another point still causes controversy. The 1860 pony express was the brainchild of the great western freighting firm of Russell, Majors & Waddell, which had prospered greatly from government hauling contracts during the Mormon War of 1857. Their partisans insist that these men alone financed, directed, and controlled the pony express; and they get downright vehement at the suggestion that Wells Fargo & Company had anything to do with it, except to act as agents in California and parts of Nevada. They insist that "the Pony" bankrupted Russell, Majors & Waddell, and that the firm deserves great and total credit for its efforts to provide fast mail communication with California in the national interest.

The opposing school, perhaps stimulated quietly by the present Wells Fargo Bank, has uncovered evidence indicating that Wells Fargo actually had a large financial interest in the firm of Russell, Majors & Waddell during much of the Pony's hoof-drumming career. Therefore, says this faction, Wells Fargo merits a share of the credit for its performance.

Without regard to who controlled this financially disastrous venture, it can truly be said that the symbolism of the pony express is fundamental to our image of the West. It embodies such figures as "Buffalo Bill" Cody and "Pony Bob" Haslam, riding three hundred miles in less than a day, changing horses every half-hour, vaulting from saddle to saddle with the mail-stuffed *mochila* in hand as they did so; not to mention out-riding, outfighting, and outwitting Indians and road agents in the process. Some facts about the pony express may not be amiss beside its legends.

At five dollars per half-ounce letter, it perhaps averaged thirty-five letters each way each trip. Its scheduled running time between terminals at St. Joseph, Missouri, and Sacramento, was ten days for the 1,966 miles. The first westbound Pony left St. Joseph on April 3, 1860; the first eastbound Pony left Sacramento on April 4 and covered the fifty-five miles to Placerville in one minute less than three hours. By July 1,

1860, the Pony's western terminus was at Folsom, and its eighteen-month life came to a close with completion of the Overland Telegraph Line, constructed with governmental assistance, which reached Sacramento on October 4, 1861.

The telegraph was another step in the moves to bind California to the federal Union, and another step in the long struggle to give California the fastest possible communication with the East. Its building is a saga in itself, and it antedates in time the building of the overland railroad.

Some historians have stated that both freight and passenger traffic along the Central Overland Route was of paramount importance to California during the Civil War, bringing the state supplies and transporting the mineral wealth of California east to bolster the exchequer of the Union government. This writer simply disagrees and believes that the sea lanes, via both Cape Horn and Panama, were of much greater importance to California and the Union cause, despite Confederate raiders.

Interestingly enough, the Alabama Hills, just west of Lone Pine in Owens Valley, commemorate the *Alabama*, most famous or notorious of these Confederate raiding ships. Just so does Kearsage Pass across the Sierra in this region commemorate the name of the Union vessel that ended the *Alabama's* career. Many a television version of life in the West-That-Was has been filmed in the Alabama Hills.

California's prolonged demands for a railroad link with the other states received an added fillip from the riches of the Comstock Lode. Its silver was of importance to the federal treasury, and this stimulus to governmental interest in a western rail line came at an opportune time for legislation to be passed. Secession had removed the South's representatives from both houses of Congress and they could no longer obstruct railroad assistance that might favor the North. In 1862 Congress passed a measure providing financial assistance to transcontinental railroad construction along the central route. The Union Pacific and Central Pacific companies were formed to put this assistance to good use.

One of the tantalizing dreams connected with this first transcontinental line was that, by providing rapid transit across the country, it would give American merchants a middleman's stranglehold on the trade between the Orient and Europe. This dream evaporated with the opening of the Suez Canal in the same year that the rails were joined in Utah, because the canal enabled maritime commerce to provide rapid intercourse directly between European and Asian ports. A portion at least of the dream seems to have come true since World War II, in that 30 percent of California's exports go to Japan, while 33 percent of her imports come from that country. In addition, another 12 percent of California's exports go to the Philippines and Australasia.

Divergent views are held over whether the government's assistance to the Union Pacific and Central Pacific was a monstrous case of capitalistic looting of the public purse, or whether the railroad builders were sincerely interested in the national welfare at a reasonable profit to themselves. The controversy seems bootless. Despite instances of flagrant corruption in the construction, the hard fact remains that the railroad link not only stimulated California's growth by making ingress easier for more people and by providing an essential access to market for the first of its high-value luxury crops, oranges; but that it also opened up the whole vast region along its course to settlement and productive development much faster than otherwise would have been possible. This first western rail link was vital to the process of creating a self-contained "continental market" out of the United States.

The story of the Sacramento merchants who became the "Big Four"—Crocker, Hopkins, Huntington, Stanford—is one of the standard subjects of California history. So is the epic of construction across the Sierra Nevada by "*Cholly Clockeh's pets*," the thousands of industrious Chinese who did the work and lost their lives in its hazards. What is not so well known is the monumental disinclination on the part of San Francisco's risk capitalists to extend financial cooperation to the Big Four. This writer has gained the distinct impression that San

Francisco's financiers were content to play the time-honored game of letting the Sacramento upstarts fail and then obtaining control of the railroad at a fraction of what an initial investment might have cost them. The game failed.

The Big Four's moves to block other rail lines from entering California, thus maintaining their monopoly of rail transportation, have been noted earlier. Certain details are added here for clarification.

The Santa Fe, building south down the Rio Grande Valley from Albuquerque and then west, met the Southern Pacific, building east, at Deming, New Mexico, in 1881. This gave Los Angeles its first direct rail link with the East.

The Santa Fe then built westward from Albuquerque to the Colorado River at Needles, Arizona, reaching that spot in 1883. Here the Espee already had constructed a line from Mojave to the west bank of the river, thus blocking the Santa Fe unless it could obtain trackage rights from the Espee, which, of course, would still give that road the whip hand regarding rail access to Southern California. Negotiations followed, including a more than idle threat by the Santa Fe to build from New Mexico to Guaymas on the Gulf of California and thus gain its own direct access to the sea routes to China and the Pacific regions.

By relinquishing these plans in favor of the Espee, the Santa Fe gained entry into California; and it appears that the Southern Pacific, which had already located a line through Cajón Pass, believed that the Santa Fe could not find another roadbed through that narrow defile. It did so in 1885, to the Espee's great chagrin, and had a linkage with tidewater at San Diego through its subsidiary, the California Southern Railway. Thereafter, the Santa Fe gained access into Los Angeles over its own tracks and gave that city competitive rail transportation to the East, a matter of great moment in the "Boom of the Eighties" in Southern California. Los Angeles gained still another rail link in 1905–6 with completion of the Los Angeles, San Pedro & Salt Lake road, now the Union Pacific.

Opposition to the Espee's monopolistic practices caused the so-called "People's Road" to be organized in the 1890's to build from Stockton through the San Joaquin Valley, giving that region access to tidewater free of Espee domination. This line encountered financial problems, and eventually was acquired by the Santa Fe, which extended it to Richmond on the deep water of San Francisco Bay. The Santa Fe then secured trackage rights over the Espee line across the Tehachapi Mountains and gave the Bay Area a competitive rail link with the East, albeit this route required a longer transit time than did the Espee mainline over the Sierra.

Northern and central California gained another rail link to the East with completion of the Western Pacific down the Feather River Canyon in 1910. The last major new rail construction in California took place during the 1930's, when the Western Pacific and Great Northern roads completed a joint undertaking in northeastern California, reaching from the Columbia River to the Feather River. This operation was designed to tap the traffic originating in the large lumber mills of this interior region.

The Southern Pacific also has a branch line into this region which wanders from Klamath Falls, Oregon, through northeastern California, and into Nevada, where it joins the overland line of the Espee at Fernley.

The rail network's long-lasting and vital importance to California's internal development and external markets has been eroded by airlines and trucks and busses, and by the ubiquitous private automobile. Short-haul and express freight, as well as all too many passengers, have been siphoned away from the rails by these more flexible and convenient forms of transportation. Since 1960 air transport of fresh fruits and vegetables to eastern markets has increased twenty-fold; shipment of high-value, perishable commodities has reached one million pounds in one day from California airports. In 1967 fifteen *tons* of cut flowers moved by air from San Francisco alone.

The railroads' success in fighting back is typified best, it

The end of the line for the transcontinental railroad: Oakland's Long Wharf in about 1900.

seems, by the "piggy-back" operations using laden truck trailers. Less visible to the general public are especially designed freight cars for specific commodities, automated and electronic improvements in train operations, the tremendously increased efficiency of the diesel locomotive, and the expansion of the railroads into other forms of common carrier activity, such as trucking and pipelines for petroleum and natural gas.

While opening of the Suez Canal destroyed the American dream of dominating the Orient's trade with Europe, rail connections with the Pacific Coast did promote a substantial growth in transpacific merchant shipping. It had gained an initial impetus from the opening of Japan to western commerce, an event almost simultaneous with the Gold Rush. Lumber was a staple item in this trade, and still is. A California lumberman, Robert Dollar, expanded his export of lumber into the famous Dollar Line of transpacific and round-the-world steamers, which operates today as American President Lines. Similarly, the Matson Navigation Company grew out of the importance of the Hawaiian Islands' commerce to California. With the Suez Canal blocked to the world's trade today, American railroads are seeking again to capture the Europe-Orient traffic by offering special rates and services across the continent between Atlantic and Pacific ports.

The adaptation of petroleum to maritime uses was a tremendous asset in the growth of transpacific shipping, and this, coupled with construction of the artificial, deep-water harbor complex at San Pedro–Wilmington, brought Los Angeles to the point of contending with San Francisco and Vancouver, B.C., as the leading tonnage-handling port on the Pacific Coast.

The opening of the Panama Canal in 1914 gave California a relatively fast maritime connection with the eastern seaboard, competitive with the railroads for the first time. This was especially vital to the transportation of bulk commodities such as lumber, which needed all the price advantage they could get. Here again, the truck has eroded the intercoastal trade, almost to the vanishing point, except for specialized commodities.

Among vessels designed for such commodities are the wine tanker *Angelo Petri,* and the bulk rice carriers operated by the rice growers' cooperatives. Special vessels have been developed to carry cement in bulk; others, to bring liquid sugar from the Hawaiian Islands to the California & Hawaiian sugar refinery at Crockett on Carquinez Strait. Bulk paper pulp is brought down from the Pacific Northwest to mills on the Bay; vessels designed for automobile-carrying are used in shipping to Hawaii, and containerization has revolutionized maritime cargo handling.

Long-distance sea transportation for bulk commodities seems destined to remain a function of the blue-water vessels that have played such a role in California's growth. But long-voyage passenger traffic has succumbed steadily to air transport; today's ocean-borne passengers, by and large, are those who can afford the time to savor the leisurely life aboard ship.

CURTIS SHAFT
SIGNALS
1 BELL HOIST.
" STOP WHEN MOVING
2 " LOWER
" 2ND
4 5 6 " 3rd "
6 " 4 "
5

The Silver Thread
in Plenty's Tapestry

DURING AND AFTER THE GOLD RUSH, immigrants to California often used the Carson River Valley to approach the granitic scarp of the Sierra from the Nevada wastes. Some found minor amounts of gold in the sands of the streams tumbling down from the snows that clung late to the slopes of a mountain above the valley. This they named Sun Peak (now Mount Davidson) because its crest caught the first glints of the rising sun before they touched the formidable pinnacles of the Sierra Nevada to the west.

More traces of gold were found by the first true settlers in the Carson, Washoe and Eagle valleys between the Sierra and Sun Peak. They were Mormons, establishing an outpost of what Brigham Young envisioned as the inland empire of the Latter Day Saints. The Mormon War of 1857 called these settlers back to Utah to defend their church on its home grounds, and drifters from California established themselves in this region. Among them were many who had found it expedient to leave San Francisco for their health; among the others were two young brothers—honest, hard-working and God-fearing Vermonters—named Hosea and Ethan Allen Grosch.

The brothers had come to California in the Rush but had not found fortune. Seeking that will-o'-the-wisp, they arrived at the Sun Peak diggings in the latter part of 1853. They found that the gold they sought was not too plentiful, and worse

"*Myriads of swarthy, bearded, dust-covered men are piercing into the grim old mountains, thrusting murderous holes through their naked bodies. . . .*" A scene in the Savage Mine, 1867.

than its scarcity was the abundance of a heavy, blue, clayish stuff that clogged the sluice-box riffles. The Grosch brothers are credited with discovering that this stuff was silver—something quite foreign to the Gold Rush in California and, indeed, new to the American experience anywhere.

It apparently took them several years to come to this conclusion, and they did not live to capitalize on their findings. One of them died of gangrene resulting from driving a miner's pick into his foot by accident. The other, after burying his brother, tried to cross the Sierra in midwinter. He succeeded, but was so exhausted by his exertions, compounded by frostbite, that he died shortly thereafter. So far as is known, they had confided their secret to none of the other inhabitants of the Sun Peak country.

In 1859 about two years after the brothers' deaths, James Finney (called "Old Virginney" for his native state) and Manny Penrod were working a claim at the head of one of the canyons that seamed Sun Peak's slopes. Here they had found a ledge of decomposed gold-bearing quartz handy to a spring of water and were making a fair haul by Sun Peak standards. This led another drifter, Henry Comstock (known as "Old Pancake" because he was too shiftless to make proper biscuits), to assert ownership of the spring and thus to a share in the claim. The two discoverers for undetermined reasons acceded to Comstock's demand. So far as the scanty records show, Comstock had nothing to do with the initial discovery of this gold claim and certainly does not appear to have done any work on it.

The ledge of quartz gave way to a stratum of the insidious blue clay, causing a decline in profits. But a sample of the clay reached Nevada City, California, in some fashion; and Mel Atwood, that town's leading assayer, found that it was worth around three thousand dollars per ton in silver. The "Rush to Washoe" was on, and the Comstock Lode took its name from "Old Pancake's" voluble and constant assertions that he, and he alone, was responsible for the whole thing.

The Comstock gave the nation its first great supply of silver

—a commodity it could use in abundance today—and it introduced bimetallism to our currency and our politics. It made Nevada a state of the Union and enhanced the Union's war-making abilities; it also gave Mark Twain his first lessons in roughing it and in western humor. More than this, it gave California a financial impetus that snapped it out of a business collapse that had occurred in 1855 and sent it on its way with increased developmental velocity.

According to its physical geography, the Comstock was in the Great Basin. According to political boundaries, it was in Nevada. Financially, commercially, and politically, however, for the years of its major productivity, 1860 to 1880, the Comstock belonged to California. It belonged to California because it was owned, developed, and exploited by Californians.

A veritable torrent of silver poured over the Sierra to enrich and expand every segment of California life. Socially, it produced the "Silver Kings," whose wives and offspring competed with those of the Big Four for supremacy atop San Francisco's Nob Hill.

The Comstock was responsible for the creation of California's first stock exchange, making Montgomery Street in San Francisco the financial heart of the Far West. It has been said that more money was made and lost speculating in Comstock shares than ever was taken out of the bowels of Mount Davidson, where the nation's basic lode-mining laws were developed.

The Comstock generated a tremendous demand for mining machinery of all kinds; the depths to which the Comstock shafts probed into the heart of the mountain required better, stronger, and more efficient hoisting and steam-generating equipment. California's heavy industry, experienced from meeting the state's own needs, met this demand and grew accordingly.

As noted earlier, the Comstock's insatiable maw devoured whole forests around Lake Tahoe, and when the railroad crossed the Sierra, the forested slopes along the Truckee River were fed into the mine mouths to shore up the workings

259

OVERLEAF: *The Diedesheimer "square-set" method of timbering the cavernous mines of the Comstock was an engineering marvel of the day.*

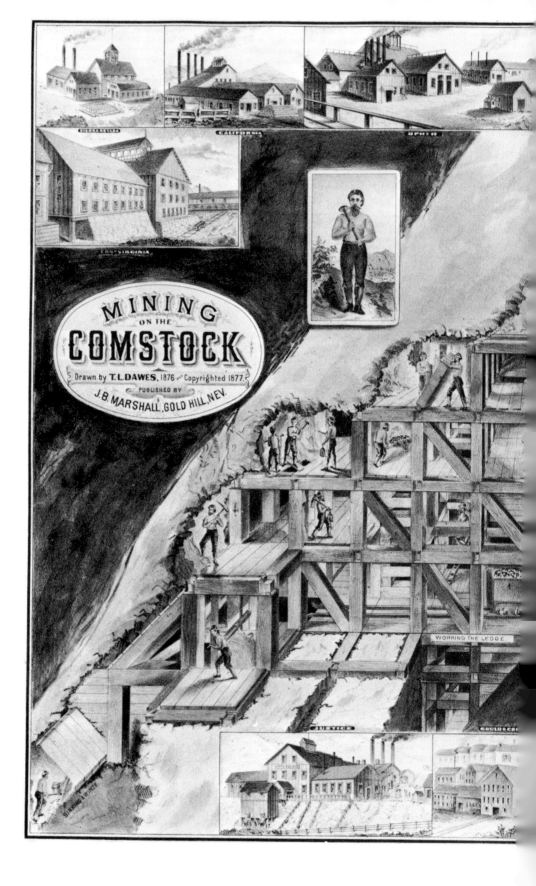

MINING
ON THE
COMSTOCK

Drawn by T. L. DAWES, 1876 and Copyrighted 1877.
PUBLISHED BY
J. B. MARSHALL, GOLD HILL, NEV.

SIERRA NEVADA

CALIFORNIA

OPHIR

CON. VIRGINIA

WORKING THE LEDGE

SINKING A WINZE

below. The underground rock formations of the Comstock were unstable, and the famous "Diedesheimer square-set" method of timbering—using timbers that were just squared tree trunks—was evolved to solve the problem. Millions of board feet of lumber and timbers were devoured by the Comstock's workings, and its fuel needs demanded more than three hundred cords of wood each day; each cord being a tightly ricked unit measuring 4 feet x 4 feet x 8 feet.

As the shafts reached deeper and deeper into the earth, temperatures increased to such a degree that ice cakes had to be used to cool the workings underground. Even so, men could work but fifteen minutes at the "face" of a crosscut, or stope, or winze, and then had to recuperate in cooling chambers thrice this long.

The Comstock provided a new and enormous market for California's basic products of agriculture and animal husbandry. The general route of today's U.S. Highway 50 from Placerville east was the principal artery of communication before the Dutch Flat & Donner Lake Wagon Road preceded the railroad across Donner Summit. Three hundred tons of freight a day left Placerville for the Comstock at rates as high as six cents per pound. Six Concord coaches daily provided "express" service to the Comstock, and the Pioneer Stage Line carried twenty thousand passengers annually at a one-way fare of twenty-seven dollars gold. The magnitude of travel between Placerville and the Comstock may be gauged by the recorded traffic that passed through one toll station in a three-month period in 1864: 6,667 foot travelers; 833 on horseback; 3,164 by stage; 5,000 pack animals; 2,564 four-horse teams, and 4,649 head of cattle. The volume and consistency of this traffic perhaps gave the Big Four the courage to undertake building a railroad across the Sierra, inasmuch as it would give their railroad a source of revenue regardless of what the transcontinental traffic might become.

Comstock profits, both from mining and from speculation, gave George Hearst the true beginnings of his financial empire. The famous Homestake Mine at Lead, South Dakota—

the nation's leading gold producer today—was acquired by Hearst with Comstock gains, and it remains a bastion of the Hearst family's income. Thus it can be said that "Hearst's Castle" at San Simeon, today operated by the Division of Parks and Beaches for the people of California, has its roots well-planted in the mined-out workings of the Comstock.

The world-famous copper mines in Montana were financed initially by California capitalists with Comstock profits. Other Comstock profits went into other ventures, of which Kern County Land Company's vast grasslands empire in the Southwest is an example.

Perched literally atop the Comstock Lode, Virginia City became the most cosmopolitan community between St. Louis and San Francisco—the beautiful, bibulous Babylon of the mining West. The Piper Opera House presented the greatest thespians of the day; and the beauteous Julia Bulette, most famous courtesan of her time and place, set the standard of elegance for the Comstock's legion of *filles de joie*. It was a town that learned to live with, and laugh at, the constant winds, dubbed "Washoe Zephyrs," which were alleged to blow laden pack mules off the street with only a minor gust. It was a town, too, that could entertain the project of blasting a tunnel clear through Mount Davidson below its crest to catch the westering sun in a system of reflecting mirrors that would not only illuminate the streets but melt the ice and snow that clogged them for many months each year. This writer was in Virginia City in the 1920's, during a major and fruitless attempt to work the Comstock's remaining low-grade ores; after World War II the late Lucius Beebe rediscovered the town and transformed it into one of the greatest tourist traps in the Far West.

The discovery of the Comstock stimulated the development of real mines and the promotion of imaginary ones all along the eastern slope of the Sierra, as well as in the contiguous portions of Nevada. What he saw and learned on the Comstock and its environs gave Mark Twain his famous axiom: "A mine is a hole in the ground owned by a liar." The strikes at Austin, Aurora, and Bodie (allegedly the toughest town of them all) fanned the speculative fever and benefited California in the process. One of the legacies to California from this mining activity east of the Sierra summit is its smallest county today, Alpine, with fewer than five hundred permanent residents. Its leading community is Markleeville, which has fewer than one hundred residents. Moreover, the county boasts no resident doctor or dentist or attorney or barber, and no motion picture theater. Its center for these amenities is Minden, Nevada.

Other mining activity farther south along and opposite the Sierra's eastern wall, at Panamint and Ballarat, and particularly at Cerro Gordo, east of Inyo-Kern, gave Los Angeles a much smaller version of the financial stimulus that the Comstock had given San Francisco. Between 1868 and 1877, some twenty-eight million dollars flowed out of Cerro Gordo alone, and steamers plied Owens Lake carrying 150 bars of silver (83 pounds each) at a time from the smelter to Remi Nadeau's freight teams, which hauled them across the Mojave Desert to Los Angeles. Lead was a by-product of the Cerro Gordo silver mines, and its occurrence here served to lessen the state's dependence upon importations of this base metal from overseas. The stimulus given to Los Angeles by Cerro Gordo was augmented by the expansion of mining interests into Arizona. The most famous of the Arizona strikes was Ed Scheifflen's find at Tombstone, perhaps more famous because of the later gunfight near the OK corral.

The Comstock's boost to every facet of California's economic and industrial life lasted long enough to keep the growth process rolling right up to the discovery of petroleum, the basis for the next big boom.

TWO OF CALIFORNIA'S PRESENT banking chains trace their origins to the Gold Rush and the Comstock Lode. Wells Fargo, which still uses the stagecoach symbol in its advertis-

"It is as if a wondrous battle raged," J. Ross Browne said
in describing the Comstock scene in 1863, "in which the
combatants were man and earth." Above, the works of the
Savage Mine in 1867. Below, making big wheels for big holes.

ing, evolved out of the express business of the Gold Rush—a business in which the eastern-born firm of Wells, Fargo & Company became supreme in California after the financial collapse of 1855. The Bank of California, on the other hand, grew out of mercantile profits amassed during the Gold Rush and combined by San Franciscans to handle the banking business of the Comstock Lode, which the bank's founders controlled for many years.

As we have seen, the rudiments of a banking system in California began with the extension of credit by resident merchants of the hide-and-tallow days. Merchants and mercantile firms were the first bankers of the Gold Rush, primarily because they were the only ones who had reasonably fireproof quarters and reasonably theft-proof safes to hold dust and nuggets, and because it was they alone, by and large, who had coin to exchange for raw gold. Too, their connections with suppliers in the East afforded the first handy means for funneling California gold into eastern coffers.

Banking in California was a business of private banks and bankers for many years after the Rush. Personal character and integrity, plus the durability of premises and resistant qualities of safes, were the basic yardsticks by which a customer could measure the probable security of his funds. The men who wrote the first state constitution prohibited state-chartered banks and prohibited private banks from issuing currency. Thus, these first banks were banks of deposit and exchange, not banks of issue. There were no state regulations governing banking practices until the Board of Bank Commissioners was established in 1878. This was not an effective agency of government because its powers extended only to state-chartered banks, which had been made possible by law in 1862, and not to private banks. These came under the commissioners' purview in 1886, but state regulation of banking did not become truly effective until 1909.

The express companies entered the banking business because of the exigencies of life in the mines and the needs of the miners for safety and service. A miner lost valuable time from digging while taking his gleanings down to San Francisco, or even to the valley supply towns. The express business followed the miners into every gulch, canyon, and river bend that attracted them. So did peripatetic merchants, who acted as agents for the express companies until the companies established their own offices and buildings, which they did only in the more stable camps. A miner could deposit his raw gold at one of these agencies or offices and receive a certificate of deposit, for which the issuing office charged a small percentage of the gross amount involved. These certificates could be cashed for their face value at any other office or agency of the issuing company, and often circulated as currency in a land that lacked it.

Thus, it can be said that the express companies pioneered a form of branch banking in California. Many years later, Amadeo Peter Giannini made branch banking and service to small depositors the keystone in the growth of his Bank of America (at first called the Bank of Italy) to its present stature as the largest bank in the world.

The express companies rendered another vital service to miner and businessman and merchant alike. It was hazardous, as well as uncomfortable to make the long journey back to the States with one's fortune encased in a money belt strapped around his waist beneath his underwear. By depositing his funds, be they in coin or dust or nuggets, with the express company in San Francisco or elsewhere, a miner could get a "bill of exchange" drawn on one of that company's correspondent bankers in almost any of the larger eastern cities, which could be cashed on arrival. Again, the express companies charged a percentage of the gross amount for taking care of a man's actual treasure and transporting it east.

The bills of exchange were payable in gold at destination, and the charges for securing such a convenient slip of paper often were more than offset when the holder could get a premium of sometimes as much as 10 percent back East for taking the face value of his bill of exchange in paper currency instead of gold. This paper premium for gold probably reflected the then ingrained distrust of Americans for the pieces of paper currency they derisively called "shinplasters." In August, 1864, the Union's inflated paper currency could be purchased in San Francisco at the rate of thirty-seven cents gold per paper dollar. California merchants and bankers, and others who could buy in the East in depreciated paper and sell what they bought for good yellow gold in California, increased the state's accumulation of surplus capital for investment.

The necessity for coin or credit is basic to the progress of any frontier or underdeveloped land. California's supply of both gold and silver gave it the means to finance the development of the state, as well as much of the Pacific Northwest and interior far western states. The need for coin or credit was illustrated in Southern California, where the lack of both is said to have been a major factor in that region's slow growth rate for more than thirty years after the Rush. When money could be borrowed in San Francisco for, say, 9 or 10 percent per annum, it commanded *1½ to 3 percent per month* in Los Angeles and contiguous territory.

Los Angeles' first bank was an outgrowth of Isaias W. Hellman's successful mercantile business. A second bank there was founded by Francisco Temple and William Workman in 1871, but succumbed to the financial panic of 1875. The first banking business capable of contributing adequately to the growth of Los Angeles seems to have been based upon men of integrity and collateral who borrowed money at "wholesale" in San Francisco and lent it at "retail" in the Southland. Even so today, savings and loan associations may borrow in large amounts, at the prime rate from the major commercial "full service" banks, and lend in smaller amounts at higher rates to individual borrowers.

In the days before government regulation of banking and government insurance of deposits, the rumor that a bank was unable to meet its obligations triggered a "run" on it to get one's deposit before it ran out of the hard coin to which a depositor was entitled. Often the rumor that any one bank was in trouble caused a stampede to withdraw deposits from all banking firms. Scenes of indescribable confusion and human anguish were registered in such instances, and nineteenth-century California survived three major financial "panics," a more bluntly expressive term than either "depression" or "recession."

The first of these in 1855 made Wells Fargo, which survived and capitalized upon it, preeminent in express and banking for many years. It also gave an economic fillip to the existing social and political conditions in San Francisco, which resulted in that city's second Committee of Vigilance in 1856.

Twenty years later, the "Panic of '75" literally shattered the state's banking businesses—the Bank of California among them—for many weeks. Many of them never reopened their doors. It was this second panic that led to the beginnings of state regulation of banking. Coupled with a severe drouth in 1876–77, which decimated the state's sheep industry, this financial collapse stimulated both agrarian and urban discontent. The result was the state's second, or "New" Constitution of 1879, under which, with all too numerous and confusing amendments, emendations, initiative and referendum measures, the state operates today. A slow resurgence of the world's markets for California's agricultural products finally overcame the cloying effects of 1875's economic slowdown.

The third financial convulsion occurred in 1893, and was precipitated by a gold problem in the national treasury very similar to that which confronts the nation today. It was not as sharply "panicky" as its predecessors, but it fanned the fires of Populism in the state which the Democrats used to capture the governorship for one of the few times since the Civil War. The long-lasting effects of the "Panic of '93" in California were alleviated by the rise of petroleum which will be discussed in the next chapter.

Insurance as an economic force affecting growth is another instance in which California benefited from an internally generated source of capital. When you *have* the funds with which to insure against risks those who have not, the profits

269

flow to you, and employment and subsidiary investments are promoted thereby. This is another prime reason for San Francisco's rise to financial dominance in the Far West. The emergence of Los Angeles as a financial center in the past twenty years cannot better be symbolized than through the selection of that city by the Prudential Insurance Company for its main offices for the Far West.

Marine insurance was the first type of risk covered in California, which is quite natural in view of the maritime trade that was so essential to the Gold Rush. Along with the later "inland marine" insurance, it was written either by foreign (largely British) companies or by eastern firms that had established agencies in California. These firms dominated the state's insurance business up to the advent of the Comstock Lode, and the profits from their underwritings flowed east or abroad. Also, their distance from the scene lent a certain detachment to the manner in which they viewed their insureds' losses.

Fire insurance was too risky for even the well-established firms to underwrite during the Rush—a most understandable conclusion, given the combustible nature of the building materials used. In fact, San Francisco experienced six disastrous fires in its first two years of Gold Rush life.

Cast-iron buildings were imported to make fireproof premises for businesses, but these were viewed with disfavor after five men were almost roasted to death inside one during the so-called "Great Fire" that swept San Francisco in May, 1851. The use of locally made brick, much of it from the prison kilns at San Quentin, and of stone quarried at Angel Island and Benicia, some even imported from China, later reduced the fire hazard. So did the use of iron doors and window shutters, which precluded, or were hoped to preclude, the fire-feeding drafts from these apertures. Mother Lode buildings that still boast such appurtenances are a favorite camera target for today's tourists.

Equally as important as non-flammable building materials in reducing fire's ravages, were the volunteer fire companies, which preceded paid municipal fire departments. These organizations performed incredible feats of fire suppression with their primitive equipment—hand-drawn hose wagons, hand-pumped waterwagons, and bucket brigades equipped with leather or canvas buckets. Membership in one of these groups was a mark of social distinction, and their Grand Balls and other functions made the outstanding social events of smaller communities for many years.

Profits from the Comstock Lode, both direct and indirect, apparently were the key to the formation of successful California-owned insurance companies that could offer a full line of policies, including life insurance, against all major risks. They were formed, in the main, during the period 1862–70, and the protection against disaster that they afforded was a contributing factor to California's growth. This was clearly demonstrated in the rebuilding of San Francisco after those April days in 1906 when "The Earth Shook and the Sky Burned." The investment and mortgage capital that their profits made available to other California enterprises, and the employment they provided, were other contributing factors to the state's progress. Opposition by the insurance companies to the use of petroleum as a fuel in urban areas was a factor in the state's slow utilization of that tremendous natural resource.

Black Gold's Propulsive Energy

IT IS VIRTUALLY IMPOSSIBLE to overstate the impact of petroleum upon California's growth and development. The miracles released from crude oil by today's refining processes affect every facet of our daily life from home cooking to national defense. Petroleum has been man's most flexible, probably his most powerful source of energy in all pre-uranium history, and his ability to use it has transformed his life—from the kerosene lamp, which was a powerful anti-dote to the terrors of darkness, down to today's air pollution by the internal combustion engine. The adaptation of petroleum to transportation wreaked havoc with established systems, both ashore and afloat, and it gave us the Jet Age, which truly ties the world together.

America's petroleum age began in 1859 with the so-called "Drake Well" at Titusville, Pennsylvania. It came to California in fledgling form shortly thereafter, and the later location of its first commercially exploited fields in Southern California gave that section of the state an economic boom equivalent to the Gold Rush in Northern California. One result was to make Los Angeles the first modern industrial city to grow horizontally because of the flexibility and utility of automotive transportation.

The existence of this fossil fuel in California was first recorded by Cabrillo in 1542, when he observed that the Chumash of the Santa Barbara Channel were using a "pitch," meaning asphaltic tar, to caulk their plank canoes. They used

Kern County oil fields, 1938.

it also to fasten arrowheads to shafts and to waterproof their carrying baskets. Notations about asphalt beds and oil springs abound in the journals and diaries of the early Spanish explorers and of the Franciscans at the missions. Captain George Vancouver, Royal Navy, recorded in 1792–93 the great oil slick that long gave iridescent hues to the ocean off Santa Barbara. However, little if any use was made of the available surface sources of petroleum and its components by the Hispanic *Californios* during the entire period of their hegemony in California.

In this regard, certain historical zealots have perpetuated the story that Andrés Pico distilled petroleum into a crude illuminating fluid at Mission San Fernando as early as 1854–55. Rather extensive research into the beginnings of the oil industry in California by this writer and by Prof. G. T. White of the University of California at Irvine has not established that this story is more than folklore.

In 1854 San Francisco became the first city west of St. Louis to light its streets by gas, which was made from imported coal. But as early as 1853–55 some of its streets and sidewalks were being paved, and its roofs coated, with asphalt. The asphalt was mined, quite literally, from deposits at Goleta and Carpinteria, near Santa Barbara. Oil that was found floating atop water springs in parts of Humboldt County seems to have been skimmed off during the latter 1850's to make a crude lubricant for the "chutes" over which redwood logs were skidded to the mills.

Illuminants imported from the East, including coal oil and the newly developed kerosene, were exported by San Francisco firms to the rest of the Pacific Basin. Most prominent among the exporters was Stanford Brothers, involving Leland Stanford and his brothers, which had branches in Lima, Peru, and elsewhere around the rim of the Pacific. The disruption of importing eastern illuminants at the time of the Civil War not only brought California its turpentine boom, it triggered the first of the state's oil booms.

The honor of being the first oil well drilled in California

generally is accorded the "Davis Well," which was put down in 1861 near Petrolia, Humboldt County. Other candidates for the title are wells near Martinez, in Contra Costa County, and near Ventura, in Ventura County. The first boom, far more speculative than productive, was concentrated in the Newhall Basin and what is now Ventura County, with its major production coming from tunnels driven by Stanford Brothers into the slopes of Sulphur Mountain near Ventura. Here the state's first well was drilled employing steam power, near Rancho Camulos in May, 1865, by Dr. Jonathan Letterman, onetime Medical Director of the Army of the Potomac, whose name is commemorated in San Francisco's Letterman General Hospital. The first recorded gusher, a well called "Ojai No. 6," was drilled in 1867 by Thomas R. Bard for the California Petroleum Company, a syndicate of eastern capital, in the Upper Ojai Valley of Ventura County. This first excitement died rapidly after 1867 because of the costs entailed.

Even if oil had been found in paying quantities during this first boom, it is *doubtful* that it would have affected California overmuch, because of refining difficulties. California crude oil was substantially harder to refine than the Pennsylvania crude that began our Petroleum Age, probably because of its excessive amount of carbon, which resulted from an asphaltum base rather than a paraffine base. The base makes it much heavier than eastern crude, as was reflected in the remark of a later California oilman when he was congratulated for bringing in a producing well: "Thank God, it wasn't a gusher," said he. "If it had been, we'd be shoveling the stuff down out of the trees."

Kerosene was the chief product derived from petroleum for many years, and it dominated the profit picture in the product-mix of that day's refineries. One of the greatest problems facing California's infant oil industry in the nineteenth century was how to refine California crude to obtain a reasonably nonexplosive kerosene, one that did not char the lampwicks and smoke the chimneys, nor stink like the back door to hell itself.

Another problem during the latter nineteenth century was developing a burner that could convert the heavy California crude into a fuel that would compete with imported coal. Four and one-half barrels of crude were the thermal energy equivalent of one ton of imported coal; oil had manifest advantages in its lack of ashes and the reduced storage space required. But until improved oil burners were designed and adapted to handle California crude, imported coal remained the state's basic energy source.

The technological improvements in refining have been continued right on down to today's petrochemical industry and its marvels. The first gasoline produced in California was marketed for paint thinner, and then for kitchen cooking in places such as Los Angeles, where other fuel was scarce or expensive. It found a market, too, in the Great Valley, where high summer temperatures made a relatively long-lasting wood or coal fire unbearable, for the housewife who could afford the initial investment required by a fast-starting, easily extinguishable, ashless gasoline stove.

Technological improvements in petroleum production, primarily in drilling equipment and techniques, make a story all their own. The first drilling equipment was the "spring-pole," a limber sapling bent over a rock or stump for fulcrum, and anchored at one end. The iron drilling bit, hand-forged and chisel-shaped, together with weights to give it impact, made the "string of tools." This was suspended from the free end of the sapling by rope, and a stirrup on each side of the rope enabled men to use their feet to "kick down" the hole. The spring of the sapling lifted the "string" back up for another downward kick. This technique apparently is as old as Chinese civilization. It limited drilling to relatively shallow depths, simply because the spring-pole could not provide adequate lift against the weight of tools and drilling line at deeper levels.

Steam came into use thereafter, utilizing a wooden derrick, perhaps forty feet tall, for which California's forests provided the raw material. A boiler-engine system powered a Pittman

By 1900, black gold was a genuine industry; derricks and tanks sprang up all over the landscape of Southern California—on hilltops, in business districts and palm gardens.

rod, which actuated the "walking-beam," and the up-and-down action of the walking-beam lifted and dropped the string of tools, which became much heavier in this method. The drilling rope was generally a two-inch hawser-laid Manila line. With these up-and-down cable-tool rigs, still using a chisel-shaped bit, which was rotated by the twist of the rope to get a reasonably round hole, maximum depth approximated five thousand feet. Below this depth, the stretch in the drilling rope offset the ability of the beam to lift the string of tools high enough to get any downward drilling impact.

The use of wire rope, larger boilers, more powerful engines, and steel derricks gave the cable-tool rigs an extension of life. The next evolution was the diesel-powered rotary drill, using alloy-faced bits. Drilling mud was pumped down the hole to prevent undue wear on the rapidly revolving bit. (Muroc Dry Lake yielded an earth that was admirably suited to this technique.) The modern rotary-rig greatly extended the depths to which man could probe for oil; it made possible the technique known as "slant" or "whipstock" drilling, whereby several holes can be put down in different directions from the same drilling platform, and it greatly speeded up the process of "making hole." Rotary-rigs are used today on off-shore drilling platforms, supplied by helicopter and boat, as well as in vessels designed for oil-drilling operations farther offshore.

Water-flooding—that is, pumping water into oil well holes to force out the oil—has increased the productive life of many wells. Also, replacing underground oil with water has halted subsidence in the earth's surface, once a problem of some concern to the city of Long Beach.

Petroleum transportation too, has a story all its own. Cans, barrels, casks, and firkins were the receptacles first used to get crude oil from well to refinery. Then came the forerunners of today's railroad tank cars, and metal tanks inserted into the holds of wooden-hulled coastwise steamers. The first vessel designed specifically for bulk oil transportation was the steamer *W. L. Hardison* built in San Francisco for the Union

Oil Company. This vessel also boasted the distinction of being the first Pacific Coast vessel to be lighted by electricity. She made several voyages before one of her officers, seeking to determine the level of the oil being pumped into her tanks at Ventura, lowered a kerosene lantern into the hold, and she burned to the water's edge. The first true tanker, in that her hull or "skin" formed the outer wall of her tankage, was the *George Loomis,* which was built in San Francisco for the Standard Oil Company of California in 1895. Her capacity was six thousand barrels. The feasibility of transporting petroleum in bulk by sea gave birth to the "Oil Coast" along an arm of San Francisco Bay between Richmond and Antioch. Here the refineries of such oil titans as Shell, Standard, Union, and others are supplied with crude from all the world by supertankers, which in turn carry the refined petroleum products to the world's markets.

California's first oil pipeline in 1879 was all of two inches in diameter and stretched all of seven miles from Pico Canyon to Newhall; thereafter, it was extended from Newhall to tidewater at Ventura. Fires had to be lighted along it in the colder months to keep the viscous crude in motion, and irate farmers tore it up when it sprang leaks in their bean fields and orange groves. Despite such drawbacks, this first pipeline possessed notable economic advantages: oil piped to Ventura could be shipped by sea from there to San Francisco for only $0.56 per barrel, whereas the Southern Pacific charged $1.10 per barrel by tank car from Newhall (Saugus) to San Francisco. Today's pipelines crisscross the state beneath its surface and move prodigious quantities of crude oil, refined products, and natural gas to meet the state's needs. Interstate pipelines bring to California natural gas from New Mexico and Texas, and an international pipeline from Alberta, Canada, brings natural gas from that province into Northern California.

Natural gas, which was "flared" or burned as a waste product in the early days, no longer is the orphan of the oil fields. In lighting San Francisco in 1854, the San Francisco Gas Company managed to manufacture 70,000 cubic feet per day from coal. Today, just one industrial consumer in San Francisco uses 1,500,000 cubic feet of natural gas per day. In 1947 the state produced its natural gas needs from its own fields, the first of which was discovered in 1864 when a water well was being dug for the San Joaquin County courthouse at Stockton. Today, California must import more than two-thirds of her natural gas supplies—dramatic proof of the contribution of natural gas to the state's productive capacity and to the convenience of daily living.

The marketing of petroleum products has come a very long way from the days when the occasional motorist was a venturesome, begoggled, often reviled curiosity in a long linen duster and a Barney Oldfield cap. In those days, gasoline was poured into the machine's tank from a can in the hands of the general-store owner, and a chamois cloth to filter it was standard motoring equipment. Today's multitudinous service stations, with their restrooms, snack machines, and soft-drink dispensers, are a far cry from the sparse, haphazard facilities of the early roadside supply points.

Application of petroleum to industrial use was slow to come about because of the difficult refining properties of the crude, the inefficiency of the first oil burners, and the opposition of the insurance companies. Breweries, ice plants, iron foundries, and isolated mining camps in Southern California's deserts were among its pioneering users. Thaddeus S. C. Lowe (for whom Mount Lowe is named) developed a new process for using petroleum to make illuminating gas that was first used in California at San Jose in 1877. A further refinement of the Lowe process in 1889 increased its usefulness for this purpose. Even so, for a quarter-century after California's first oil boom collapsed in 1867, the state's petroleum industry progressed at a snail's pace.

The Pacific Coast Oil Company, a forerunner of today's Standard Oil Company of California, operated in that slack period in the Newhall Basin. One of its drillers, C. A. "Alex" Mentry, brought in the state's first truly commercial well in near-by Pico Canyon in September, 1875. This well's produc-

The age of the automobile helped California become the nation's leading oil-producing state between 1900 and the 1930's.

tion, together with the company's other output, was sent to a refinery at Alameda—an indication that the state's principal market then was the San Francisco Bay Area. Exploration and development, as the terms are used today, were unknown; production seems to have been held down deliberately to keep the price up. By and large, the Pacific Coast Oil Company was the mainstay of the state's oil industry well into the 1880's.

Its first real competition was provided when three small companies operating in Ventura County combined to form the Union Oil Company in 1890. Here again, production was determined by what the slowly expanding market could absorb at prices that permitted a profit to the oil men. The same limitation applied to Lacey & Rowland, which operated in the Puente Hills Field east of Los Angeles. Refining was a hit-and-miss proposition, and fuel oil was sold just as it came from the well, sometimes being mixed with the inferior California kerosene to reduce its viscosity and improve its thermal properties.

The real breakthrough in petroleum stemmed from a well put down on West Second Street in Los Angeles by a wandering, down-on-his-luck prospector, who sank it by the shaft technique he had learned in mining. It burgeoned into the Los Angeles City Field between 1892 and 1894 and turned West Second Street into a raucous, oil-soaked little gulch, which created demands from citizens near by that the state's attorney-general abate the nuisance. This field laid the foundation of the wandering prospector's enormous fortune, his name being E. L. Doheny, and it marked a watershed in the state's production and use of petroleum and its products. As these lines are being written, a new multimillion-barrel "pool" has been discovered beneath downtown Los Angeles. Drilling operations using a tastefully camouflaged and noiseless derrick, and the "whipstock" or "slant drilling" technique, are expected to probe beneath the city's sprawling municipal complex to tap this pool.

In 1891 the state's total crude production had been 326,600 barrels; in 1895, with the Los Angeles City Field in full flow, it was 1,208,482 barrels. This plentitude of oil forced the price from $1.25 per barrel at the wellhead to but $0.29. At this time, coal was selling in Los Angeles for $5.00 to $7.00 per ton. Given the ratio of 4.5 barrels of oil to one ton of coal, users could get the same energy from oil for only $1.31. The economics of this equation literally forced the state's railroads to take advantage of it.

Petroleum had been used to fire locomotives in Russia and in Peru before it was tried in this country. The Pennsylvania Railroad had used it successfully in 1887, between Altoona and Pittsburgh, but coal still was cheaper for the Pennsylvania's operations. Then, in October, 1894, a Santa Fe locomotive burned oil in trial runs over the Espee tracks between Santa Paula and Ventura, with a burner adapted for moving use by the knowhow of Union Oil's mechanical staff at its Santa Paula headquarters. Before the year was out, the Santa Fe was using oil successfully over Cajón Pass, at a substantial saving over coal. Within two years, the Espee had followed the Santa Fe in a major conversion from coal to oil, and the industrial market expanded accordingly. Today's diesel locomotives, of course, use petroleum products for their application of increased adhesive efficiency to tractive effort.

The first adaptation of petroleum for maritime fuel was either in the aforementioned *W. L. Hardison* or in a coastwise lumber carrier, the *Pasadena*, operated by Kerckhoff & Cuzner of Los Angeles, one of the largest lumber firms in the Southland. Petroleum utilization in the transpacific trade eliminated the danger of running out of fuel at sea during adverse weather—a problem that had plagued the coal-burners. A concomitant of increased maritime use was the development of San Pedro Harbor by construction of a breakwater there between 1893 and 1903. San Franciscans referred to it as an "irrigated port," which did not affect its growth in the least. The availability of cheap fuel at San Pedro gave the initial push that made the present-day harbor complex there among the top ranked tonnage-handling ports on the Pacific Coast. The opening of the Panama Canal in 1914 also helped; vessels

OVERLEAF: *"It is plain to the least instructed persons that the amount of oil capable of being produced here is almost without limit." Standard Oil's Sunset-Midway field, 1931.*

transiting the canal on voyages from all over the world put in at San Pedro to refill their fuel tanks.

The lands and islands of the Pacific Basin made a growing export market for California petroleum products. And the industrial growth of Los Angeles, of all Southern California, was due primarily to the availability of cheap energy in the form of petroleum and its by-products.

After the Los Angeles City Field had sparked the major industrial breakthrough of petroleum, fields were brought in at such places as Coalinga, Santa Maria, Kettleman Hills, Santa Fé Springs, and Signal Hill. Great gushers ran wild, spewing thousands of barrels of oil into the surrounding countryside, excavating holes large enough to swallow a county, it seemed, and sometimes catching fire in titanic outbursts of uncontrollable waste. These fields and others enabled California to rank as the nation's leading oil-producing state between 1900 and 1936, and to hold second place in this category until 1958.

California's distances and generally smooth gradients made the automobile peculiarly suitable for individual transportation; its climate permitted a much greater year-round automobile activity for personal enjoyment and recreation. By 1927 California had the highest proportion of automobiles to people of any state in the nation, or any country in the world. "Good roads!" became the cry; the Automobile Club of Southern California became a power in this drive and the largest automobile club in the world. Asphalt was used for road-paving, with the process invented by the Scotsman, MacAdam; and then concrete, for which California had ample supplies of raw material. Automobile assembly plants were located in California, as were tire and accessory plants. These were attracted by the market California's population afforded. They in turn attracted more people, spawning service industries as they did so, and the cycle has kept feeding upon itself ever since. The automobile's more noxious side effects should be obvious to today's residents of California's more urbanized areas.

286

Today, nuclear-powered generating plants are being constructed or proposed for construction at several locations along the California coastline. If the application of nuclear energy to industry has the same multiplying effect that petroleum did, California's growth would seem destined to keep accelerating until the sheer weight of civilization west of the Sierra Nevada will cause a crack along the San Andreas Fault and slide everything into the sea! This would be the ultimate happening in what has been termed the "Westward Tilt."

A final note to the petroleum story is its connection with the citrus fruit industry by providing the most effective fuel to "smudge" against frost. There have been times in the past, before smog became a household word, when the whole of Southern California was smudge-bound for days on end by the outpourings from thousands of orchard heaters. Improved versions of these heaters are still used where air pollution has not become a major problem to public health and convenience.

J UST ENOUGH DIAMONDS were found in the hydraulic workings around Oroville in Butte County to enable that fact to be briefly noted here. More importantly, California was blessed with other mineral resources that lacked the impact of oil, but which have played and continue to play a tremendous role in the state's prosperity.

The enduring vermilion with which the California Indians colored their rock carvings was derived from cinnabar, the raw ore of quicksilver, and one of the world's few substantial sources of this shimmering, restless metal was found in California. The first important discovery was at New Almadén, near San Jose, while the other major find was at New Idría, in San Benito County. Smaller deposits were found and worked in the Coast Range folds of Lake County. The New Almadén deposits were uncovered just prior to the American acquisition of California, and their production was of great value to the extractive processes for gold and silver that followed.

As fulminate of mercury, quicksilver ignited the small arms of the nineteenth century, contributing to the Union's victory in the Civil War, to the slaughter of buffalo on the Great Plains, and to the subjugation of the horse-riding Plains Indians, "the finest light cavalry the sun ever shone on." It also began the powder-smoke fog that shrouds the deeds of the gunfighters within and without the law in the Old West. Fulminate caps also fired the black powder and smokeless powder and dynamite produced by the state's explosives industry, and thus served to advance the pace of mining and heavy construction.

The "twenty-mule team" of Death Valley fame actually consisted of two horses and eighteen mules, and in the popular fancy the livestock loom larger than the borax they hauled. The borax they hauled is also overshadowed by the numerous boron compounds that today come out of the state's southeastern Basin and Range province. Modern society hardly could exist without the products that these compounds make possible. Before the state's borax riches were unlocked, the bulk of the world's supply came from Tibet and from Tuscany in Italy; today California produces about 90 percent of the Free World's needs.

The center of the state's borates production today is the great dry lake that John Searles discovered in 1862. Once the Southern Pacific line to Los Angeles came within hauling distance of Searles Lake, a borax company was formed to work its deposits in competition with the more publicized operations in Death Valley. It was not until this century that our level of technology was able to tap all the riches contained in and below the saline crust, ten feet thick, of the lake bed.

Among these are the gasoline additive made famous by Atlantic-Richfield's "Boron" slogan; additives for glass and glazes; cleansing agents for detergents; components of weed and insect killers; fire-extinguishing compounds for home and industry, and for forest fire fighting by "borate bombers." Other compounds are used for alloying steel and for giving

Signal Hill, Los Angeles City, Summerland—all the great strikes of the century increased California's oil production from 4,329,950 barrels in 1900 to more than 300,000,000 in 1925.

the grit to abrasives, of which boron carbide is one of the hardest known. As if this roster was not enough, they also yield gypsum for plasterboard, and "Bristol Salt" for softening the Colorado River water supplied to Southern California by the Metropolitan Water District. Air-conditioning enables the towns of Boron, Borosolvay, Trona, and Argus to remain oases of production when the white hell of summer descends upon their Mojave Desert locale.

California leads the nation in the production of cement. Its widely distributed supply of raw materials spans the length and breadth of the state, including shells dredged from San Francisco Bay, where long ago the *Costanoan* tribelets depended upon shellfish as their granary. The utility of cement, its availability, statewide distribution, and concomitant cheapness have made it also a powerful factor in California's ability to construct not only highways but also the dams, aqueducts, and canals of its major water distribution and storage system. Further use in irrigation pipe and systems, and in industrial and residential construction makes cement one of the state's most valuable natural assets.

Available hand in hand with cement are rock, sand, and gravel—aggregates—which cement binds together by criss-crossing interlocking crystals as the liquid mass sets into concrete. The role of gold-dredging debris in constructing the Oroville Dam is a dramatic example of this correlation of assets, while the rotating "ready-mix" truck that delivers the makings of a new patio relates it directly to the individual Californian.

California's clay products and ceramic tile industries utilize clays that the California Indians were unable to transform into pottery. Millions upon multiplied millions of single-celled sea plants called "diatoms" were laid down on California's coastal lands as they subsided and emerged with the rhythms of geologic time. California leads today in the world's production of diatomaceous earth, which is essential to industrial filtration processes and to the swimming pools that are so much a part of the "outdoor syndrome" in California living.

The state's purest deposits of this earth are worked near Lompoc.

Iron ore from Eagle Mountain enabled the Kaiser interests to build the state's first integrated steel complex near Fontana during World War II. In pelletized form, this raw ore also makes an export commodity. Tungsten and vanadium mines perch high on the eastern reaches of the High Sierra, and copper gave its name to Copperopolis on the Mother Lode. Other copper deposits were worked in Shasta County and in the intramontane reaches of Plumas County, though copper was never a major item in California's cornucopia of natural resources. It did not need to be.

As this book went to press, escaping crude oil from offshore drilling played havoc with the manifold attractions of Santa Barbara's beaches. Hence it should be noted that escaping crude from natural fissures once spangled the sea off Santa Barbara with a shimmering iridescence. This sight was recorded in fulsome fashion by a passenger aboard the steamer *Senator* in June, 1864:

"Often for hundreds of acres square at one view . . . the sea boils like effervescing soda water, with the escaping gas which accompanies the oil, and great globules of pure oil rising with the gas flash out on the surface of the water, tossing it up in jets, and then breaking into films of rainbow hues like the tints of a dying dolphin [*sic*]. The effect is wonderfully beautiful and exciting."

Man's changed and changing environmental web makes yesteryear's exciting natural phenomenon a monstrous calamity today. It is a lesson to be taken to heart.

Sun-Seekers

T HE HEALTH INDUSTRY, TOURISM, HOLLYWOOD, aircraft manufacture, and space-age technology — each of these seemingly disparate elements of California's social and economic life owe their beginnings to the beneficent qualities of the state's climate. In this wise, they accentuate the opening portion of this narrative, which was devoted to an exposition of the state's physical geography.

Just as California's distances and gradients made the automobile peculiarly appropriate for California living, its climate provided more good days per year for personal enjoyment of the "sputterbuggy" and its descendants. In 1908 the *Los Angeles Times* called a road race between Los Angeles and Phoenix, Arizona, via Blythe, the "most hazardous" ever undertaken. It was won by a Stanley Steamer in a running time of thirty hours for the 455 miles. Today, Los Angeles assembles more automobiles than any other American city save Detroit; it bakes more tires than any other city except Akron, Ohio.

In 1966 the state tallied some 14,300,000 out-of-state visitors, of whom more than two-thirds arrived by automobile. The forecast is for this total to reach 37,000,000 by 1975. In 1966 California residents made approximately 60,000,000 one-day trips and 24,000,000 overnight trips by automobile within the state. When it is considered that the cash return to a community from just twenty-four tourists per day equals that from an annual payroll of $100,000, the economic impact of tourism becomes apparent.

"Not only are the sights grand, wonderful, and surprising in the highest degree, but the climate is exhilarating and favorable to an active life. . . ."

The other, less attractive, impacts are all too apparent to both resident and out-of-state travelers during the height of the summer season.

The therapeutic qualities of California's climate received their first boost from Sebastian Vizcaíno, the Basque mariner who rediscovered California for Spain in 1602. At San Diego [he reported] an Indian woman had a navel that "protruded like a gourd," and the wrinkles in her stomach resembled those of a "blacksmith's bellows." These were marks of great age to Vizcaíno, and he attributed the woman's longevity to the salubriousness of the climate in which she lived.

Early travelers and explorers wrote glowingly of this same climate, and as noted earlier, it was John Marsh's reports on the climate of Northern California that prompted the first avowed party of overland emigrants to quit Missouri's chills and fevers. The gospel of the climate was spread by returning gold-seekers, but until the overland rail link was forged, travel remained too difficult for significant numbers of simple health-seekers or sun-lovers to make the journey. The railroad promoted the travels of journalists, such as Charles Nordhoff and Frank Leslie's editors, and their accounts in books and periodicals encouraged health-seeking tourism in the 1870's. Southern California, the "Italy of America" — where the plaster-and-lath beach community of Venice sought to re-create its Italian counterpart, complete with Grand Canal— was the beneficiary of most of this eastern publicity.

The town of Ojai, in Ventura County, once an exotic haven for Theosophists and long an exclusive residential community, got its start as a health resort named Nordhoff. Other Southern California communities were similarly favored by doctors who prescribed the mild, sea-tempered climate for patients suffering from pulmonary ailments. Mineral springs throughout the state, such as Warner Hot Springs behind San Diego, were added attractions for health-seekers, as this was the heyday of balneology, the science of the therapeutic use of baths. Direct rail connection of Southern California with the East in the 1880's gave further impetus to this traffic, and it continued in a flood tide well into the period of World War I. In the meantime, California's natural wonders, such as the Big Trees, the Redwood Groves, Yosemite, and all the rest, became sightseeing and honeymoon havens with the advent of improved external and internal communications.

The mild winter climate, which often fills the northern and central coast of California with sunshine, in contrast to the fog-shrouded summers there, spawned the stately pleasure domes of the Hotel Del Monte near Monterey, the Hotel Del Coronado near San Diego, and the Potter Hotel at Santa Barbara. These, admittedly, were not for lower-income visitors. Most had an array of spur tracks for the private-railroad-car trade, and beginning at the turn of the century, they competed successfully with Florida for the winter resort custom of such monied easterners as the Rockefellers, du Ponts, Cudahays, and their ilk.

Southern California attracted hosts of the less affluent citizenry from the East and Middle West who came to bask in the sun and avoid the rigors of severe winters. In fact, San Diego attracted so many of the elderly infirm that it was known at one time as the "city of suicides." One of Southern California's largest annual gatherings long was the picnic of expatriate Iowans at Long Beach; and Lodi, near Stockton, became a favored winter rendezvous for South Dakotans.

California today is a favorite spot for summer tourists, as the number of out-of-state licenses on the freeways inescapably attest. Yosemite Valley entertains "wall-to-wall" people all through the season to the traditional Labor Day weekend. Such widely publicized attractions as Disneyland and Marineland-of-the-Pacific and their imitators exert a powerful pull among peoples of all the world, Khrushchev included, and they benefit from the low construction costs and the greater number of operating days per year made possible by the climate.

The Sierra Nevada, where the Donners perished, where Snowshoe Thompson did his deeds, gives California a tremendous winter sports region for devotees of *"skeeing"* or

"*sheeing*" as you prefer. California's first organized ski races were staged at La Porte [Rabbit Creek] in the 1850's, and outsiders were invited to compete in these events for the first time in 1860. Snowshoe Thompson is said to have cost his backers five hundred dollars by losing to the LaPorte racers, when the latter invited his participation. Today, the roads into the ski country are as thronged on winter weekends as ever they were in the days of traffic to the Comstock Lode. And today, whenever the winter storms do not perform as they should, a ski resort in the Donner Lake area uses more than five hundred thousand gallons of water per night to make artificial snow for the enjoyment of skiers and snow-bunnies.

California's coast lacks the great combers of Makaha Beach on the windward side of Oahu, but the cry of "Surf's up!" attracts thousands of devotees at all seasons of the year—even when, to this thin-blooded, over-thirty reporter, the water seems so gelid as to make an Antarctic-born penguin demand a battery-heated wet suit. The first surfboard used by the recently deceased Duke Kahanamoku was fabricated from California redwood; today, California leads the nation in the manufacture of light, be-ruddered polyurethane surfboards. Surfing has become a virtual way of life for its fanatics, and this has given rise to the cry, "Would you want your daughter to marry a surfer?" among those who seek to disparage all things Southern Californian.

Far less strenuous recreation than surfing or skiing, and one perhaps more aesthetically rewarding than watching those who do, is to be found in awaiting the return each year of the swallows to San Juan Capistrano. These birds find their counterparts in the insect world in the hosts of monarch butterflies (*Amosaie plexipus*) that migrate each autumn from east of the Rocky Mountains to warm themselves through the mild coastal winter by clustering on two tall pines at Asilomar, near Pacific Grove. These are the only members of the order Lepidoptera known to make annual migrations; and they have the singular status, so far as is known to this writer, of being the only insect protected by a municipal ordinance.

297

"*The fields are full of flowers, the grass is green, and Nature is in her most inviting garb.*"
OVERLEAF: *The Good Life of the Gilded Age—Hotel del Coronada, San Diego.*

THE CAMERA WORK OF EADWEARD MUYBRIDGE—there are those who accent the last syllable of his surname—in capturing the action of a running horse at Leland Stanford's farm south of San Francisco is held by some to be the birth of the motion picture. Other sources hold, apparently with more reason, that modern cinematography stems from pioneering work by French inventors.

America's pioneer picture-makers moved from the East Coast to California shortly after the turn of the century. One view is that they did so to escape their creditors. A stronger, long-range reason for the move seems inherent in the climate, which afforded more shooting days outdoors and thus reduced studio-use expenses, and in the terrain and scenery which offered variety without expensive set construction. Too, the cost of building studios was much lower in a climate that did not require, for example, steam heating or the burying of water pipes three feet below ground level to prevent freezing.

One of the first major sites for movie-making in California was at Livermore, where Essanay made the "Broncho Billy" Anderson Westerns, a genre that has remained a staple in films even unto television. Livermore's status as the new center of motion pictures was short-lived; between 1910 and 1914 the industry became concentrated in a Southern California community that had been founded in 1887 as a temperance colony. When the film makers discovered Hollywood, it had fewer than five thousand people and boasted a civic ordinance against driving more than two thousand sheep at a time down what became Hollywood Boulevard. The big event of its daily life was the arrival of the stage from Los Angeles to Toluca Lake.

Why the infant industry chose to leave the environs of sophisticated and cosmopolitan San Francisco for the more rigidly conventional, evangelical atmosphere then enveloping the City of the Angels and its suburbs seems best explained by the latter's superior scenic and climatic conditions. An added inducement may have been the proximity of the Mexican border, which, before extradition closed the door, offered swift sanctuary via automobile from creditors and strict interpretationists of other statutes.

The rise of the motion picture industry was sparked by the "feature" film, meaning one of more than two reels; and its development of the "star" system turned Gladys Smith into Mary Pickford at $10,000 per week. The impact of these developments upon the American public made Los Angeles a news source rivaling the world's greatest cities. Even such grubby stories as the "Fatty" Arbuckle scandal, or Wally Reid's destruction by dope, made news for America and the world at large. And publicity was publicity, for the industry and for California, following the old maxim, "I don't care what they say about me, as long as they spell my name correctly!"

Hollywood and its environs became a tourist attraction *par excellence*; more importantly, it became the entertainment capital of America, and it has retained this position as the industry moved away from movies into radio and then into television. Today, 90 percent of all feature films and 75 percent of *all* the films made in America come from the producing center known loosely as Hollywood. (These figures are accurate when written; they may not be when read, so swiftly does change affect the cinema-television production matrix.) The effects of this industry on California's economy cannot be measured accurately but they most certainly have been most substantial.

A by-product of the movie industry in the "Home of the Stars" has been to give a most prosperous fillip to the fashion world, or garment trade, if you prefer. Los Angeles now is second only to New York City in clothing production. Another by-product was the rise of a cosmetics industry out of the wizardry of the Max Factors and Perc Westmores who prepared filmdom's greats for their celluloidal roles.

Technologically speaking, the foundation laid down by this variegated industry also contributed to the rise of the electronics industry which today is so important to California.

301

THE AIRCRAFT INDUSTRY HAS COME a very long way from the days when the correct way to determine whether a biplane was rigged to airworthiness was to release a sparrow between its wings: if the bird escaped, you needed more wire! The full measure of its growth has been due in large part to California's physical attractions, and prominent among these was the climate, which has provided more flying days per year and lower plant construction costs.

Only very recently has the work of California's aviation pioneers come to the fore. Twenty years before the Wright brothers got off the ground at Kittyhawk, John Joseph Montgomery made a heavier-than-air glider flight off Otay Mesa, near San Diego, on August 28, 1883. Montgomery now has been dubbed the "Father of Basic Flying" (apparently with some reason) because of his discovery of the lifting principle of an airfoil, which was the vacuum above it. He was killed in 1911 during another glider experiment at what is now Montgomery Hill in the community of Santa Clara.

The bewhiskered semi-mythical Lyman Gilmore is another Californian accorded stature as a pre-Wright-brothers pioneer. Born in Calaveras County about 1874, Gilmore is said to have made a heavier-than-air flight in a glider he designed and built himself in 1891 when a precocious seventeen years of age. In May, 1902, near what is now Lake Almanor in the northernmost Sierra Nevada, Gilmore seems to have made a truly significant heavier-than-air flight of two minutes' duration. The plane was of his own design and construction, was powered by a steam engine, and launched into the air down a chute. Five years later, he is said to have built, again to his own design, the world's first cabin monoplane, which did not fly. With another of his designs he won a race from Grass Valley to San Francisco in 1918 at an average speed of 125 miles per hour. Thereafter, he faded into obscurity, and his exploits never have been as solidly documented as have those of John J. Montgomery.

The state's commercial aircraft industry began in 1906, when Glenn Curtiss, an emigré from Long Island, is said to

The age of flight brought with it a touch of romance not unlike that of the great days of sail. Above, an intrepid airman pioneers sea-going flight from the deck of the U.S.S. Pennsylvania in San Francisco Bay, 1910. Below, a China Clipper passes over an incomplete Golden Gate Bridge on the first leg of a trans-Pacific flight to Manila.

have built the first airplane in the state at Santa Ana. By 1909 another great aviation pioneer, Glenn L. Martin, had left the hazards and expenses of eastern weather for the more favorable surroundings of Santa Ana. Between January 10 and 20, 1910, what is said to have been the first air meet in the United States was held at Dominguez Hill, between Compton and Long Beach. And on May 10, 1912, Glenn Martin made the first water-to-water flight in aviation history, from Balboa to Avalon Bay at Catalina Island.

World War I, of course, gave a tremendous boost to aviation, and between the two world wars Southern California blossomed as the home of the nation's most noted aircraft. The first planes to fly around the world were the products of Donald Douglas's talents, which he had developed as chief designer for Glenn Martin before breaking away to start his own firm at Santa Monica.

In the between-wars period, too, the Navy established its aviation headquarters for the Pacific at North Island, in San Diego Bay, where Glenn Curtiss had moved his flying school earlier. The "Spirit of St. Louis" was built at San Diego, and in 1927 Lindbergh flew from San Diego to New York before his epic transatlantic crossing. In this same year, Maitland and Hegenberger won the disastrous Dole transpacific air race to Hawaii from Oakland, and the first airmail was flown from California to New York. The mail flight began at a forgotten field near Concord, east of San Francisco, and required almost thirty-three hours and fifteen stops to its completion. The fare was $404 per passenger. Finally, in 1928 a wealthy "Angeleno," G. Allan Hancock, financed the 7,800-mile flight between California and Australia that gave Charles Kingsford-Smith a knighthood and his plane, the "Southern Cross," a place in aviation history.

These examples point the premise that the productive heart of America's air capacity was beating in Southern California between the wars. During World War II, it became *the* difference between air supremacy and defeat. Economically, the aircraft industry has been of incalculable value to California, and together with its offshoots, it created a reservoir of highly skilled technicians who could and did adapt to the needs of space-age production and contracting.

The airplane is ubiquitous in California's daily life. Its use for seeding, fertilizing, and insecticide application in agriculture has been noted; so has its use in forest-fire fighting. It is also used for pest control and reforestation in this vital industry, for aerial surveying and mapping, and for swift patrol of long-distance electrical transmission and telephone lines. Few radio disc jockeys can earn their salt without a traffic-spotting helicopter to keep their audiences abreast of what is happening during the rush hours on the state's assorted freeways and other urban arterials.

Muroc Dry Lake is a testing ground for supersonic aircraft, and Edwards Air Force Base encompasses three hundred thousand acres and boasts three hundred and fifty good flying days per year. The Mojave Desert community of Palmdale has mushroomed because of the space and flying days it offered the aircraft and space-age industries of the Los Angeles Lowlands. The vast air terminals are an integral part of (and annoyance to) the state's great urban centers, but without such terminal facilities, these urban centers probably could not exist.

The climate and terrain of California add one soothing factor in the air age: the sport of gliding. The best sailplane currents in the world, it is said, are found on the east side of the Sierra in the Owens Valley region; there the "Sierra Wave" permits superlative soaring and swooping, and offers silent, soul-resting communion with the primeval forces that have made California what it is. These same forces permit less spectacular but equally soul-satisfying gliding virtually throughout the state.

IT WAS BECAUSE OF THE CLIMATE that purse science, which is here defined as the pursuit of scientific knowledge for its own sake, first came to California. Astronomical observatories, such as those at Mount Wilson, Mount Hamilton, and Palomar Mountain, were so located because the clarity of the atmosphere made observations clearer and longer than elsewhere; and here again, the climate reduced construction costs far below those where the winters were more severe. What these began, today produces space probes fired from the Vandenberg Missile Range that light up the evening sky upon occasion as far north as San Francisco, and clog police department switchboards with queries.

The human link between past and present explorations of space in California seems personified in the bewhiskered, shrewd, and crafty realist named James Lick. A piano-maker from Pennsylvania, Lick came to California by way of South America, where he prospered, and arrived in San Francisco in 1847 with perhaps thirty thousand dollars in his possession. He eschewed the Gold Rush and its attendant mercantile pursuits, and concentrated his energies in real estate investment. He was reputedly worth some four million dollars by the early 1870's, when Professor George Davidson, then president of the California Academy of Sciences, introduced him to star-gazing through a homemade telescope atop one of San Francisco's famous hills. For whatever reasons—perhaps because their lonely, pristine beauty stirred his soul—James Lick fell in love with the stars. At his death in 1876, he bequeathed seven hundred thousand dollars (a colossal sum in those days) to build an observatory for the advancement of science. Mount Hamilton, 4,261 feet above sea level, was selected as the site, and Lick Observatory atop its crest was completed in 1888. The first true study of the nebulae was made here, and today its 120-inch reflector telescope is second in size only to that atop Palomar Mountain in Southern California.

Intertwined with the advent of science has been the growth of what properly can be called technological "knowledge centers." By this is meant such institutions as California Institute of Technology, whose evolution from Amos "Father" Throop's private school for boys and girls was stimulated by the first solar research conducted atop Mount Wilson, high

The age of intrepid airmen was succeeded by the profoundly complicated Space Age, but California's industries re-tooled to take a major role in a future beyond imagination.

above the then smog-free residential community of Pasadena. Not to be overlooked are such other assets as the development of major scientific research centers at Stanford University, the University of California at Berkeley, and UCLA. The world's longest linear accelerator at Stanford, the Livermore Radiation Laboratory operated by UC-Berkeley, and the Jet Propulsion Laboratory at Cal Tech—all bear witness to the cross-fertilizing effects of the growth of scientific activity and its translation into applied technology by the reservoir of trained talents which such institutions have made available.

California has pioneered in the development of the "community college" concept ever since the city of Fresno established the state's first public junior college in 1910. Commitment to public higher education has been of incalculable value in maintaining and stimulating the state's growth. The expansion of this commitment at every level—universities, state colleges, community colleges—is the *sine qua non* in maintaining California's allure for those who seek to better their condition in life beside the Golden Shore.

Today's electronics industry had its beginnings on what had been a grainfield on Leland Stanford's favorite farm. In 1912, at Stanford University, Lee de Forrest began his experiments that made him the inventor of the oscillating vacuum tube, the precursor of the wonders of solid-state and miniaturized electronics, not to mention whatever advances may be made after these lines are written. Concurrently with de Forrest's experiments, Dr. Charles Herold's wireless laboratories at San Jose made the first radio station broadcast—using a "carpet" antenna comprised of eleven thousand feet of wire strung back and forth between two seven-story buildings.

This evolved first into radio station KQW, which secured the first U.S. government license for radio telephony, and then into station KFRC, which originated the first audience show in radio history with Al Pearce's "Blue Monday Jamboree." Radio's first dynamic speaker, the Magnavox, was produced at Oakland in 1922, and the first radio drama—the ineffably soapy "One Man's Family"—began its generation-spanning run over San Francisco's KGO in 1932.

The growth of specialist firms engaged in conceiving, designing, producing, and marketing space-age hardware and its civilian offshoots has been of the utmost value since World War II to California's economy. This is attested most tangibly by the fact that the aerospace industry, including electronics and aircraft, employs six hundred thousand Californians today, and that over fifteen thousand firms in this industry are located in Southern California alone.

It is in the space industry and its most sophisticated products that the whole complex of pure science is coupled with, and utilizes, the skills and knowhow previously accumulated through the cinema, communications, and aircraft industries. Before the National Aeronautics & Space Administration was located at Houston, Texas (through, it would appear, political divination) California far outstripped the rest of the nation in the value of governmental "prime contracts" for space-age research and development. Now Texas is crowding California for this position and, in fact, passed California in the value of prime contracts awarded during the second quarter of the current fiscal year.

In this context, it should be noted that federal spending in California during World War II (1940-45) approximated thirty-five billion dollars. We must face the sobering fact that California's economy today is dependent in very large part upon federal spending: in prime contracts and their concomitant subcontracts, and in basic military and other agencies' payrolls and procurement disbursements.

From Dang-Na
to Megalopolis

THE SHAPE OF THE FUTURE, according to demographers, is the "megalopolis," the overpowering urban concentration that will make today's greatest cities seem no more than the rustic villages of a bygone time. Three of these are foreseen for California. One will cover the southern coast with a solid mass of humanity from San Diego to San Luis Obispo.

Another will dominate the Great Valley from above Sacramento to Bakersfield. The third will encompass the San Francisco Bay region as far south as Salinas-Monterey.

It is in this context that the rise of Los Angeles has been the most significant California development of the twentieth century. Reapportionment of the state legislature has given political domination of the state to Southern California, with the key being held by the City and County of Los Angeles. This allocation of political power has been justified on the grounds that it provides the greatest good for the greatest number, which is a version of the older saying that "might makes right." It has been justified as well on the grounds that approximately 70 percent of the state's total tax revenues are derived from Southern California. The tax base reflects the status of Los Angeles as an economic power within the state, equaling if not surpassing the long-established eminence of San Francisco in this respect.

History reveals a pendulum-like swing between power centers in California. During the Mexican period, 1822–46,

"We are different in pursuits, in tastes, manner of thought and manner of life. We call ourselves, not Californians but Southern Californians." Highland Park, Los Angeles, in 1900.

Southern California held the edge, in humanity and in property. The Gold Rush swung the power center to San Francisco and north-central California. The rise of Los Angeles has returned it to the southern region, where it seems destined to remain for a very long time. The population growth of the City and County of Los Angeles is shown starkly by the following: in 1860, it had 11,333 inhabitants; in 1967, 7,000,000. And it must be noted that 97 percent of the region's population has come there since 1900. Before that date, the evolution of Indian village into *pueblo* into city had proceeded with almost glacial speed.

In 1781 the *Gabrieleño* village of *Dang-Na* provided the site for the second and last true *pueblo* established by Spain in California. Its first settlers, eleven *pobladores* and their families, had made the overland trek from Sinaloa; they were the Indian, Negro, and *mestizo* admixture of Spain's northern frontier. By 1797 the village had grown to perhaps three hundred persons, who still dwelled in habitations of brush-and-tule construction because they were kept too busy keeping alive by farming to build better *adobe* abodes.

The settlement did not get *ciudad* (city) status until 1835, after secularization of the missions; when the American forces occupied it in 1846, it had a population of perhaps three thousand *mas ó meños*. Its chief claim to fame in the early American period was as a haven for undesirables from San Francisco and the Mother Lode, and its usual tally of a killing per day brought it the cognomen of *El Pueblo de los Diablos* in 1854. Its true growth began when its comparative isolation was ended by transportation facilities.

The mild climate made the citrus industry possible, and the export market that made it profitable was created by the advent of the Southern Pacific in 1876.

About the same time, silver strikes in the Cerro Gordo region of Inyo County gave Los Angeles a much smaller version of the Comstock Lode's stimulation of San Francisco. This furnished surplus investment capital and expanded the agricultural and commercial economy of the region.

Connections between the Espee and Santa Fe at Deming, New Mexico in 1881, coupled with the arrival of the Santa Fe via Needles in 1885, gave Los Angeles a much larger trading hinterland in the Southwest than it had enjoyed previously. This greatly stimulated its basic agricultural economy, and further expanded its position as a distribution and investment center. And it set in motion the first great boom in Southern California's history.

In 1886–87 competition between the Espee and Santa Fe for westbound passenger traffic briefly drove the price of a one-way fare from St. Louis to Los Angeles down to the ridiculous level of just one dollar per person. However, this rate war, coupled with extensive railroad advertising in the East, brought people of all ages, conditions, and economic assets to Southern California in a lemming-like display unseen since the Gold Rush. Towns were platted even in the dry bed of the Los Angeles River, and on the ridge ribs of the adjacent mountains whence only a mountain goat or a hot-air balloon could provide transportation. The "Boom of the Eighties" fizzled out in 1887, but its enduring impetus is shown in the population growth of Los Angeles and Orange counties from 33,400 in 1880 to 190,000 in 1900.

This growth was aided and abetted by the upsurge in petroleum production in the 1890's. The improvement, actually the construction, of the harbor at San Pedro, which had been the "hellhole" of the California coast in the hide-and-tallow days, began in this period. In 1906 today's Union Pacific line between Los Angeles and Salt Lake City was completed. The cinema industry moved south before World War I; the Panama Canal was opened in 1914, and the aircraft industry began to grow after the first world war.

The Southern California Edison Company began Los Angeles' imperial expansion northward in the early 1900's by reaching across the Tehachapi Range to develop hydroelectric power in the Sierra near Huntington Lake. As this is written, construction crews are stringing a 500,000-volt transmission line from John Day Dam on the Columbia River—a part of

313

OVERLEAF: *An aerial view of Megalopolis.*

the Bonneville Power Administration—into the Great Valley near Redding, where it will feed into the system that already carries power to Los Angeles.

Fundamental to Los Angeles' northward expansion was the "good roads" program it boosted so ardently. The old road between Los Angeles and the San Joaquin Valley had meandered across the Mojave Desert and Tehachapi Pass. This was replaced in 1915 by the Ridge Route motor highway (the "Grapevine" of infamous memory), which boasted a curvature equal to 110 full circles in its forty-eight miles. With this artery across the Tehachapi "knot," Los Angeles began to function as a magnet pulling the upper San Joaquin Valley southward. This effect has been reinforced and increased by successive highway improvements, U.S. 99 in 1933, and more recently Interstate 5. Good roads and San Pedro Harbor also determined Los Angeles' ability to gain the trade of the Imperial and Coachella valleys as they developed under irrigation, a trade which San Diego had anticipated would be hers. The overpowering growth of "automobility" in the Southland now sends 350,000 vehicles per day past a single point near the Los Angeles Civic Center. Instead of creating "autopia," this has spawned a new definition of Los Angeles as "1,000 miles of freeways and 10,000 miles of cars."

The growth these happenings both evidenced and increased enabled Los Angeles to make its political power felt significantly during the first decade of this century. Southern California in general, and Los Angeles in particular, was the bastion of strength that enabled Hiram Johnson to cleanse the Republican Party and purge the state of the almost monolithic power of the Southern Pacific's political apparatus.

Interstitial with every facet of the Southland's growth was the necessity of water to meet the needs this growth engendered. Los Angeles' claim to the waters of the Los Angeles River stemmed from its status as a *pueblo,* and these rights finally were confirmed by the state supreme court. The decision enabled Los Angeles to sustain its initial growth spurt, but kept the San Fernando Valley in unirrigated grain-

"God made Southern California," Charles F. Lummis said, "and made it on purpose." God made Southern California; man subdivided it. Above, a view of the virtually unchanged San Fernando Valley in 1853. Below, Westlake Park, one of the many mushrooming subdivisions of the 1880's.

fields for many years by the loss of its share of Los Angeles River water. In fact, the Los Angeles Farm and Milling Company raised 500,000 bushels of wheat annually on its 55,000-acre holdings until 1910, when they were sold to the Los Angeles Suburban Homes Company for sixty dollars per acre. The communities of North Hollywood, Studio City, Universal City, Sherman Oaks, Toluca Lake, and Van Nuys have taken root on this acreage, thanks to the availability of water from outside the Los Angeles Lowlands.

A dry cycle between 1892 and 1904 drove home the need for outside water if the Southland was to continue growing. Extra water, without which Los Angeles could not have burgeoned beyond five hundred thousand people, was first provided by Owens Valley. Whether this acquisition was the "rape of Owens Valley" or simply "aggressive vision" depends upon which side one prefers. The controversy still heats emotional fires around Bishop and Lone Pine, despite the fact that Owens Valley today gets far more income, summer and winter, from Los Angeles tourists than ever it could from alfalfa, sheep, and cattle.

Possession of this Sierra-stored water gave Los Angeles a powerful lever in absorbing many of the independent civic entities within its sphere, thus enhancing its growth. This water also produced California's greatest man-made disaster on March 12, 1928, when the San Francisquito Dam above the Newhall Basin collapsed and sent its capacity rushing down the Santa Clara River to meet the sea below Ventura. While the total loss of life remains unknown, it has been estimated at about five hundred persons.

The possession of adequate water supplies was vital to the growth of the aircraft and cinema industries between the world wars, and without it the tourist trade would not have kept on growing. Fish-canning and women's apparel added new economic muscle. Automobile assembly plants, and tire manufacturing plants, and oil refineries, and salt-evaporating ponds grew apace.

These attracted people, and people stimulated construction,

and service industries multiplied to meet the needs of multi-plying urban residents.

More water was obtained from the Colorado River Project in the 1930's, and the Los Angeles Department of Power and Light then became the largest municipal utility district in the nation. To distribute the Colorado River water, the Metro-politan Water District was formed, and became almost a law unto itself throughout the Southland.

Southern California is now regarded inaccurately by over-enthusiastic Angelenos as encompassing fourteen counties reaching as far north as Fresno in the San Joaquin Valley, and Sun Luis Obispo on the coast. Whatever its extent, it is re-garded as an ever-thirsty *bête noire* by many in central and Northern California because of the throbbing vitality, as palpable as smog, that emanates from Los Angeles.

It is the second largest Mexican center in the world; has the largest proportion of Negroes of any city in this country, after Washington, D.C.; is second only to New York City in its Jewish population; and has the largest Japanese population in the nation. It constitutes the largest consumer products marketing area west of the Mississippi; has the most bank-ruptcies; and is a national leader in fashions—both in clothing styles and in ways of outdoor living. It is at once a showcase for the superficial and a serious challenger to San Francisco's self-proclaimed cultural superiority. It is truly the New York-of-the-Pacific, a city of worldwide influence.

Cries for a separate state have arisen many times from Southern California and from other portions of the state. In 1859 one of the Southland's separatist pleas actually passed the legislature but was buried in Congress because of the crisis of the impending Civil War. These cries are heard today from both South and North, but the umbilical cord that neither can afford to sever is the massive water distribution system (the Feather River Project), born at Oroville, which will enable Los Angeles and its satellites to slake their thirst for a little while longer. In the 1930's Los Angeles voted two to one against the Central Valley Project, which the federal

government later assumed when the state could not afford it. In 1960 the Los Angeles vote assured passage of the bond issue that began the Feather River Project. That this project had other economic considerations—irrigation, flood control, power generation, and recreation—was incidental to its promise of water for the Southland.

Upon completion in 1990 the Feather River Project will comprise 16 dams, 25 power-generating plants, and 650 miles of aqueducts. These components will transport 4,230,000 acre-feet annually to California's water-short areas, which include the San Francisco Bay Area, the southern coast counties, and the upper San Joaquin Valley, as well as Southern California. What one acre-foot of water (326,700 gallons) means to California may be seen in the fact that each inhabitant requires 150 gallons per day, that it takes 100,000 gallons of water to process one ton of steel, and that more than 2,000 gallons of water are needed in refining one barrel of petroleum.

Water and taxes are ties which neither section of the state can afford to sever, because neither section of the state can live without the other's contributions to these essentials of today's society.

"The West is the most American part of America. . . ."

The Water of
Life and Growth

T HIS INTRODUCTION TO THE "world of California" thus
must end very much as it began—with the realization
that the natural forces that created California will
continue to affect, perhaps control, California's future,
just as they have dominated its past.

Man is a subaerial creature, living between water and air.
We need both to sustain life, but air pollution will not kill us
as quickly (despite the upsurge of emphysema) nor limit the
state's growth as surely as will lack of water. This already has
been demonstrated by the growth of Los Angeles.

Water from the Colorado River explains the present size of
Los Angeles. These same waters created the Salton Sea when
the Colorado overflowed its banks one disastrous season. A
court decision has settled the long dispute between California
and Arizona over proper allocations of Colorado River water
—in Arizona's favor. California's loss in this dispute is actually
only Southern California's loss. It will be compensated for by
the Feather River Project, but only until 1990, when the San
Joaquin Valley alone will require an additional four million
acre-feet of water annually. The developing science of "sky
farming" hopefully will meet some of this demand by causing
a long-term annual precipitation gain of five percent on the
watersheds that feed the major streams of the southern Sierra
Nevada. "Sky farming" involves the use of radar to track
incoming, cold Pacific storms, and the seeding of these storms
by silver iodide particles distributed both by aircraft and by

323

*The Coastal Aqueduct, 1968. "The Yankees are a wonderful
people," said Mariano Vallejo. "If they emigrated to hell
itself, they would somehow manage to change the climate."*

"It is impossible to forecast all of the good things, the fruitage which must follow the reclamation of our arid lands. . . ." The bleak wastes of the Imperial Valley were some of California's most arid lands, until Colorado River water made them "blossom as the rose."

propane-burning ground generators at high elevations.

Diversion of the north coastal streams (such as the Eel, Mad, and Russian rivers) through tunnels into the Sacramento River will increase the capacity of the overall California Water Plan and will help assuage Southern California's thirst, but not forever, perhaps not for very long. There is the threat that even the state's adjudicated diversionary share of Colorado River water cannot be met by that stream.

California's congressional servants now are demanding that the federal government find water elsewhere and construct facilities to divert such water to the Colorado River drainage. This leads logically to the idea of diverting some of the flow of either the Snake River or the Columbia River, or both, across the wastes of the Great Basin into the tributaries of the Colorado.

The citizens of Oregon, Washington, Idaho, and Canada, too—for the Columbia is an international waterway—will not favor this plan. Nor shall we be allowed to forget, and we should not be allowed to forget, that Mexico has demands upon the waters of the lower Colorado which we guaranteed by solemn treaty and cannot now fulfill.

An idea more grandiose than diverting waters from the Pacific Northwest is the North American Water Alliance plan. This proposes to take water from Canadian rivers flowing into the Arctic Ocean and divert some of it southward across the land to the Colorado. Others of these waters would be diverted southeastward to the Great Lakes region to remedy their water shortage and water pollution problems. This plan makes any past construction feat in man's history seem rather puny by comparison.

The use of nuclear energy to desalinate salt water cheaply is held by many to be the answer to the water problem in California. A consortium of private and federal agencies has scheduled such a plant to begin in 1969 near Huntington Beach, at a cost of $500,000,000. It is projected to produce 1,800,000 kilowatts of electricity daily at a cost of 3.5 mills per kilowatt, which is cheaper than in natural-gas-fired plants

325

OVERLEAF: *Water for land, water for people:
The opening of the Owens Valley Aqueduct in 1913.*

Water power: Above, a 1905 view of Main Street, Brawley, before "white gold" enriched the land of the Imperial Valley; below, an aerial panorama of Brawley today.

today. This plant also will produce 150,000,000 gallons of good water daily, enough for a city of 750,000 persons, at an estimated cost of twenty cents per thousand gallons. That is cheap enough for domestic and industrial use, it is said, but not for agriculture, which depends upon irrigation.

Desalination enthusiasts say that the cost will be lowered with larger plants, which will make more efficient use of nuclear energy. If these costs still are too high for agricultural use, at least water presently committed to urban needs under the master California Water Plan will be freed for agriculture.

There are even more roseate prognostications. Multipurpose nuclear plants are envisioned that would produce 1,000,000 kilowatts and 400,000,000 gallons of water daily, at estimated costs substantially lower than those cited above. In addition to their power and water capacities, these plants would process the salt-water residue to extract 2,000 tons of ammonia and 360 tons of phosphorus daily. One such plant would produce enough water and fertilizer to serve 200,000 acres, which in turn would yield in one year 1,000,000,000 pounds of grain, enough to feed almost 2,500,000 people at the level of 2,400 calories per day. Moreover, such a plant also could export annually enough fertilizer to underdeveloped lands to cultivate another 10,000,000 acres.

In this view, California's water problem and the world's hunger are capable of solution, and the length of California's coastline affords numerous suitable sites for such multipurpose plants.

Man has enjoyed just enough short-range successes in tinkering with his environment to make these plants millennially attractive. But, and a very big *but* it is indeed, would such a large-scale intrusion upon the ecology of the sea so affect our climate that normal weather patterns would become something else again? In such an event, could even desalination offset the resultant loss of water storage in the Sierra Nevada? And what would become of the lumber industry, and the whole web of life in California that radiates from its sea-born climate?

While we await better answers to the problems posed by a millennial solution, why don't we reprocess our sewage? There is no chemical reason why this cannot be done to make water as potable as the purest mountain spring products extolled by the beer commercials on television. Los Angeles does, in fact, reprocess some sewage, and it is used for agricultural purposes in and around Orange County. Notwithstanding, Los Angeles continues to discharge other sewage daily into the Pacific in an amount equal to its daily importation of water from Owens Valley. San Francisco and the other Bay Area communities are even more wasteful, and they are joined by virtually every name on the roster of urban enclaves in California. The water problem, in all its ramifications and continental magnitude, may well prompt the question: What boots it to reach the moon if we are thirsty on earth?

I<small>N</small> *the days when the* Californios *lived their uncomplicated lives as the Will of God dictated they should be, the wayfarer was expected to give courteous thanks for hospitality received. In turn, the host expressed the wish that his guest would have good of what he had received. That wish is here expressed in the olden phrase:*

Buen Provecho!

Wind Gap Pumping Plant of the Feather River Project—the most ambitious water plan in American History. It will not be enough. "Time seems too short for what they have to do," James Bryce wrote of Californians in 1889, "and results always seem to come short of their desire."

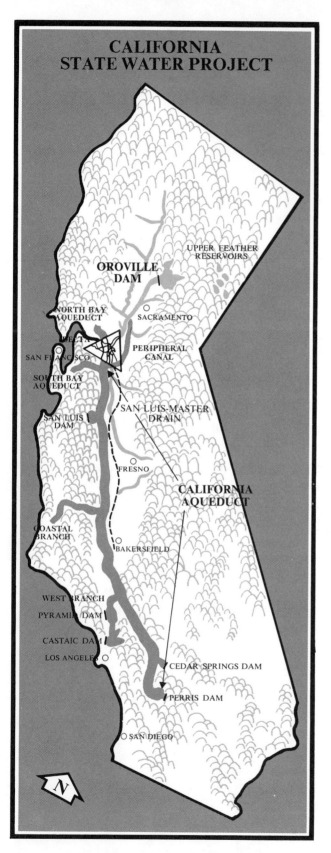

CALIFORNIA STATE WATER PROJECT

UPPER FEATHER
RESERVOIRS

**OROVILLE
DAM**

NORTH BAY
AQUEDUCT

SACRAMENTO

DELTA

SAN FRANCISCO

PERIPHERAL
CANAL

SOUTH BAY
AQUEDUCT

SAN LUIS-MASTER
DRAIN

SAN LUIS
DAM

FRESNO

**CALIFORNIA
AQUEDUCT**

COASTAL
BRANCH

BAKERSFIELD

WEST BRANCH
PYRAMID DAM

CASTAIC DAM

LOS ANGELES

CEDAR SPRINGS DAM

PERRIS DAM

SAN DIEGO

N

The California
Water Project,
begun in 1957 and not
expected to be complete
until the year 2020,
is an $11,000,000,000
plan to bring water
from Northern California
to Southern California
through hundreds of
miles of canals,
tunnels, siphons, and
penstocks. The biggest
single part of the plan
is "the world's largest
dam"—the Oroville Dam
on the Feather River,
completed in 1967.

Map reproduced courtesy of
Cry California.

Appendices

THE GOVERNORS OF CALIFORNIA

Spanish Governors

GASPAR DE PORTOLA

Governor of *Las Californias*, residing at Loreto from December 17, 1767, until his departure for Alta California, May 13, 1769. He was the new land's military commander, rather than civil authority, until July 9, 1770.

FELIPE DE BARRI

Governor of *Las Californias*, 1770–1775, residing at Loreto. Pedro Fages and Fernando Rivera y Moncada exercised military command in Alta California during this period. Moncada later was killed in the uprising at the Yuma Crossing that closed the overland route from Sonora and Sinaloa.

FELIPE DE NEVE

Governor of *Las Californias* residing at Loreto until the provinces were separated and thereafter at Monterey, February 3, 1777, to September 10, 1782.

PEDRO FAGES

September, 1782, to April, 1791. His domestic difficulties provided Monterey with its choicest gossip and exacerbated the normal friction between the military and religious factions.

JOSE JOAQUIN DE ARRILLAGA

Interim governor, April, 1792, to October, 1794.

DIEGO DE BORICA

October, 1794-January, 1800. A Basque, Borica ameliorated the laws that applied to *los Indios*.

JOSE JOAQUIN DE ARRILLAGA

Interim governor, 1800–1804; constitutional governor, 1804–1814. Russian penetration began during his administration.

JOSE DARIO ARGUELLO

Acting-governor, 1814–1815, at Santa Barbara.

PABLO VICENTE SOLA

August 15, 1815, to November 22, 1822, was the last of the Spanish governors; his term carried over into the Mexican period.

Mexican Governors

LUIS ANTONIO ARGUELLO

Acting-governor, 1822–1825, was the first native Californian to hold the post.

JOSE MARIA DE ECHEANDIA

1825–1831, moved the capital to San Diego; the first overland penetration of California by Americans occurred during his administration.

334

MANUEL VICTORIA
   1831–1832, served for about three months.
PIO PICO
   1832, served for about three weeks. He represented the *hijos del país* of
   Southern California.
JOSE MARIA DE ECHEANDIA
   1832–1833, resided in the south.
AGUSTIN VICENTE ZAMORANO
   1832–1833, resided in the north. He was the first printer to ply the trade
   in California. (The turnover of governors between 1831–1833 reflects
   internal strife ignited by sectionalism and secularization of the missions.)
JOSE FIGUEROA
   1833–1835. Had he not died on September 29, 1835, this most capable
   of the Mexican governors might have alleviated the plight of the ex-
   mission Indians and have prevented the political turmoil that followed.
JOSE CASTRO
   Acting-governor, 1835–1836.
NICOLAS GUTIERREZ
   Acting-governor for four months, 1836.
MARIANO CHICO
   Who served three months, 1836.
NICOLAS GUTIERREZ
   Who returned as acting-governor for another three months later in 1836.
   Agitation for home rule explains these short administrations.
JUAN BAUTISTA ALVARADO
   Revolutionary governor, 1836–1838. Recognized as governor by Mexico,
   August 8, 1838, he served until 1842. In actuality, Mariano G. Vallejo
   was co-governor during the period of alleged independence from
   Mexico.
MANUEL MICHELTORENA
   1842–1845, was the last governor appointed by Mexico.
PIO PICO
   1845–1846. José Castro exercised military command in the north during
   this time and met Frémont's junketing in that region.
JOSE MARIA FLORES AND ANDRES PICO
   1846–1847, were provisional governors in Southern California during
   that section's revolt against United States occupation forces.

United States Military Governors

Commodore John D. Sloat
          July 7, 1846
Commodore Robert F. Stockton
          July 23, 1846
Captain John C. Frémont
          January 19, 1847

General Stephen W. Kearny
          March 1, 1847
Colonel Richard B. Mason
          May 31, 1847
General Persifor F. Smith
          February 28, 1849

General Bennett Riley, April 13, 1849

Governors of the State of California

The original term of office was two years, to begin the first Monday after the first day in January. The term was extended to four years by constitutional amendment in 1862, and was to begin the first Monday after the first day of December. The constitution of 1879 restored the January date for inauguration and limited the term of the first governor serving under this constitution to three years. From 1850 to 1880, California's general elections were held on the first Wednesday in September, with a separate judicial election held thereafter. The new constitution provided for state elections to coincide with national election dates, beginning in 1880.

NAME	BIRTHPLACE	PARTY	INAUGURATION
Peter H. Burnett	Tenn., 1807	Ind. Dem.	Dec. 20, 1849
			(Resigned Jan. 9, 1851)
John McDougal	Ohio, 1818	Ind. Dem.	Jan. 9, 1851
John Bigler	Pa., 1805	Dem.	Jan. 8, 1852
(First two-term governor)			
John Neely Johnson	Ind., 1825	Amer. (Know Nothings)	Jan. 9, 1856
John B. Weller	Ohio, 1812	Dem.	Jan. 8, 1858
Milton S. Latham	Ohio, 1827	Lecompton Dem.	Jan. 9, 1860
			(To U.S. Senate)
John G. Downey	Ireland, 1827	Lecompton Dem.	Jan. 14, 1860
(Only naturalized governor; first governor from Southern California)			
Leland Stanford	N.Y., 1824	Rep.	Jan. 10, 1862
Frederick F. Low	Maine, 1828	Union	Dec. 10, 1863
(First four-year-term governor)			
Henry H. Haight	N.Y., 1825	Dem.	Dec. 5, 1867
Newton Booth	Ind., 1825	Rep.	Dec. 8, 1871
			(To U.S. Senate)
Romualdo Pacheco	Calif., 1831	Rep.	March 4, 1875
(First native-born state governor)			
William Irwin	Ohio, 1827	Dem.	Dec. 9, 1875
(The new constitution of 1879 gave him the longest four-year term)			
George C. Perkins	Maine, 1839	Rep.	Jan. 8, 1880
(Only governor elected to a three-year term)			

Name	Birthplace	Party	Inauguration
George Stoneman	N.Y., 1822	Dem.	Jan. 10, 1883
Washington Bartlett	Ga., 1824	Dem.	Jan. 8, 1887
			(Died, Sept. 12, 1887)
Robert W. Waterman	N.Y., 1826	Rep.	Sept. 13, 1887
Henry H. Markham	N.Y., 1840	Rep.	Jan. 8, 1891
James H. Budd	Wis., 1851	Dem.	Jan. 11, 1895
Henry T. Gage	N.Y., 1852	Rep.	Jan. 4, 1899
George C. Pardee	Calif., 1857	Rep.	Jan. 7, 1903
James N. Gillett	Wis., 1860	Rep.	Jan. 9, 1907
Hiram W. Johnson	Calif., 1866	Prog. Rep.	Jan. 3, 1911
(First four-year governor to be re-elected)			*(To U.S. Senate)*
William D. Stephens	Ohio, 1859	Rep.	Mar. 15, 1917
Friend W. Richardson	Mich., 1865	Rep.	Jan. 9, 1923
Clement C. Young	N.H., 1869	Rep.	Jan. 4, 1927
James Rolph, Jr.	Calif., 1869	Rep.	Jan. 6, 1931
			(Died, June 2, 1934)
Frank F. Merriam	Iowa, 1865	Rep.	June 2, 1934
Culbert L. Olson	Utah, 1876	Dem.	Jan. 2, 1939
Earl F. Warren	Calif., 1891	Rep.	Jan. 4, 1943
(Only three-term governor to date)		*(Appointed to Supreme Court, 1953)*	
Goodwin F. Knight	Utah, 1896	Rep.	Oct. 5, 1953
Edmund G. Brown	Calif., 1905	Dem.	Jan. 5, 1959
Ronald Reagan	Ill., 1911	Rep.	Jan. 5, 1967

Of the thirty-three governors to date, only six have been born in California.

THE SPANISH TRIPOD OF SETTLEMENT

The Twenty-One Missions

San Diego de Alcalá, July 16, 1769.

San Carlos Borroméo (Carmel), June 3, 1770.

San Antonio de Padua, July 14, 1771.

San Gabriel Arcángel *(the mother of Los Angeles)*, September 8, 1771.

San Luís Obispo de Tolosa,* September 1, 1772.

San Francisco de Asis (Dolores), October 8 (or 9), 1776.

San Juan Capistrano,* November 1, 1776.

Santa Clara, January 12, 1777.

San Buenaventura, March 31, 1782.

Santa Barbara, December 4, 1786.

Purísima Concepción, December 8, 1787.

Santa Cruz, August 28 (or September 25), 1791.

Nuestra Señora de la Soledad, October 9, 1791.

San José de Guadalupe (distinct from the *pueblo* of San Jose),
June 11, 1797.

San Juan Bautista,* June 24, 1797.

San Miguel Arcángel, July 25, 1797.

San Fernando Rey de España, September 8, 1797.

San Luís Rey de Francia, June 13, 1798.

Santa Inés (or Ynéz), September 17, 1804.

San Rafael Arcángel, December 14, 1817.

San Francisco Solano* (Sonoma, the only Mexican-established
mission), July 4, 1823.

*Pueblo status was granted the civilian communities that grew up around
these missions.*

Presidios

San Diego, July 16, 1769
Monterey, June 3, 1770
San Francisco, September 17, 1776
Santa Barbara, April 21, 1782

Pueblos

San José, November 29, 1777
Los Angeles, September 4, 1781
Branciforte, 1797
(virtually still-born)

Pueblos also grew up around each of the military posts.

THE COUNTIES OF CALIFORNIA

Almost half of the state's fifty-eight counties retain the names, if not the size, that they were given in 1850, when the state was first divided into political subdivisions. These "original" counties are: Butte, Calaveras, Colusa, Contra Costa, El Dorado, Los Angeles, Marin, Mariposa, Mendocino, Monterey, Napa, Sacramento, San Diego, San Francisco, San Joaquín, San Luis Obispo, Santa Barbara, Santa Clara, Santa Cruz, Shasta, Solano, Sonoma, Sutter, Trinity, Tuolumne, Yolo, and Yuba.

The "new" counties were created because of economic and population shifts during the years that followed:

Nevada	1851	Tehama	1856	Modoc	1874
Placer	1851	Fresno	1856	Orange	1889
Siskiyou	1852	San Mateo	1856	Glenn	1891
Sierra	1852	Del Norte	1857	Madera	1893
Tulare	1852	Mono	1861	Riverside	1893
Alameda	1853	Lake	1861	Kings	1893
San Bernardino	1853	Alpine	1864	Imperial	1907
Humboldt	1853	Lassen	1864		
Plumas	1854	Inyo	1866		
Stanislaus	1854	Kern	1866		
Amador	1854	Ventura	1872		
Merced	1855	San Benito	1874		

(The standard work on the state's counties is Owen C. Coy's *California County Boundaries*)

The transverse ranges, with Tehachapi Pass for datum point, made the traditional northern boundary of Southern California, which thus contained San Diego, Imperial, Riverside, San Bernardino, Orange, Los Angeles, Ventura, and Santa Barbara counties. Water quests and improved communications brought Inyo, Mono, and Kern counties properly within its orbit. Enthusiasts also claim Tulare, Kings, and San Luis Obispo counties for the Southland, while extremists add Fresno County as well.

Separatists have cried for two states since California's entry into the Union—basing the division on North-South spheres of interest. Another separatist demand arose in 1956 among the state's northernmost counties, out of, it is believed, a desire for publicity, as well as, a desire to secure more highway appropriations from Sacramento. It should be noted, as well, that the southern Oregon counties have separatist inclinations of their own.

Intermittently for more than a century, the counties east of the Sierra summit have protested their inclusion in California, and Nevada has on occasion encouraged these outcries for its own purposes. "Geographical inhumanities" still afflict portions of California, to a diminishing degree, but it is not believed feasible, let alone desirable, to start dismembering the state. A possible exception might be the cession of California's trans-Sierra territory to Nevada, reserving the water potential of Mono and Inyo counties for Los Angeles, in return for an outright grant of Nevada's share of the Colorado River water.

AIDS TO UNDERSTANDING

Bibliography

Any attempt to compile even a reasonably comprehensive listing of Californiana would consume more paper and ink and reader time than seems warranted here. The few books mentioned below hopefully fulfill the dual function of expanding understanding and providing a base for further reading.

Four college-level histories are available either by purchase or library loan, at this writing: *California* by John Walton Caughey; *California: A History* by Andrew F. Rolle; *California: An Interpretive History* by Walton Bean; and *Everyman's Eden* by Ralph J. Roske. Each of these contains an extensive bibliography. The first two are complemented by books of selected readings on specific aspects of California history: *California Heritage* by John W. and LaRee Caughey and *Readings in California History* (paperback) by N. Ray and Gladys Gilmore. *Everyman's Eden* probably will appeal more than the others to the general reader, who must be warned that it contains numerous minor errors.

Earl Pomeroy's *The Pacific Slope* places California in perspective with other Far Western states, and Richard G. Lillard's *Eden in Jeopardy* should be required reading for every resident of California. Oscar Lewis's *The Big Four* and *The Silver Kings* are sparkling interpretations of the men who built the Central Pacific Railroad and those who snatched their fortunes from the Comstock Lode. Dwight L. Clarke's *Stephen Watts Kearny* rescues its subject from the animosities of the pro-Frémont faction, and Bernard DeVoto's *Year of Decision* explains the compulsions encompassed in the catch phrase, "Manifest Destiny." The importance of Theodora Kroeber's *Ishi in Two Worlds* has been mentioned in the text, and her *Tales of the Inland Whale* is worthwhile as a beautiful and sensitive interpretation of the mystical legends of the California Indians; both are available in paperback.

Personal opinion holds two books indispensable to the enjoyment of intrastate travel—even by air. The first of these, *California: Land of Contrast* by Lantis, Steiner, and Karinen, is a college-level geography, which will astonish those who persist in regarding geography as a simple exercise in "bounded-on-the-east-by" memorization. The second, Rev. William N. Abeloe's revision of *Historic Spots in California*, comes as close to a true compendium of each county's human history as we are ever likely to see.

Place names are more evocative to this Californiac than the remembered kisses of a long-past youth. For this reason alone, and disregarding the panorama of the past it contains, I have an abiding regard for Erwin G. Gudde's monumental *California Place Names*.

Some readers may object that this opinionated selection of books has overlooked both the Hispanic period and its people; the college histories mentioned above devote quite adequate space to these subjects.

Historical Societies

Unlike other states — Texas, for example — California has no state-sponsored or -supported historical society. Unfortunately, too, despite the textbooks mentioned above, state and local history has fallen into disrepute in recent years among the intellectual mandarins of the state's system of higher education. These weaknesses have been offset, in part, by privately organized, supported, and directed historical societies at both the state and local levels.

The *California Historical Society* maintains research materials, genealogical archives, and exhibition facilities in its handsome quarters at 2090 Jackson Street, San Francisco 94109. The importance of Southern California to a privately supported society has been recognized by the establishment of a branch headquarters at 1120 Old Mill Road, San Marino 91108. A quarterly journal devoted to California history is distributed to members.

The *Historical Society of Southern California* maintains its offices at 200 E. Avenue 43, Los Angeles 90031, and publishes a quarterly journal for its members. The limited research materials and facilities of this society are alleviated by the resources available at the Los Angeles County Museum of Natural History, 900 Exposition Boulevard, Los Angeles 90007.

The *Conference of California Historical Societies* is the statewide, central organization made up of more than one hundred and fifty county and local societies in the state. Information about specific county and local societies may be obtained from the executive secretary of the conference, Dr. R. Coke Wood, University of the Pacific, Stockton 95204.

The *American Indian Historical Society* is not concerned with the original inhabitants solely of California, but its publications contain much material on them. Information may be obtained from their headquarters at 1451 Masonic Street, San Francisco 94117.

Museums and Reconstructions

No more is claimed for the places below than that they may repay your time if you have leisure in their vicinity and some interest in what they have to show and say. With the possible exception of Adam, this world has never known an exclusively "now" generation, and museums are one means of reminding ourselves of this fact. Admittedly the choices below are selected by the same personal opinion that compiled the preceding bibliography. This roster is by no means complete and the categories overlap one another.

Indian and prehistoric exhibits are found at the Southwest Museum and the Los Angeles County Museum of Natural History in Los Angeles. Other Indian materials are displayed in the Eastern California Museum, Independence; the Clark Museum, Eureka; and the state-maintained Indian Museum in Sacramento.

Hispanic life — the restored and unrestored missions excluded — is depicted at the *Casa de Adobe* in Los Angeles where an early ranchero's residence is reproduced and operated by the Southwest Museum. Mariano G. Vallejo's home at Sonoma is maintained by the Division of Beaches and Parks; and Vallejo's ranch headquarters, the largest surviving example of adobe construction in the state, is being restored by that same agency between Petaluma and Sonoma. The museum of the Santa Barbara Historical Society has a strong Hispanic flavor, and Sutter's Fort at Sacramento and the restored Russian outpost at Fort Ross—both maintained by the Division of Beaches and Parks— retain the flavor of the Hispanic period in which they were built.

The *Gold Rush*, naturally enough, is well represented in this roster. The Division of Mines and Geology has an extensive display of minerals in San Francisco's Ferry Building, augmented by a working-model stamp mill and a three-dimensional reproduction of the famous Idaho-Maryland Mine.

The mother lode town of Columbia, "Gem of the Southern Mines," has been restored by the Division of Beaches and Parks; while Bodie, on the eastern fringe of Mono County, is preserved in the state of decay that gripped it when this same agency took it over. A replica of Sutter's sawmill and the museum at Coloma, where the Rush began, are more of the Beaches and Parks' operation.

The sleepy hamlet of Murphys in Calaveras County is held by many to be the finest Gold Rush town *au naturel*, while others opt for Downieville, where a gold display is housed in one of the old stone buildings.

The *Chinese* presence in the mines is commemorated in the well-kept Joss House in Weaverville and the Chinese Temple in Oroville. Residents of Coulterville have restored Sun Wo's store as a local museum.

Pioneer Life, for want of a more definitive category, is represented at the Beaches and Parks' museum at Donner Lake, and is the theme of the Pioneer Village and Kern County Museum at Visalia. The Kelly-Griggs House in Red Bluff, the Lott House in Oroville, and the Bidwell Mansion in Chico (the latter maintained by the Division of Beaches and Parks) provide glimpses of life in the interior during the agricultural heyday of the last century. The Haggin Museum in Stockton houses exhibits of nineteenth-century life in California.

Other museums reflecting local heritages include the Junípero Serra Museum, San Diego; Museum of the Desert, Palm Springs; San Bernardino County Museum, San Bernardino; Bowers Museum, Santa Ana; Ventura County Museum, Ventura; San Mateo County Museum, San Mateo; Old Timer's Museum, Murphys; Plumas County Museum, Quincy; Lassen County Museum, Susanville; Trinity County Museum, Weaverville; Siskiyou County Museum, Yreka; and the museum housed in the lighthouse at Crescent City, but readily accessible at low tide.

Transportation in the shape of a Concord coach is the central theme of the Wells Fargo Bank's History Room in San Francisco, which also contains an extensive firearms collection. A specialized exhibit of Yosemite transportation is housed at El Portal.

Maritime displays, appropriately enough, are clustered within easy walking distance of Ghirardelli Square and Fisherman's Wharf in San Francisco. These include the San Francisco Maritime Museum and its restored square-rigged *Balclutha*, as well as the four-vessel fleet—bay ferry, sailing schooner,

342

steam schooner, and hay-hauling scow-schooner—maintained by the Division of Beaches and Parks.

The San Diego waterfront boasts a museum housed in the restored blue-water sailing vessel, *Star of India*, while a portion of the former Cunard liner *Queen Mary*, now owned by and moored at the City of Long Beach, is slated to become a museum of the sea.

Petroleum, despite its importance in the state's history, is served by only two museums known to this writer—neither of which is truly comprehensive. One is sponsored by the Standard Oil Company of California at its complex at 555 Market Street, San Francisco; the other is maintained by the Union Oil Company in its first headquarters building in Santa Paula, Ventura County.

Lumbering boasts no exhibit in California comparable to the one at Collier State Park in Oregon, on U.S. 97 between Klamath Falls and Diamond Lake Junction. *Railroads*, too, are ill served, with only the Lomita Railroad Museum meriting mention. These are woeful shortcomings in a state that has benefited so greatly from both industries.

Plans for a truly comprehensive Transportation Museum with the acquisitions of the late Gilbert Kneiss, to be directed by the Division of Beaches and Parks in conjunction with its existing maritime display in San Francisco, are snarled in political maneuverings and the project's future is uncertain.

Money used for museums and other means of preserving the past may to some seem ill spent in this day of urban crises. In rebuttal it is suggested here that such reminders of the continuity between generations would help man to identify to his land and thus alleviate the rootlessness that afflicts so many of California's urban residents.

PICTURE CREDITS

AMERICAN GEOGRAPHICAL SOCIETY: pages 242-243.

MORLEY BAER: page 31 (top).

BANCROFT LIBRARY, *University of California:* pages 10, 23, 25, 27 (top), 33 (both), 39 (both), 53, 66, 71 (both), 74 (top), 82-83, 87 (top), 91 (bottom), 100, 104-105, 113, 118, 121 (both), 123, 126 (both), 133, 135 (bottom), 138 (both), 140-141, 147 (both), 154, 156, 160, 169 (both), 183 (top), 187 (Dorothea Lange photo), 191 (top), 200 (top), 210 (both), 214, 229, 238, 247 (both), 256, 260-261, 265 (both), 303 (top), 307, 317 (both).

CALIFORNIA REDWOOD ASSOCIATION: page 171 (bottom).

CALIFORNIA STATE DEPARTMENT OF WATER RESOURCES: pages 189 (top), 322, 330.

CALIFORNIA STATE LIBRARY: page 76.

B. A. GUSTAFSON CO., *La Mesa:* page 328 (bottom).

LOS ANGELES COUNTY MUSEUM OF NATURAL HISTORY, *History Division:* pages 14, 50 (photo by Adam Clark Vroman), 59 (photo by Adam Clark Vroman), 62-63, 74 (bottom), 167 (top), 174, 183 (bottom), 191 (bottom), 194-195, 222, 236, 277, 281, 289, 296, 326-327.

JOHN HOWELL BOOKS: pages 82-83.

HUNTINGTON LIBRARY, *San Marino:* pages 87 (bottom), 129 (both).

PHILIP HYDE: frontispiece (from *The Last Redwoods,* Sierra Club).

ROBERT LEE *(A. O. Carpenter Collection):* pages 163 (both), 171 (top).

LIBRARY OF CONGRESS: pages 27 (bottom), 31 (bottom), 73, 272 (Dorothea Lange photo).

OAKLAND MUSEUM: pages 44-45, 96, 135 (top), 226 (top).

PACIFIC AIR INDUSTRIES: page 220.

PAN AMERICAN AIRWAYS: page 303 (bottom).

DAVID PARI: page 42.

P. G. & E. NEWS BUREAU: pages 232-233.

SAN FRANCISCO MARITIME MUSEUM: pages 91 (top), 150-151, 153, 167 (bottom), 206, 217, 253.

SAN FRANCISCO PUBLIC UTILITIES COMMISSION: page 226 (bottom).

SOUTHWEST MUSEUM, *Los Angeles:* pages 36, 47.

STANDARD OIL COMPANY: pages 18-19, 284-285.

STATE OF CALIFORNIA, DIVISION OF HIGHWAYS: pages 94, 314-315, 320.

SUNKIST GROWERS: page 203.

CURT TEICH & CO., *Chicago:* page 310.

TITLE INSURANCE AND TRUST COMPANY, *San Diego:* pages 149, 292, 298-299, 324, 328 (top).

U. S. BUREAU OF RECLAMATION: pages 178, 189 (bottom).

ROBERT A. WEINSTEIN (from a private collection): page 108.

344

Index

345

This book was printed and bound in Menlo Park, California
by Peninsula Lithograph Co. Body type is Caledonia,
composed by Hazeltine Typesetting, Inc., Oakland, California.
Type for the chapter headings is Bembo, furnished by
Los Angeles Type Founders, Inc. The paper is Capstan Vellum,
cream white, furnished by Zellerbach Paper Co., San Francisco.
The cloth is Renee from the Columbia Mills, Inc., Syracuse, New York.

Jacket color photograph by Josef Muench; frontispiece photograph
by Philip Hyde (from "The Last Redwoods," Sierra Club).